THE CASE THAT SHOOK INDIA

The case that shook India

Prashant Bhushan

VIKAS PUBLISHING HOUSE PVT LTD
New Delhi Bombay Bangalore Calcutta Kanpur

VIKAS PUBLISHING HOUSE PVT LTD
5 Ansari Road, New Delhi 110002
Savoy Chambers, 5 Wallace Street, Bombay 400001
10 First Main Road, Gandhi Nagar, Bangalore 560009
8/1-B Chowringhee Lane, Calcutta 700016
80 Canning Road, Kanpur 208004

© Prashant Bhushan, 1978

ISBN 0 7069 0594 6

1V02P2501

First Published, 1978
Second Impression, 1978

Printed at India offset Press, Mayapuri, New Delhi

ACKNOWLEDGEMENTS

It is difficult for me to imagine how I could have written this book without the help and encouragement of a large number of well-wishers and relatives. I would, however, like to mention my special debt to a few individuals.

I am grateful to my cousins Sumati and Bhagwant Bishnoi who sacrificed much of their vacations for doing the preliminary editing. I also wish to thank my brother-in-law Kenneth Waldron, cousin Ashok Mittal, and family friends R.N. Verma and V.K. Khanna, for giving me valuable suggestions which made substantial improvements in the book.

My thanks are also due to J.P. Goyal, Advocate, who secured my entry in the court room during the hearings in the Supreme Court and otherwise helped me, and to M.C. Gupta, Advocate, who furnished me with much valuable information.

Last but not the least, I am profoundly grateful to M. Hidayatullah who spent several hours of his valuable time in going through the manuscript and writing a foreword for the book.

FOREWORD

Elections to Parliament and the Legislatures of the States are regulated in two ways by law. The first relates to the conduct of the elections by the Election Commission and the second to the personal conduct in it of the candidates. Unlike in other countries the duty of deciding whether the election was fair and free and if the candidate was guilty of a corrupt practice is entrusted to the High Court and finally to the Supreme Court.

After the election is over the defeated candidate or a voter can challenge the election of the successful candidate by proving irregularities in the conduct of the election by the authorities and/or by proving corrupt conduct on the part of the candidate. In no other way can the result of the poll be challenged. The courts apply to such cases the standards which they usually apply in trials before them. Such cases are like any other case. The allegations made must be strictly proved. Some judges call these quasi-criminal proceedings. This is not an apt description. They rather resemble the trial of allegations of fraud, subject to this that the benefit of a doubt goes to the successful candidate.

Ordinarily I have found more perjury in these cases than in others. Political motivation often colours evidence and courts have to be very careful in assessing partisan testimony. This task becomes even more difficult when the actions of the candidate are also partly referable to his official position. Such was the case dealt with here.

The book deals with the election petition filed by Raj Narain to challenge the election of Mrs Gandhi in the last but one election to Parliament. The author has recorded the day-to-day progress of the case through all stages. He is the son of the Counsel for Raj Narain and was presumably present at conferences and in the courts. He has first-hand knowledge of all facts. He has narrated them in a very readable form, describing the proceedings objectively. He has also outlined the many steps by which legislative interference righted what was found wrong at the trial. So much so that the Supreme Court was not even allowed to decide the case in appeal. This was an unusual and undesirable feature of the case. Only one case (*Mc Cardle* case) was withdrawn from the Supreme Court of the United States. It was not an election case but never afterwards was a pending case withdrawn from the courts. All the events are told without acrimony by the author and the comments that one finds are legitimate.

I have had may share of election trials as a judge of the High Court and the Supreme Court. Twice I unseated ministers and once upheld an election. There is no doubt that Justice Sinha proved equal to the task. He decided every issue adequately and his reactions during arguments were also relevant and proper. Whether one agrees with his conclusions or not none can accuse him of taking a strained view of facts. It must be remembered that a person in authority can and should always prevent from acting overzealously the officials who go out of their way to act in aid of such a candidate. The higher the position of the candidate and the more the availability of official aid, the more the risk of allegations.

Justice Sinha, in my judgment, has rightly been strict. Although I do not say that I agree with him on every point *pro* or *con*, this much I can say that my approach, by and large, would have been similar. In any event Justice Sinha and Judge Sirica of Watergate case have much in common just as there is a parallel between Shanti Bhushan and Jaworski in the same case.

I have enjoyed reading the book and have found much that was not in the newspapers and I recommend it to the reader.

M. HIDAYATULLAH
MA. (Cantab); LL.D.
Bencher Lincoln's Inn and Former
Chief Justice of India

Bombay
1 October 1977

INTRODUCTION

The day had hardly begun on 26 June 1975. The streets of Delhi should rightfully have been resting at that time after the previous day's hectic political activities. But this morning they were witnessing a strange kind of activity. Hundreds of police cars were moving silently along the streets in search of their prey. Their prey were no ordinary men. A list of those who were to be nabbed in the midnight operation made up a "who's who" of those who had asked Mrs Gandhi to quit office. The operation was totally successful. In a coup planned and executed with ruthless military efficiency, Mrs Gandhi that night transformed the country from a working democracy into a dictatorship.

The apparent reasons for this sudden transition are fairly obvious. They perhaps lay in something which took place in a small, inconspicuous courtroom of the Allahabad High Court, just two weeks earlier. On that day, a lone judge, sitting in the High Court, had pronounced a verdict, setting aside the election of the respondent on charges of corrupt practices. This by itself was not unusual. The High Court almost every year set aside elections on charges of corrupt practices. What made the case unusual was the fact that the respondent here was no ordinary person. She was the Prime Minister of the country.

The rumblings set off by the judgment had their culmination in the midnight coup of 26 June. But the story does not end there. With remarkable swiftness, in less than two years, history has completed a full circle. The night which began on 26 June 1975 ended on 20 March 1977, with a resounding defeat of Mrs Gandhi and her Congress Party, at the polls.

Most people will dispute that it was the "case" that had brought about this remarkable political revolution. They will say that the "case" has become the scapegoat for the political revolution which was bound to take place, seeing the political dynamics of the country at that time. Their argument would be that Mrs Gandhi was bound to strike as ruthlessly as she did, whenever her power was threatened. The author entirely agrees with this analysis. But no one will deny that the case at least expedited the process, and made the country go through in a flash what it would normally have gone through in a much longer time. Therein lies the political importance of the case. It was the immediate, though not the real cause of the ensuing revolution.

People will wonder what this history-making case was. What were the charges against Mrs Gandhi? What happened inside the courtrooms? What were the manoeuvrings behind the court? This book is intended to provide the answers to all these questions. It deals with the entire case right from the time the petition was filed in the High Court in April 1971, till it was finally disposed of by the Supreme Court in November 1975. Thus, viewed from a political perspective, this can be regarded as a historical book which focuses on a legal event, which had grave political consequences. However, viewed from a wholly legal perspective, it can be regarded as a case history of one of the most important court battles of our times. There are really two cases involved here. The case in the Supreme Court had become entirely different from the one in the High Court. While in the High Court it was an ordinary election petition, in the Supreme Court, because of the constitutional and election-law amendments made to influence the case, it became an entirely constitutional case.

The Supreme Court arguments would be of special interest, as most of them went unreported in the newspapers due to pre censorship. The arguments have been presented as the author heard and interpreted them, and therefore the account must necessarily have a bias. The author has tried to avoid bias as much as possible, and whatever bias remains is unavoidable in the circumstances.

Another matter needs to be clarified. As there are no verbatim records of court proceedings, it is impossible to record the exact wordings of the arguments and observations which took place in the court. Therefore, while the account of most of the arguments and observations are given in the first person, they are not necessarily the exact words used by the counsel and judges on those occasions. The first person has been used so that the account remains more lively and interesting, though care has been taken to see that there is no misrepresentation.

PRASHANT BHUSHAN

CONTENTS

1
PRELIMINARY COURT PROCEEDINGS

1. From Electoral Battle to Court Battle — 3
2. The Petition — 7
3. The PM in Court — 20

2
IN THE HIGH COURT

4. The Petitioner's Opening Arguments — 29
5. Attorney-General Defends the Amendment — 54
6. The PM's Counsel — 58
7. The Petitioner's Rejoinder — 80
8. The Verdict — 93

3
THE REPERCUSSIONS

9. Rumblings after the Judgement — 107
10. The Stay Order — 116
11. Law? What law? — 128

4
VALIDITY OF THE CONSTITUTIONAL AMENDMENT

12. "It Destroys Democracy" — 143
13. "PM can be above the Law" — 155

14. "Amendment is like a Firman" 168
15. Emergency Measure or Tranquillizer? 173

5
VALIDITY OF THE ELECTION LAWS AMENDMENT

16. Rules of the Game Changed Retrospectively 185
17. "Rules not Changed, Merely Clarified" 197
18. "Parliament Cannot Interpret the Law" 211
19. The Supreme Court Judgement 220
20. Epilogue: From Court Battle to Electoral Battle 240

APPENDICES

1. Testimony of Yashpal Kapoor 243
2. Testimony of Mrs Indira Gandhi 249
3. Supreme Court Reviews the Keshavananda Bharati Case 256
4. Review Application against Justice Beg's Judgement 268
5. Representation of People Act, 1951—Part VII, Section 123 274
6. Representation of People (Amendment) Act, 1974 278
7. The Election Laws (Amendment) Act, 1975 280
8. The Constitution (Thirty-ninth) Amendment Act, 1975 285

INDEX 289

1

Preliminary Court Proceedings

1

FROM ELECTORAL BATTLE TO COURT BATTLE

If any year signifies the beginning of Mrs Indira Gandhi's ascendance to power, it would probably be 1969, when the Congress split took place. Though at that time the faction led by Mrs Gandhi was reduced to a state of minority in the Lok Sabha, she started looking for an early opportunity to consolidate her power. She had to rely on the support of the Communist Party of India—which she did not like —to get Bills passed in the Lok Sabha. However, when the Privy Purses Abolition Bill was stalled by the combined Opposition parties in the Rajya Sabha where they had a majority, Mrs Gandhi was given the opportunity she needed.

On 27 December 1970, the President dissolved the Lok Sabha at the advice of Mrs Gandhi and called for elections in early March. This was one year before the normal scheduled elections which were due in 1972. Although the Opposition parties were somewhat taken by surprise, they recovered quickly and announced they would form an alliance to fight the election against Mrs Gandhi's Congress Party. The members of this alliance, which Mrs Gandhi called the "grand alliance," were all the major non-communist Opposition parties, which included the Congress (Organization), the Jan Sangh, the Swatantra Party and the Samyukt Socialist Party.

On 29 December 1970, Mrs Gandhi held a Press Conference regarding the elections. At the Press Conference, someone told her that "a short while ago in a meeting of the Opposition parties, the opposition leaders said that Mrs Gandhi was changing her constituency from Rae Bareli to Gurgaon." To this, she replied emphatically, "No,

I am not." (Mrs Gandhi had fought and won her first election to the Lok Sabha from Rae Bareli in the 1967 General Elections.)

Meanwhile the opposition parties were also choosing their candidates for various constituencies. On 19 January 1971, the opposition parties which had forged an alliance against Mrs Gandhi's Congress Party announced Raj Narain's candidature from Rae Bareli to oppose Mrs Gandhi. He would be their jointly sponsored candidates and even other opposition parties like the Bhartiya Kranti Dal, which were not members of the alliance, decided not to put up their own candidate from Rae Bareli. The next day Mrs Gandhi, giving a speech in Coimbatore, lashed out against Raj Narain's candidature from Rae Bareli. She said that "Mr Narain had been chosen by the Opposition parties to contest from Rae Bareli because he was a well-known Nehru hater and baiter."

On 25 January, the Election Commission allotted the symbol of a cow and calf to the ruling Congress Party of Mrs Gandhi and the symbol of a lady with a *charkha* to the Congress (Organization) Party led by Morarji Desai.

A few days later, Shanti Bhushan received a telegram from C. Rajagopalachari which expressed his dissatisfaction at the allotment of the cow and calf symbol to the ruling Congress party. He asked Bhushan to challenge this allotment in the court on the ground that it was a religious symbol. Bhushan replied that as the election process had already started with the issue of the Presidential notification on 27 January, it was not possible to challenge the allotment of the symbol till the elections were over.

The polling dates were 3, 5 and 7 March and the last date for filing nomination papers was 3 February. Meanwhile, on 25 January, Mrs Gandhi's tour programme for Rae Bareli was issued for 1 February. In the tour programme, 11 A.M. was marked out for filing her nomination papers in the District Magistrate's office. In accordance with her tour programme, Mrs Gandhi went to Rae Bareli on 1 February and filed her nomination papers. She appointed Yashpal Kapoor as her election agent. Kapoor was earlier working as Officer on Special Duty in the Prime Minister's Secretariat and he had resigned just a few days before. It is noteworthy that Kapoor who was Mrs Gandhi's Private Secretary earlier, had resigned at the eve of the 1967 elections and had worked in Mrs Gandhi's election campaign. Immediately after the elections, he had rejoined Mrs Gandhi's Secretariat as Officer on Special Duty.

With the last date for filing nomination papers over, the din for getting party tickets died down and the election campaign of the parties started in a big way. The Opposition parties' slogan was "*Indira Hatao*" and their main charge against her was that she was responsible for the corruption which had crept into the Government in the past two years. Mrs Gandhi who had earlier nationalized the 14 major banks of the country and had tried to abolish the privy purses of the erstwhile Maharajas was successful in projecting her image as a radical socialist, who was seriously interested in bridging the gap between the rich and the poor as quickly as possible. In reply to the Opposition's slogan of "Indira *Hatao*," she coined her own simple slogan "*Garibi Hatao*." In every election speech, she said "All that the Opposition wants is the removal of Indira, and all that I want is the removal of poverty. Now, it is upto you to decide what you want." The effectiveness of this rhetoric can only be guaged by the election results.

The polling date for Mrs Gandhi's constituency was 7 March. The day went off uneventfully and counting of votes started on 9 March. Meanwhile on 8 March, before the votes were counted, Raj Narain led a victory procession through the streets of Rae Bareli, thanking the people for their support and for having elected him.

The results started coming in by 10 March and early returns showed that the Congress was heading for a landslide victory, even beyond the most optimistic estimates of the Congress supporters. In her own constituency, Mrs Gandhi routed Raj Narain by more than 1,10,000 votes. Mrs Gandhi polled 1,83,309 votes while Raj Narain could get only 71,499 votes. The only other candidate Swamy Adwaitanand who had fought as an independent candidate, did not get any significant number of votes.

Raj Narain is a very optimistic man and the victory procession was taken out by him on his firm belief that he would indeed win. The results, however, shook him, and he started believing the stories which were being circulated about the chemical treatment of ballot papers. The results were so surprising that some other Opposition leaders also started believing that the ballot papers might indeed have been treated chemically so that the ink of the actual stamp mark disappeared after some time, and an invisible stamp mark which had been put on the ballot papers at the time of their printing, appeared on the paper just before counting. If it was true that the marks had been manipulated, then they should have been identically placed on the ballot papers. But the only way in which this could be determined, was by examination of the ballot papers, which could only be done by means of an election petition. The fear that such rigging had taken place was perhaps the main reason why Raj Narain decided to file petition challenging Mrs Gandhi's election. The charges of corrupt practices were at that time regarded as only subsidiary issues. This was the background of the court battle which was destined to create history.

2

THE PETITION

The Representation of Peoples Act, 1951, specifies that the result of an election announced by a Returning Officer can only be challenged by an election petition brought before the High Court in whose jurisdiction the election was contested, and that the petition must be filed within 45 days of the announcement of the result. It was, therefore, some time in mid-April that Raj Narain went to Ramesh Chandra Srivastava, a lawyer of Allahabad known to him, for the handling of the petition. Raj Narain also decided to engage Shanti Bhushan as his Senior Counsel in this case. Although Raj Narain did not know Bhushan personally, he chose him, as apart from being an active member of the Congress (Organization) he was regarded as a very competent lawyer, who did most political cases without charging any fee. After some junior lawyer had done the initial drafting of the petition, Raj Narain took the draft to Bhushan on 22 April. The initial draft which was brought to Bhushan contained several allegations, and the chief ones were:

1. that the ballot papers had been chemically treated;
2. that Yashpal Kapoor (Mrs Gandhi's Election Agent) had induced Swamy Adwaitanand to stand as a candidate by bribing him to the tune of Rs 50,000;
3. that Mrs Gandhi's agent had distributed quilts, blankets, dhoties, liquor, etc., to induce voters to vote for her;
4. that a large number of voters had been conveyed to and from the polling stations in vehicles provided by Mrs Gandhi's agent;

5. that Mrs Gandhi had incurred expenditure much above the prescribed limit of Rs 35,000;

6. that Mrs Gandhi had procured the help of Yashpal Kapoor for her election while he was still a Gazetted Officer in the Government.

All these, except the first, were made out to be corrupt practices under the Election Laws (see Appendix 5). If a corrupt practice is proved against a returned candidate his election is declared void and he is disqualified from holding any public office for six years.

To Bhushan the petition seemed to be more of a vehicle for propaganda than an election petition. He also did not believe the first allegation, which was the main charge in the petition. So he told Raj Narain that he would only argue the case if it was treated as a serious election petition and not as a propaganda stunt. Moreover, the charge of chemical treatment of ballot papers would have to be deleted from the petition, he said. At that time Raj Narain, though reluctantly, agreed to the conditions. Bhushan also added three more charges to the petition. These were:

1. that Mrs Gandhi had procured the assistance of a number of gazetted officers and members of the police forces for furthering the prospects of her election by erecting barricades for her visits and constructing rostrums for her speeches;
2. that she had procured the services of members of the Armed Forces for the furtherance of her election prospects by flying in Air Force planes flown by them;
3. that the symbol of cow and calf used by Mrs Gandhi was a religious symbol.

At this time, Bhushan was asked about the chances of the success of the petition. "Negligible" was his reply. Firstly, the case was not strong enough, and secondly, few judges would have the courage to unseat the Prime Minister. "Nevertheless, we must fight it, on the off chance that it succeeds."

Next day, Raj Narain came back to Bhushan and told him that he could not sleep the whole night on account of Bhushan's deleting the issue about the chemical treatment of ballot papers. Very reluctantly Bhushan agreed to restore it, though in a different form. Instead of alleging that the ballot papers were chemically treated, the petition now alleged that a large number of ballot papers counted in Mrs Gandhi's favour were not actually cast by the voters and that the

The Petition

markings on these papers were made surreptitiously by some mechanical process. The petition alleged that this would be clear from the fact that the seal marks on these papers were in exactly identical places.

So the final draft of the petition contained the following charges:

1. that Mrs Gandhi had procured the assistance of Yashpal Kapoor for the furtherance of her election prospects while he was still a gazetted officer;
2. that at the instance of Mrs Gandhi, Swami Adwaitanand was bribed to stand as a candidate from Rae Bareli;
3. that Mrs Gandhi procured the assistance of members of the armed forces of the Union for furthering her election prospects by ordering them to fly her to her election meetings in Air Force planes;
4. that she procured the assistance of the District Magistrate and the Superintendent of Police of Rae Bareli and other police officers for erecting barricades and rostrums and making loudspeaker arrangements for her election meetings;
5. that her agent freely distributed liquor, quilts, blankets among the voters of Rae Bareli with the object of inducing them to vote for her;
6. that by using the symbol of a cow and calf she appealed to the religious sentiments of the voters for the purpose of getting votes for herself;
7. that Yashpal Kapoor and other agents of Mrs Gandhi hired a number of vehicles for the free conveyance of voters to and from the polling stations;
8. that Mrs Gandhi and her election agent incurred, or authorized expenditure, much beyond the prescribed limit of Rs 35,000 for the purpose of the election.

All these, the petition alleged, were corrupt practices under the Election Laws on the basis of which Mrs Gandhi's election was liable to be declared void. The last allegation in the petition was about tampering with ballot papers.

THE PETITION IS FILED

This petition was presented to the Additional Registrar, Allahabad High Court, on the night of 24 April by Raj Narain along with Ramesh Srivastava. This was, incidentally, also the last date for the filing of the election petition. The petition was listed before Justice W. Broome. He directed the court to issue notices to the first respondent, Mrs Gandhi, and the second respondent, Swami Adwaitanand.

Mrs Gandhi's Reply

The written statement of Mrs Gandhi was filed on 5 August 1971. In that she denied that Yashpal Kapoor did any election work for her before resigning. She also denied the bribery of Adwaitanand.

It was stated that Mrs Gandhi travelled in Air Force planes on the basis of the Standing Instructions of the Government of India regarding the travel arrangements for the Prime Minister. The instructions stipulate that the Prime Minister should travel by Air Force planes even when she is not on official duty.

She further denied that the use of Air Force planes by her was a corrupt practice. She said that this facility of Air Force planes for the Prime Minister was like a commercial service created exclusively for her. Further, she denied soliciting the use of the planes; these were provided merely on the basis of her tour programmes.

She also denied that the construction of barricades and rostrums was for furthering her election prospects. These were merely for law and order purposes, she said.

She also denied the allegation of bribery and the conveyance of voters to and from the polling stations.

She further denied that the cow and calf symbol was a religious symbol and that she exceeded the limit on election expenditure.

She dismissed the charge of tampering with ballot papers as fanciful and ridiculous.

The Issues are Framed

After the written statement was filed, Justice Broome framed the issues for the petition on 19 August 1971. The main issues framed were:

1. Whether Mrs Gandhi procured the services of Yashpal Kapoor for the furtherance of the prospects of her election while he was still a gazetted officer.

2. Whether Yashpal Kapoor had bribed Swami Adwaitanand for the purpose of inducing him to stand as a candidate in the election.

The Petition

3. Whether at the instance of Mrs Gandhi, members of the armed forces arranged Air Force planes and helicopters for her, flown by members of the armed forces to enable her to address election meetings, and if so, whether this amounted to a corrupt practice under Section 123(7) of the R.P. Act.

4. Whether at the instance of Mrs Gandhi and Yashpal Kapoor the District Magistrate and Superintendent of Police of Rae Bareli arranged for the erection of barricades and rostrums and loudspeakers for Mrs Gandhi's election meetings, and if so, whether this amounted to a corrupt practice under Section 123(7) of the R.P. Act.

5. Whether quilts, blankets, dhoties and liquor were distributed by agents and workers of Mrs Gandhi in order to induce voters to vote for her.

6. Whether by using the symbol of the cow and calf, Mrs Gandhi was guilty of making an appeal to religious sentiments and committed a corrupt practice under Section 123(3) of the R.P. Act.

7. Whether on the polling date voters were conveyed to the polling stations free of charge on vehicles hired by Yashpal Kapoor or with his consent.

The Judge also said that regarding the charge of tempering with ballot papers, he would carry out an investigation of a sample of papers to see whether there was any substance in it.

THE INTERROGATORIES

A few days later, an application was filed on behalf of Narain making a plea to deliver interrogatories to Mrs Gandhi under Order 11 of the Civil Procedure Code. Interrogatories are written questions for which the petitioner can ask the respondent to provide written answers. This was strongly objected to by Mrs Gandhi's Counsel on the ground that Order 11 of the C.P.C. which permits interrogatories to be delivered in a civil suit does not apply to an election petition. After hearing arguments of both sides in this matter, Justice Broome granted leave to Raj Narain for delivering interrogatories to Mrs Gandhi.

Mrs Gandhi had engaged S. C. Khare, a senior lawyer of the Allahabad High Court, and a staunch member of the Congress Party, to be her senior counsel in this case. Khare, however, was not satisfied by Justice Broome's decision on the interrogatories and he decided to appeal to the Supreme Court.

In the Supreme Court, the case went before Justices Hegde, Khanna and Vaidyalingam. After some arguments were heard by the Bench on this matter, the appeal was withdrawn by Khare on the advice of the Bench.

"Tampering Charge Baseless"

Raj Narain was not happy with Bhushan's attitude towards the charge of tampering with ballot papers. Bhushan was not taking it seriously, while Raj Narain was convinced that the papers had been chemically treated. When Bhushan was in Delhi at that time, Raj Narain took him to a scientist from Bombay who, he said, would convince him that the ballot papers were chemically treated. Bhushan met the scientist at the house of Balraj Madhok, a Jan Sangh leader. The scientist had with him infra red and ultra violet lamps. He showed Bhushan two identical ballot papers and then projected ultra violet rays on them. The paper now appeared to have different colours. This, the scientist claimed, proved Raj Narain's charge that some ballot papers were chemically treated. Bhushan, however, was not convinced. He said that these papers were printed in different printing presses, so the texture of the papers might have been different which could account for difference in colour when observed in ultra violet light.

Regarding this issue, Justice Broome carried out an investigation of a sample of ballot papers.

On 15 November 1971, he inspected 200 ballot papers cast in favour of Raj Narain and 600 cast in favour of Mrs Gandhi. He found that the seal marks on the ballot papers were in different places and hence there was no reason to believe that they had been tampered with.

"Unreasonable, Vexatious, Oppressive and Irrelevant"

A few days later, a set of 31 interrogatories were delivered to Mrs Gandhi by the petitioner. As soon as the interrogatories were delivered, Mrs Gandhi's counsel took objection to these saying that they were "unreasonable, vexatious, oppressive, unnecessary and irrelevant." All the interrogatories related to the issues about Yashpal Kapoor and Swami Adwaitanand. Mrs Gandhi's counsel also pleaded that the particulars set out in the petition did not afford a basis for these issues and hence these issues should be deleted.

COURT DELETES SOME ISSUES

The Judge then heard arguments on this matter. Khare contended that since the petition did not specify the date on which Mrs Gandhi became a candidate (as the R.P. Act specified that the corrupt practice must be committed by the "candidate") nor did it specify the date from which the assistance of Kapoor was procured, corrupt practice on account of Yashpal Kapoor was not made out. Regarding the issue of Swami Adwaitanand's bribery, Khare contended that since the date on which the money was paid was not mentioned, the issue was not made out.

Bhushan in his arguments did not press the issue of bribery of Adwaitanand. He, however, contended that since the petition alleged that Kapoor's services had been procured while he was a gazetted officer, and Mrs Gandhi was a candidate, it did make out the charge of corrupt practice.

Justice Broome, however, agreed with Khare and deleted this issue too from the petition.

The petitioner then filed an application for making some amendments to the petition, under Section 86(5) of the R.P. Act, which says, "the High Court if it deems fit may allow the particulars of any corrupt practice alleged in the petition to be amended or amplified to ensure a fair and effective trial of the petition, but shall not allow any amendment of the petition which will have the effect of introducing particulars of a corrupt practice not previously alleged in the petition." In the proposed amendment, it was sought to be stated clearly that Mrs Gandhi had been holding herself out as a candidate right from 27 December when the Lok Sabha was dissolved and that Yashpal Kapoor had started doing election work for her right from that time. The allegation that she began holding herself out as a candidate from 27 December was necessary because it is normally held that a person starts attracting charges of corrupt practices only after becoming a candidate. The R.P. Act specifies that a person becomes a candidate when he starts holding himself out as a candidate.

The amendment application was strongly opposed by Khare on the ground that the proposed amendment would have the effect of introducing particulars of a corrupt practice not previously alleged in the petition and hence was not permissible. Justice Broome accepted the argument of Khare and rejected the amendment application on 23 December 1971.

Case goes to the Supreme Court

Raj Narain was not satisfied with Justice Broome's decision and he appealed against the order to the Supreme Court. The special leave petition was heard by a Bench consisting of Justice Hegde, Justice Jagan Mohan Reddy and Justice Mathew.

The judgment in this case was delivered on behalf of the Bench by Justice Hedge, who allowed the appeal. In his judgment, he said:

> But if the petition is read reasonably, as it should be, it is clear that the allegation of the petition is that the services of Yashpal Kapoor were obtained by the respondent when she had already become a candidate and when Shri Yashpal Kapoor was still a gazetted officer. It is true that the ingredients of the corrupt practice alleged is not specifically set out in the petition but from the allegations made it flows as a necessary implication. While a corrupt practice has got to be strictly proved it does not follow that a pleading in an election proceeding should receive a strict construction.... Moreover, no objection was taken to the issue about Yashpal Kapoor when it was originally framed by the trial judge. Objection was only taken when the petition to set aside the interrogatories was heard. Therefore, it is clear that the respondent was not in the dark about the allegation of this particular corrupt practice.

He therefore ordered that the petitioner be allowed to amend the petition. He also ordered that the issue about Yashpal Kapoor which had been deleted by Justice Broome be restored and recast in the following manner:

> Whether respondent No. 1 obtained and procured the assistance of Yashpal Kapoor in furtherance of the prospects of her election while he was still a gazetted officer in the service of Government of India. If so, from what date?

In his judgment, Justice Hegde found it necessary to mention one other fact. Justice Broome when deciding on the amendment application had come to the conclusion that Yashpal Kapoor ceased to be in the employ of the Government of India from 14 January 1971. The facts were that Yashpal Kapoor appears to have tendered his resignation on 13 January 1971. The President accepted his resignation on 25 January 1971, but with effect from 14 January 1971. Justice Hegde said that normally the services of a Government servant stood terminated from the date on which the letter of resignation is accepted by the appropriate authority. Since in this case it was accepted on 25 January therefore it could not be easily concluded that the resignation was effective from 14 January with retrospective effect. He ordered that this question be re-examined with reference to Yashpal Kapoor's conditions of service. Regarding the interrogatories, Justice Hegde allowed some of them, those which related to the issue of Yashpal Kapoor.[1]

Meanwhile, Justice Broome had retired in December 1971 and for a few days the case was with Justice B.N. Lokur. He too, however, retired a few months later and the case was then taken up by Justice K.N. Srivastava.

On 27 April 1973, Justice Srivastava framed three additional issues consequent to the amendment made in the petition. Additional issue No. 1 was the issue of Yashpal Kapoor which had been recast by the Supreme Court. Additional Issue No. 2 was, "whether Respondent No. 1 held herself out as a candidate from any date prior to the 1st of February 1971 and, if so, from what date." Additional Issue No. 3 was "whether Yash Pal Kapoor continued to be in the service of the Government of India from and after 14 January 1971 and till which date."

THE STATE PRIVILEGE

Oral examination of the petitioner's witnesses started from 10 September 1973.

One of the witnesses summoned by the petitioner was S.S. Saxena, Under Secretary in the Confidential Department, U.P., who was directed to produce certain documents before the court. He appeared on behalf of the Chief Secretary on 10 September 1973 with the documents, but he objected to produce: (1) The "Blue Book" entitled "*Rules and Instructions for the Protection of the Prime Minister When on Tour or Travel*, (2) Correspondence exchanged between the

---

[1] This judgment was delivered on 15 March 1972. About a year later came the appointment of Justice A.N. Ray as the Chief Justice of India and the supersession of the three judges—Justices Shelat, Hegde and Grover. It might be of interest to know that in an interview with Kuldip Nayar on the eve of the supersession Justice Hegde is reported to have said that he was superseded because of this judgment which he had delivered in Mrs Gandhi's case.

Government of India and the Government of U.P. in regard to the police arrangements for the meetings of the Prime Minister, and (3) Correspondence exchanged between the Chief Minister of U.P. and the Prime Minister in regard to the police arrangements for the meetings of the latter.

The objection was made on the ground of a State privilege, claimed under Section 123 of the Evidence Act. Bhushan objected to the claim of privilege and Justice Srivastava heard arguments on this issue for three days. He argued that the privilege could not be claimed as no affidavit, stating that the documents related to matters of State and that their release would injure public interest, was filed by the Minister or the Head of the Department. This, he argued, was mandatory under Section 123 of the Evidence Act for a claim of privilege to be sustained. He further argued that since portions of the Blue Book had been published, it was not an unpublished official record relating to affairs of the State and hence no privilege could be claimed in that respect.

Khare on behalf of the respondent and Kackar on behalf of the State argued strongly for the claim of privilege to be upheld. They argued that although no affidavit was filed by the Minister or the Head of the Department, the affidavit filed on 20 September 1973 by R.K. Kaul, Home Secretary, served the same purpose.

Justice Srivastava, however, rejected the claim of privilege and allowed the production of the three sets of documents. At this stage, Khare told him that he would be appealing against this order to the Supreme Court, so he was granted two days time to produce a stay order from the Supreme Court.

A Special Leave Petition against this order was admitted in the Supreme Court in April 1974 and the production of those documents was stayed. Thereafter, a joint application was filed by both parties for the adjournment of the case, till the Supreme Court finally disposed of the claim of privilege. The case was thus adjourned.

While the case was in the Supreme Court, pending disposal of the appeal, Justice Srivastava also retired, and the case was taken up after the summer vacations by Justice Jag Mohan Lal Sinha. It might be noted here that this case had already been going on for more than three years and recording of the oral evidence had barely started. This was because of neglect by both parties; possibly, they never expected anything to come of it. However, as soon as Justice Sinha took it up, he gave it top priority. Although the Supreme Court was yet to dispose of the appeal on the privilege matter, Justice Sinha told the petitioner to start producing evidence on other issues which were unconnected with the privilege matter or else give them up. If not for Justice Sinha, the case might still have been in the High Court today.

Between August 1974 and January 1975, the entire oral evidence of the petitioner was recorded.

Chawla's Case

Meanwhile on 3 October 1974, a Supreme Court Bench composed of Justices Bhagwati and Sarkaria gave an important decision on the law of election expenses, in what has come to be known as Amar Nath Chawla's case. The decision in this case was to have far-reaching consequences. Justice Bhagwati, delivering the judgment on behalf of the Bench, comprehensively analyzed and interpreted the law as it stood on election expenses. He laid down that the expenditure incurred by any person with the consent or acquiescence of a candidate, or any expenditure of which a candidate takes advantage, or fails to disavow, shall be treated as expenditure impliedly authorized by the candidate within the meaning of the section and has to be included in his return of election expenses. As the facts in Mrs Gandhi's case were that most of the election expenditure was incurred by the Congress party on her behalf, with the express or implied authorization of her election agent, the decision in this case was bound to influence the decision in Mrs Gandhi's case on the expenses issue.

Raj Narain's counsels were very happy with this decision and they felt that now they had a very strong case on the expenses issue. Their joy was, however, shortlived as only a few days later, an Ordinance[2] was promulgated by the Government which amended the law on election expenses retrospectively. This was clearly an attempt to nullify the law laid down in Chawla's case. The amendment added an explanation to Section 77 of the R.P. Act which deals with election expenses. It was now provided that any expenditure incurred or authorized by a political party, friends or supporters of the candidate, or any other person (except the candidate or his election agent) shall not be deemed to be and shall never be deemed to have been expenditure in connection with the candidate's election. This amendment was given retrospective effect so as to apply to all cases which were pending before the courts.

---

[2]An Ordinance is a law which can be passed by the executive when Parliament is not in session. It has to be ratified by Parliament within six months or it lapses. The text of the amendment appears in the Appendix.

It was greeted by howls of protest in Parliament and elsewhere. The timing of the amendment was such that it fooled no one. Almost every one interpreted it as an attempt to interfere with the decision in Mrs Gandhi's case. It was formally enacted into law by the Congress-controlled Parliament on 21 December 1974.

THE SUPREME COURT HEARS THE PRIVILEGE ISSUE

The appeal on the privilege matter came up for hearing in the Supreme Court in January 1975, before a five-member Constitution Bench composed of Chief Justice Ray and Justices Mathew, Untwalia, Sarkaria and Alagiriswamy. It was argued on behalf of the state by the Attorney-General, Niren De, and on behalf of the petitioner by Bhushan. There were two issues involved here:

1. Whether privilege could be claimed even if no affidavit was filed at the time of the presentation of documents by the Minister or Head of the Department concerned.

2. Was such privilege absolute and whether the court could examine the document to see whether they related to matters of State so that their disclosure would injure public interest.

De submitted that the court could not reject the claim of privilege merely on the basis of some technical irregularity, as public interest would be seriously injured by the disclosure of the documents. When he was asked by the Bench as to how the court would know whether the documents really related to matters of State and that their disclosure would injure public interest, De replied that the executive was the best judge of whether certain documents related to matters of State or not. He cited cases from England to show that certain classes of documents, such as Cabinet papers and minutes of Cabinet meetings were privileged *per se*. Even the court could not look into those to determine whether their disclosure would injure public interest.

The claim of the Attorney General was strongly contested by Bhushan, who argued that the State could not be the sole Judge to decide whether the disclosure of certain documents would injure public interest as the State was a prejudiced party in this matter. To support his claim, he cited the decision of the US Supreme Court in the then recently decided case concerning President Nixon's presidential tapes. In that case, too, the US Supreme Court had rejected the claim of privilege of Nixon with regard to his tapes and had allowed the trial judge to hear the tapes to decide whether they should be brought on record or not. As Nixon's case had not been reported till then, a typed copy of the judgment had been hurriedly procured by Raj Narain's counsel from the US. Bhushan, therefore, submitted that it would be open to the court to inspect any documents regarding which privilege could be accepted or rejected by the judgment on the merits of each document.

The judgment in this case was delivered by Chief Justice Ray on behalf of the Bench. Justice Mathew gave a separate though concurring judgment. The Bench allowed the appeal of the State, on the ground that the privilege was not lost merely because of the technical lacuna that an affidavit of the Minister or the head of the Department had not been filed at the first instance. They directed that the High Court should call for an affidavit of the Minister or the Head of Department. If on the basis of the affidavit the Court was satisfied that the documents belonged to a class, the disclosure of which would injure public interest, then the privilege should be upheld. However, if the court was not so satisfied by the affidavit, it could took into the documents itself to determine whether they belonged to the privileged class.

3.

THE PM IN COURT

Recording of the oral evidence on behalf of the respondent started on 12 February 1975. P.N. Haksar, then Deputy Chairman of the Planning Commission, was the first witness to be examined by Khare. He had come to give evidence on the issue of Yashpal Kapoor's resignation. In his examination, he deposed that Kapoor had submitted his letter of resignation on 13 January 1971 and he had accepted the resignation orally at that very time. Thus a new twist was given to the issue of Yashpal Kapoor's resignation. In his cross-examination, Haksar deposed that he had assumed charge of the office of Deputy Chairman of the Planning Commission of India on 4 January 1975 on a verbal order of the Prime Minister. He was asked by the cross-examining Counsel, Bhushan, as to whether Government servants could be appointed by orders given orally. Haksar replied that as far as he was aware temporary Government servants could be appointed orally and that a formal order in writing could follow later. In reply to another question, he said that he was not aware of any rule under which it was permissible to make appointments by word of mouth, but claimed that it was known that every appointing authority could appoint a person and terminate his services orally. As in 1971, Haksar was the Secretary-in-Charge of the Prime Minister's Secretariat, Bhushan asked him whether he was aware of any rule authorizing the Secretary-in-Charge of making appointments to the post of Officer on Special Duty (the post which Kapoor held). Haksar replied that he was not aware of any rule, but he believed that a Secretary in the

Government of India had very wide powers and that he could make appointments of persons to such a post.

The key witness of the respondent was clearly Yashpal Kapoor. His testimony would be of vital importance to the issues about his resignation, the assistance which he provided to Mrs Gandhi during the elections, and also to the issue of election expenses and the way he fared in his cross-examination would be of crucial importance to the final decision. Kapoor was produced in court on 18 February 1975. His examination and cross-examination lasted for about eight hours and went on till the end of the next day. Perhaps it was his being key witness that made Kapoor don an air of swaggering arrogance when he was being cross-examined. The way he paced back and forth in the witness stand with his hands in his pocket was unmistakably a display of arrogance. His face wore a smile of condescending power. He probably thought the proceedings to be of minor importance—for him at least.[1] Kapoor certainly did not fare well in his cross-examination. For, in his anxiety to conceal certain things he made several blunders and revealed himself to be a man of extremely doubtful integrity.

The fact that Kapoor had not put up a good show was clearly perceived even by Mrs Gandhi's lawyers. This was, perhaps, one of the main reasons why it was decided that Mrs Gandhi should herself come to give evidence. For only a few days later, on 26 February a request was made by Khare to Justice Sinha, that a Commission be set up for the recording of her evidence in Delhi, and that the Commission should have the power to disallow questions which it considered irrelevant for the case. Justice Sinha, however, refused this request mainly on the ground that the Commission could not be given the power to disallow questions at its discretion. It was then decided that Mrs Gandhi herself should come to the Allahabad High Court to be a witness in the case. It is a common misconception that Mrs Gandhi was summoned to adduce evidence before the court. The fact is that Mrs Gandhi had decided to appear as a witness of her own will and on the advice of her lawyers. Whether this advice was sound or not is still a matter of debate. In this context it is of interest that a few days before his death, Pandit Kanhaya Lal Mishra, the former Advocate-General of UP,[2] told Bhushan that when he heard that Mrs

---

[1] A detailed summary of the main substance of his evidence appears in Appendix I.

[2] Pt Kanhaya Lal Mishra could have been Mrs Gandhi's senior counsel in this case had it not been for his frail health. In fact he had argued some parts of the case during hearings about preliminary matters.

Gandhi was coming to the witness stand, he had written a letter to her strongly advising her, in the best interest of her case not to appear in court. Needless to say, his advice had been ignored.

The dates fixed by the court for the recording of Mrs Gandhi's evidence were 18, 19 and 20 of March.

Meanwhile there was hectic activity among the lawyers on both sides. Mrs Gandhi's lawyers were busy preparing the questions that they would ask her in order to get on record whatever they thought was useful to them.

The activity was even more intense on the petitioner's side. Raj Narain along with a number of other workers who had worked for him during the Rae Bareli election, went every day to Bhushan's house for lengthy discussions. R.C. Srivastava and the other assisting lawyers, M.C. Gupta and T.C. Porwar, would also be present. Meanwhile word had been sent to the Congress (O) office at Jantar Mantar in New Delhi to try to unearth any documents which could be used in the court to shake the credibility of Mrs Gandhi. (Jantar Mantar had been the central office of the undivided Congress party before the split in 1969. After the legal division of property took place, Jantar Mantar was given to the Congress (O). It housed a vast pile of old documents, letters and other material.)

The people at Jantar Mantar sent a fair amount of documents and papers for Bhushan's examination. Although a number of them were very interesting and revealed curious things about Mrs Gandhi, Bhushan found only one paper that could be used in the court. It was a letter written by the Lieutenant-Governor of Himachal Pradesh, the Raja of Bhadri, to Mrs Gandhi who was then the Congress President.

In the letter the Lieutenant-Governor informed Mrs Gandhi that the Congress candidate had been successful in the Lok Sabha by-election held in Himachal Pradesh. He said that he had thus passed the toughest test that Mrs Gandhi had put him through. This was a devastating letter, as it implied that Mrs Gandhi had asked the Lieutenant-Governer who is supposed to be a neutral observer to help the Congress candidate in the election.

Mrs Gandhi arrived in Allahabad on 17 February. Until then the case had received very little publicity. Although the local newspapers were covering the significant events in the case (like the cross-examination of P.N. Haksar and Yashpal Kapoor) no one gave much importance to the case itself. They regarded it as a futile election etition filed by a poor loser, just to harass the Prime Minister. But cross-examination of Mrs Gandhi, the case exploded into the limelight. It was a big event in itself. Never before had a Prime Minister of the country gone to a court to testify. The former President, V.V. Giri, had however once testified before the Supreme Court in his election petition.

There were massive security arrangements outside the court that day. All the gates were manned by policemen and entry inside the Court premises was restricted to lawyers and litigants accompanied by lawyers. Apart from these, only a few news reporters, *pairokars* (special attorneys who are acquainted with the facts of the case and who can help counsel in some aspects of the case, and pass holders were permitted inside the court premises. Entry inside Court No. 24, where the cross-examination took place was severely restricted (Justice Sinha's court room was Court No. 5, but Court No. 24 was chosen for the cross-examination because it was at one end of the court, and the restriction of entry around it would not hamper the working of other courts).

People had started pouring into the court room from as early as 9.00 A.M. that day. The security staff had installed a metal detector in the passage leading to Court No. 24 where the evidence was to be recorded.

Just before the proceedings in the court were about to begin, a drama took place outside the court. A man carrying a plastic briefcase was apprehended by the security staff at the metal detector. His briefcase allegedly contained a loaded country-made pistol. His name was Govind Misra and he was the editor of a two-page newspaper *Vijay*, published from Allahabad. The exact circumstances in which he was caught are still not clear, but the version of the security men was that he was carrying the pistol in his briefcase, when the metal detector picked it up. When he was interrogated, he revealed that for the past four months, he had always carried a revolver with him, as he feared violence from some enemies. He did not have a licence for his weapon but had applied for one. He was kept in police custody for a few days and later released as he was found to be harmless.

The Govind Misra affair however caused quite a sensation in Parliament. Accusations were hurled across the floor. Many legislators demanded a high-level probe into the matter and urged that the security arrangements for the Prime Minister be further strengthened.

Meanwhile, Court No. 24 was completely packed by the time the judge arrived. Among those people who were present in the court were high ranking Opposition leaders like Madhu Limaye, Shyam Nandan Mishra, Piloo Mody, Jyotirmoy Bosu and Rabi

Ray. They had come all the way from Delhi to witness the cross-examination. They had been cited as *pairokars* by Raj Narain. Among those present were also Mrs Gandhi's son, Rajiv Gandhi, and his wife Sonia Gandhi.

Raj Narain himself was also present in the court. Earlier when he had told Bhushan that he wanted to be present during the cross-examination, Bhushan had objected to it, knowing the volatile temperament of Raj Narain. Bhushan, however, reluctantly agreed to Narain being present when he undertook not to utter a word during the proceedings.

The Judge arrived two minutes before 10 o'clock. Everybody in the court room rose when the Judge came in. After taking his seat, he announced that the court conventions dictate that no one should rise when a witness comes in. This however did not prevent some people from rising when Mrs Gandhi came in.

Mrs Gandhi took a seat which was specially provided for her. The normal practice is that witness stands in the witness box. The deviation from convention was made by Justice Sinha after consultation with Bhushan. Her chair was on a raised platform to the right of the Judge so that she was on level with the Judge. She looked composed and unruffled as she sat down. If she regarded the ordeal before her as something of great significance, she did not give the slightest indication of it. Her appearance was of one who was performing yet another routine task.

Khare was called upon to lead the examination, and he was visibly excited. He was the first person to question the Prime Minister in court. The main issues which could turn on Mrs Gandhi's evidence were (1) whether she held herself out as a candidate prior to 1 February, and (2) whether Yashpal Kapoor actually resigned on 13 January. Khare's questions were mainly focused on these issues.[3] His examination lasted about an hour.

It was now Bhushan's turn. He was inwardly excited, though outwardly calm, when he got up to begin the task before him. It was a big event for him. Apart from the fact that he would be cross-questioning the Prime Minister, with the whole country watching at least through newspapers, he was also fully aware of the far-reaching political consequences of the outcome of this case. This cross-examination could be crucial to the outcome of the case.

Most people who are not familiar with courts visualize a cross-examination as something dramatic where the counsel is supposed to

---

[3] The highlights of Mrs Gandhi's testimony are given in Appendix 2.

give a theatrical display, Perry Mason style. Most cross-examinations are, however, incredibly dull where little happens in the nature of drama.

The cross-examination had not finished when the court rose that day. That evening all the Opposition leaders who had come from Delhi to witness the cross-examination, were invited for tea to Bhushan's house. Opinion there was almost unanimous, that Mrs Gandhi had fared well on the first day of her cross-examination. She had maintained her composure and was convincing in the manner in which she had answered the questions. " Piloo Modi did not enjoy the cross-examination. "Why don't you heckle her? Annoy her a bit!" he told Bhushan. Bhushan smilingly remarked that on the first day he had only given her the bait and made her feel confident. "Tomorrow she will walk into the trap," he said. Little did anyone know that he was indeed serious and was about to spring a surprise.

Pandit Kanhaya Lal Mishra wrote to Mrs Gandhi at the end of the first day's cross-examination, "I hear that today's cross-examination has gone off very well. I am pleased about that. But that still does not alter my opinion that you should not have appeared for the cross-examination." His words were indeed prophetic, and later Mrs Gandhi was to regret not having followed his advice.

Bhushan took only 90 minutes to complete his cross-examination the next day. The tables had indeed turned. The additional written statement containing the decision of the All India Congress Committee about her constituency had caught her off guard. Till the previous day she had been maintaining that she had taken a final decision to contest from Rae Bareli only on 1 February. Her additional written statement said that a final decision regarding her constituency was announced by the AICC on 29 January. When confronted with this statement she said that the statement was drafted in legal language which she had difficulty in understanding. Bhushan did not give her time to recover her composure. Although he had some more questions, he decided to end at this point, not taking the chance of losing his advantage.

The people at large, who were following the cross-examination did not however, catch on to Mrs Gandhi's blunder till the arguments stage, when it was fully exploited by Bhushan. But the more astute observers caught on. The report of the second day's cross-examination was headlined in some of the newspapers as: "Prime Minister did not know of AICC decision about her constituency," and "PM cannot follow legal language."

Mrs Gandhi was the last witness of either side to give evidence.

The stage was now set for the main battle, the final arguments. The arguments were to start on 21 April. Both sides started preparing for them.

Meanwhile some of the documents, mainly the controversial Blue Book were examined by Justice Sinha on 2 April. There were the documents on which privilege had been claimed. The Supreme Court, it will be remembered, had ruled that the Judge could examine them and then either uphold or reject the privilege as he thought fit. The judge accepted the claim of privilege in respect of some documents and rejected the claim in respect of others, which were then exhibited and admitted as evidence.

One further development took place before the arguments started On 16 April, a writ petition was filed in the court by Raj Narain's lawyers, challenging the constitutional validity of the R.P. (Amendment) Act. It was challenged mainly on the ground that it was discriminatory and thus violative of Article 14 in its retrospective effect.

The stage was now set for the arguments. Raj Narain was in jail at this time because of his participation in a civil disobedience movement. This was not a novelty for him as it was his 52nd trip to jail since Independence. He had spent more than half the post-Independence period in jails. He, however, was brought every day to Bhushan's house in police custody, to allow him to brief his Counsel on the case. Being of a religious bent of mind, he gave Bhushan a queer stone to keep in his pocket during the arguments as a good luck charm. Although Bhushan is not superstitious, the stone remained in his pocket during the entire arguments.

2

In the High Court

4

THE PETITIONER'S OPENING ARGUMENTS

Opening his arguments on behalf of the petitioner, Bhushan said that he would first address the court on the issue of Air Force planes.

THE ISSUE OF THE AIR FORCE PLANE

The issue read as follows: "Whether at the instance of Respondent No. 1, members of the armed forces of the Union arranged Air Force Planes and Helicopters for her to be flown by members of the armed forces to enable her to address election meetings on 1.2.71 and 25.2.71 and, if so, whether this constituted a corrupt practice under Section 123(7) of the R.P. Act."

The corrupt practice outlined in Section 123(7) of the Act is the "obtaining or procuring or abetting or attempting to obtain or procure by a candidate or his agent or by any other person (with the consent of the candidate or his election agent) any assistance (other than giving of votes) for the furtherance of the prospects of that candidate's election from any person in the service of the Government and belonging to any of the following classes, namely, (a) Gazetted Officers, (b) Stipendary Magistrates and Judges, (c) Members of the Armed Forces of the Union, (d) Members of the Police Forces, and (e) Excise Officers.

Bhushan said that the facts of this issue were undisputed and it was admitted by the respondent that she flew by an Air Force plane from Delhi to Lucknow on 1 February, from where she went to Rae Bareli by car to file her nomination papers. He submitted that in order to prove the charge of corrupt practice on this issue, he would have to establish two facts: (1) That Mrs Gandhi "obtained" or "procured" the assistance of Air Force personnel, and (2) that this assistance was availed for furthering her election prospects.

Counsel argued that there was no doubt that Mrs Gandhi obtained or procured the assistance of Air Force personnel by asking them to fly her from Delhi to Lucknow in an Air Force plane. He said, "the other side contends that Mrs Gandhi did not solicit the supply of the plane and it was supplied to her under the standing instructions which exist for the Air Force, in respect of travel arrangements for the Prime Minister. These rules were amended in 1968, and Mrs Gandhi was party to the amendment. Previously the rules provided that Air Force planes were to be placed at the Prime Minister's disposal only for official tours, but after the amendment, the planes are to be supplied even for non-official and election purposes. The procedure now is that whenever the tour programme of the Prime Minister is communicated to the Air Froce, it is their duty to place an Air Force plane at her disposal.

"So first she had issued instructions that whenever her tour programme is communicated to the Air Force, they must supply her with an Air Force plane and then she issued her tour programme. This clearly amounts to asking for the plane to be supplied to her. Moreover, even if it can be said that the rules existed from before, they cannot obliterate the responsibility of the candidate to abide by the R.P. Act. An administrative order cannot override a statutory provision about corrupt practices. Moreover, no one could force her to board the plane. The very fact that she boarded the plane knowing that it would be flown by members of the Air Force makes her liable for a corrupt practice."

Moreover, Counsel submitted, *mens rea* (criminal intent) is not essential for a corrupt practice to be proved. "Take the Supreme Court's decision in Y.S. Parmar's case.[1] The court held that the very fact that the polling agent was a member of the Armed Forces was enough to attract a corrupt practice even though the candidate at that time was ignorant of the fact."

Counsel then contended that this assistance rendered by the Air Force did further the election prospects of Mrs Gandhi. He argued, "The other side says that an Air Force plane is provided for the Prime Minister's security. My Lord, there is no limit to the extent of this argument. Even the rostrum and loud-speaker arrangements are said to be for her security. If this can be done for the Prime Minister,

---

IR 1959 SC 244, *YS Parmar* v *Hira Lal Paul*.

The Petitioner's Opening Arguments

then such things can also be done for every Minister, State Minister, Deputy Minister, in fact, for every member of the ruling party. They are also important because they take part in the law-making process. If this were done, the election would become grossly unfair, as the ruling party would enjoy tremendous advantages over the other parties. It is because Government servants cannot ignore the orders of the ruling party that Section 123(7) expressly prohibits the procuring of their assistance. The holders of high offices are already in an advantageous position by virtue of their offices. Why should they be allowed to derive any further advantage on the pretext of security?"

Counsel further submitted that mobility was a very important part of the electioneering of a candidate, and said how some leaders once demanded that this facility must also be provided to Opposition parties on payment but were refused by the Government.

"She cannot escape the charge of corrupt practice here by saying that her flight to Lucknow was not for her election work but for party work. It is true that from Lucknow she flew to other places for party work and also addressed some meetings outside her constituency on her way to Rae Bareli, but the fact remains that her main purpose for stopping at Lucknow was to file her nomination papers at Rae Bareli. No one can deny that the filing of nomination papers is not election work, for without filing the nomination papers, a person cannot even contest the election."

THE ISSUE OF ROSTRUMS AND LOUDSPEAKERS

Bhushan then took up the issue of rostrums and loud-speakers which was framed as follows.

"Whether at the instance of Respondent No. 1 and her election agent, Yashpal Kapoor, the District Magistrate of Rae Bareli, the Superintendent of Police of Rae Bareli and the Home Secretary of U.P., arranged for rostrums, loudspeakers and barricading to be set up, and for members of the Police Forces to be posted in connection with her election tour on 1.2.71 and 25.2.71 and, if so, whether this amounts to a corrupt practice under Section 123(7) of the R.P. Act." Counsel said, "the District Magistrate and the Superintendent of Police of Rae Bareli have deposed that they did arrange for rostrums, loud-speakers and barricading to be set up in connection with Mrs Gandhi's election tour but they did so in pursuance of the instructions contained in the Blue Book. The question here is whether these arrangements amount to assistance for furtherance of prospects of Mrs Gandhi's election and whether this assistance was procured at the instance of Mrs

Gandhi or her election agents. Another question is, can she escape the rigour of Section 123(7) because this assistance was provided because of the Blue Book instructions. Regarding the second question, I submit, that administrative orders cannot by-pass statutory provisions. If it is provided in the statute that certain acts are illegal, they cannot be made legal by any administrative order."

Counsel then turned to the question of whether this assistance was procured at Mrs Gandhi's instance. Here too, the instructions contained in the Blue Book were amended in February 1969 with Mrs Gandhi's consent. Before November 1969, the arrangements were only to be made for the Prime Minister's official or non-official meetings excluding election meetings. The amendment provided that the arrangements would also have to be made for election meetings.

"Blue Book—The Indirect Mean"

Bhushan said, "even if the assistance was not directly procured, it has been indirectly procured through a circuitous procedure of Blue Book instructions. If this sort of thing is permissible, then the whole Government machinery can be used by Ministers for their elections. Moreover, even if the arrangements were made without her instructions, she should have refused to use them knowing that they were arranged by Gazetted Officers of the State Government. She could have asked her party to make arrangements for her rostrums."

Justice Sinha: Suppose she had only asked the people to vote for the Congress in her meetings. Then would it be "her" election meeting?

Counsel: She was the Congress candidate there. Therefore, a vote for the Congress means a vote for her.

Counsel told the court that it was not that the State Government was making these arrangements on its own. He said that, in fact, the State Government had protested against the burden which it had to bear. He displayed a letter from the Chief Minister of U.P. to the Prime Minister, in which he had said that an expenditure of Rs 35.08 lakhs was incurred in less than two months on security arrangements for the Prime Minister's visits. This, the letter said, was an extremely heavy burden for a poor State like U P. which got no benefit from these political tours.

Bhuhan then came to the question of whether these arrangements furthered the prospects of Mrs Gandhi's election. He argued, "The other side contends that these arrangements were for the security of the Prime Minister. Security seems to be their magic word for explaining away all the corrupt practices. I can understand that barricading can be said to be for the Prime Minister's security, but I totally fail to understand how rostrums of particular dimensions are necessary to ensure her security. In fact, the higher the rostrum the less secure she is because it is easier to shoot upwards in a crowded public meeting."

Justice Sinha: Then why is it that the Blue Book says that the rostrum should be of particular dimensions?

Counsel: Because the bigger the rostrum the better is the image of the person projected. All these are image-projecting devices. Moreover, even if by some stretch of imagination, one reaches the conclusion that the rostrum is for security purposes, I submit, is it impossible to conclude that loud-speakers are for security purposes. Whatever do loud-speakers have to do with security?

Counsel argued that if security was the only consideration involved in the instructions about the rostrums and loud-speakers, then there should also have been similar instructions for public meetings of Opposition leaders.

Justice Sinha: This might be because the Prime Minister's election meetings are expected to be the largest.

Counsel: That might be, but it cannot be said that the smallest meeting of the Prime Minister is larger than the largest meeting of a top Opposition leader. After all, security of Opposition leaders is also very important in a democracy.

Khare at this point got up and stated that two truck loads of policemen were provided for the protection of Raj Narain when he went around. Bhushan replied that the police protection was only to deal with law and order. Bhushan showed the court an issue of *Current*, the weekly news magazine, in which it was reported that Bahuguna, then Chief Minister of U.P., had ordered exactly the same arrangements for his public meetings as existed for the Prime Minister. "All this," Counsel said, "was being done to project an image equal to that of the Prime Minister's. There was no question of security involved."

THE ISSUE OF EXPENSES

Bhushan then turned to the issue of election expenses which was "whether respondent No. 1 and her election agent, Mr Yashpal Kapoor incurred or authorized election expenses in excess of the amount prescribed by Section 77 of the R.P. Act."

Section 77 prescribes a limit of Rs 35,000.

Counsel told the court that since he was submitting that a lot of expenditure incurred by the District Congress Committee of Rae Bareli was impliedly authorized by Kapoor, the R.P. (Amendment) Act of 1974 would become relevant. The Amendment added an Explanation to Section 77 of the Act. Explanation was "any expenditure incurred or authorized in connection with the election of a candidate by a political party or any other association or body of persons or by an individual (other than the candidate or his election agent) shall not be deemed to be and shall not ever be deemed to have been expenditure in connection with the election incurred or authorized by the candidate or his election agent." This amendment was given retrospective effect so as to apply to all cases pending before the courts.

Counsel said that before going to the expenses issue he would first challenge the validity of the amendment.

The Supreme Court decided Chawla's case[2] in October, 1974. In that case, the interpretation given to Section 77 of the R.P. Act was, "when a political party sponsoring a candidate incurred expenditure in connection with his election as distinguished from expenditure from general party propaganda and the candidate knowingly takes advantage of it and participates in the activity or fails to disavow the expenditure, or consents to it or acquiesces in it, it would be reasonable to infer, save in exceptional circumstances, that he impliedly authorized a political party to incur such expenditure and he cannot escape the rigour of ceiling by saying that he has not incurred the expenditure but his political party has done so."

Counsel said that the validity of this amendment would have to be decided in the light of the interpretation given to Section 77 in Chawla's case.

INTERPRETATION OF THE AMENDMENT

Bhushan told the court that he would first advance his interpretation of the amendment, and if the interpretation found favour with the Judge, he would have no quarrel with the amendment. He said, "The amendment lays down that if any expenditure was incurred or authorized by a political party or a friend or supporter of a candidate, (without being incurred or authorized by the candidate or his election agent), then it will not be treated as the candidate's expenses. The bracketed words "except the candidate or his election agent"

[2] AIR 1975, SC 308, *K.L. Gupta* v. *A.N. Chawla*.

are of crucial importance here. It seems clear that the intention of the Parliament was only to exclude that expenditure which was incurred or authorized by a political party or any other person but which was not authorized by a candidate or his election agent.

Counsel submitted that a correct interpretation of the amendment would only exclude that expenditure which was both incurred and authorized by a third party, without any hand of the candidate. He argued, "If we accept their interpretation, we would reach the rather absurd conclusion that even if some expenditure was incurred by the candidate himself, it would not have to be included in his return merely because it was authorized by some other person. This makes the provision for a ceiling on election expenses absurd and ridiculous. There would be no difficulty at all in evading the ceiling. All that the candidate would have to do would be to get a letter of authorization from his political party or friend for any expenditure which he wishes to incur in his election, and it would then be excluded from his return. In fact, usually, a candidate does not spend money on his election from his own pocket; it is provided by his political party or friends and supporters. If their interpretation of the amendment is accepted, nobody would ever come within the rigour of the ceiling."

Counsel read out the following passage from Justice Bhagwati's judgment in Chawla's case: "A small man's chance is the essence of Indian democracy and that would be stultified if large contributions from rich and affluent groups are not divorced from the electoral process."

Counsel submitted that this virtual abolition of the ceiling would convert democracy into moneycracy where only moneyed people would have a chance of sitting in Parliament. He argued, "When such drastic and unpleasant consequences flow from the rejection of my interpretation, then I see no reason why my interpretation should not be accepted. I quote the well known principle of law that when two interpretations of statutory provisions are possible, the interpretation which harmonized with the other provisions of the statute should be accepted."

Bhushan told the court that if, however, his interpretation did not find favour with the court, he would challenge the constitutional validity of the amendment. He outlined the four main grounds of his challenge:

1. That it infringed Article 14 of the Constitution by discriminating against the candidate who abided with the law in the election.
2. That it was beyond the power conferred by Article 327 of the

Constitution which only conferred power to make prospective laws relating to elections.

3. That it had the effect of destroying democracy which was the basic feature of the Constitution.

4. That is was a colourable piece of legislation designed solely to secure a particular result in a particular case.

Amplifying his first ground of challenge that the amendment infringed Article 14 (Art. 14 guarantees the fundamental right of equality), Counsel said that since the amendment was given retrospective effect, it did not provide an equal opportunity to all the candidates. "If Mr Narain also knew that the law would be that any expenditure could be incurred by his political party or his friends and supporters, he too could have asked his political party to spend a lot of money for him. He did not do so as he was a law abiding citizen. But Mrs Gandhi did not care about the law. After she has contravened the law, this amendment is passed in her favour. It involves an absurd classification, a classification between law abiding citizens and citizens who have no respect of the law, in which the advantage is given to the latter. Where is the free and fair election? One candidate works under an injunction which restricts him from spending more than Rs 35,000 and the other spends several lakhs and later the law is amended with retrospective effect to legalize this illegality."

Justice Sinha: Have there been other retrospective amendments to the R.P. Act?

Counsel: Not a single one, my Lord. How can we contemplate retrospective changes in the rules of contest in any civilized country.

Counsel then cited a case[3] in which the Maharashtra State Electricity Board had issued an advertisement for the post of an Engineer. There were certain conditions for applicants. The person who was finally selected did not fulfil those conditions but the conditions were later relaxed for him. The Bombay High Court held that the selection was void as it discriminated against other persons who could not apply for that post as they did not fulfil the conditions in the same way as the person selected did. The Judges in that case observed, "When such is the case, it is not permissible for the Appointing Authority to relax or condone any of the conditions to the detriment of equal opportunity being made available to other candidates whose cases for similar condonation or relaxation could not be

[3] AIR 1968, Bombay, 65, *MSEB Engineers* v. *MSEB*.

considered by the selection committee for want of proper advertisement."

Counsel submitted that in the present case too, the rules had been relaxed with retrospective effect to the detriment of Raj Narain.

Coming to his second ground of challenge, Bhushan submitted that the amendment was also unconstitutional on the ground that it was beyond the powers conferred on the Parliament under Article 327 of the Constitution. Article 327 reads thus:

> Subject to the provisions of this Constitution, Parliament may from time to time by law make provisions with respect to all matters relating to or in connection with elections to either House of Parliament or to the House or either House of the Legislature of the State including the preparation of electoral rolls, delimitations of constituencies and all other matters necessary for securing the due constitution of such House or Houses.

Counsel said that Article 327 had been interpreted by the Supreme Court[4] and their Lordships had observed that before an election machinery could be brought into operation, one of the requisites which had to be attended to, was that: "There should be a set of laws and rules making provisions with respect to all matters or in relation to or in connection with elections. . . ."

Counsel argued that according to this interpretation Article 327 contemplates that there should already be a pre-existing law determining the conduct of elections before the election is held. He contended, "Thus their Lordships have held that law making power of Parliament under Article 327 was only prospective. Article 327 does not contemplate any retrospective law relating to elections. Since the amendment is given retrospective effect, I submit that it is void to that extent."

Coming to his third ground of attack on the Amendment, Counsel argued that it was also invalid on the ground that it destroyed democracy which was the basic feature of the Constitution. He said that the Supreme Court in Keshvanand Bharati's case[5] had laid down that there were implied limitations to the Parliament's power of amending the Constitution.

Justice Sinha: Do these limitations also extend to ordinary legislations?

[4] AIR 1952, SC 64, *Ponnuswamy* v. *Returning Officer, Nammakal.*
[5] AIR 1973, SC 1461, *Keshvananda Bharti* v. *State of Kerala.*

Counsel: The constitution amending power is a much bigger power than the power of ordinary legislation. If this limitation applies to the constitution amending power of the Parliament, then it must also apply to the legislative powers of Parliament.

The author here would like to explain that in Keshvanand Bharati's case which was decided in April 1973, the question before the court was whether the constitution amending power of Parliament was plenary, and if not, what were its limits. The arguments in this case had gone on for four months before a Bench consisting of all the thirteen Judges of the Supreme Court. Eleven separate judgments were delivered in this case which rendered the decision fairly ambiguous. Eminent jurists are still in dispute over the details of the majority view. The operative order, however, lays down that although the amending powers of Parliament are wide, they do not extend to damaging or destroying the basic structure or identity of the Constitution. Nine of the thirteen Judges had signed the operative order; four Judges, Justices Ray, Mathew, Dwivedi and Beg had refused to sign it. This case also became controversial due to the fact that it led to the supersession of the three seniormost Judges who had decided in favour of the majority view.

Quoting from the judgment of the majority, Counsel showed that all of them were agreed that Parliament's power could not extend to damaging or destroying democracy.

Counsel argued that even if this amendment was not retrospective, it would still have the effect of destroying democracy in the country. He argued that as this amendment virtually abolished the ceiling on election expenses, it completely negated the small man's chance of being elected to Parliament. He said that in a country like India, where most people were uneducated, money played a tremendous part in the election and unless this money influence was divorced from the election process, democracy would be a distant dream.

Arguing on the retrospective aspect of the amendment, Bhushan submitted that if this power was granted to Parliament, then the party in power could perpetually remain there by manipulating the laws retrospectively. He said, "They could make retrospective laws to validate the invalid elections of members of their party and invalidate the valid elections of members of the Opposition parties. Has anyone ever heard of retrospective laws regarding the conduct of elections? The idea itself is ludicrous."

Justice Sinha: This amendment cannot invalidate a valid election. All that it can do is to validate an invalid election.

Counsel: My Lord, if they can validate an invalid election, what

The Petitioner's Opening Arguments

prevents them from invalidating a valid election? There is no difference in principle between them. The situation is just like a cricket match which is played first and the rules are made later. Not even that, the rules are made by one of the playing teams. If most of the players of that team were bowled and most of the players of the other team were caught, they could retrospectively frame the rule providing that those who have been caught would be out and those who had been bowled would not be out. Thus the team framing the rules could easily ensure the victory of their team.

Counsel then argued that this amendment had been manifestly enacted to save the election of Mrs Gandhi. He said that since it had been enacted with a view to secure a particular result in a particular case, it was a colourable piece of legislation.

Justice Sinha: There are other people who can benefit by this amendment.

Counsel: It has been couched in general terms merely to avoid embarrassment, although it is clearly done with a view to benefit Mrs Gandhi. All the other people who benefit by this amendment would be just subsidiary beneficiaries.

With this, Counsel ended his arguments on the validity of the amendment.

Bhushan then turned to the merits of the issue of expenses. The return of the election expenses filed on behalf of Mrs Gandhi showed that a total expenditure of Rs 12,892.79 had been incurred in her election. The petitioner had alleged that the return did not include lakhs of rupees which were spent on vehicles used by the Congress Committee for Mrs Gandhi's election, rostrums constructed for her by the State Government, loudspeakers installed at her meetings, Air Force planes used by her and payments made to election workers.

Taking up the item of construction of rostrums for eleven meetings addressed by Mrs Gandhi on 1 and 25 February, Bhushan showed a letter from the U.P. Police Headquarters to the UPCC in which it was stated that a total expense of Rs 17,600 was incurred on the rostrums constructed for those public meetings of Mrs Gandhi.

Justice Sinha: The amendment excludes this expenditure.

Counsel: I am submitting that since the expenses were incurred by the State Government, even the amendment does not exclude them. Even if my interpretation of the amendment is rejected and the amendment is not struck down, the expenses incurred by the State Government would still have to be included if they were authorized by the candidate. The amendment only excludes expenditure by a political party, an association, or any other person. A Government is neither a political party nor an association nor any other individual.

Taking up the expense on the Air Force plane, Counsel told the court that the amount actually paid by Mrs Gandhi for her travel in that plane was at the rate of .33p per mile (that was the commercial air fare at that time). He produced a document to show that the chartered rate of these planes was Rs 16 per mile. He said, "There is no reason why she should pay less than this. At the rate of Rs 16 per mile, her fare from Delhi to Lucknow works out to Rs 5,000, which must be added in the return."

THE TWENTY-THREE VEHICLES

Counsel then turned to the crucial issue of expenses incurred on the 23 vehicles used by the District Congress Committee of Rae Bareli during the elections. He contended, "All these vehicles must have been used for the election campaign of Mrs Gandhi and their use was authorized by Yashpal Kapoor. The return of expenses by Mrs Gandhi, however, shows the expenditure on only one jeep which was in the personal use of Mr Kapoor. It is ridiculous that the election campaign of the Prime Minister was carried on with the use of only one jeep. The other side admits that 23 jeeps were used by the District Congress Committee in the three constituencies of that district. They, however, say that since they were used by the District Congress Committee the expenditure on these could not be included in the return."

Counsel showed the court a letter written by Kapoor to the District Magistrate of Rae Bareli. In that letter, Kapoor had requested the District Magistrate to release these vehicles which had been requisitioned because they were to be used for the election of Mrs Gandhi. The respondent had also filed a letter written by the President, District Congress Committee to Kapoor. In the letter, the President had asked Kapoor to write a letter to the District Magistrate requesting the release of the vehicles which were needed for the use of the DCC. During election time, the District Magistrate can requisition, i.e., call for, any vehicle which is registered in that area, for the use of the Government, on payment. If a vehicle has been requisitioned, it can only be derequisitioned, i.e., released, on the request of a candidate or his election agent. He has to state that it is being used in his constituency.

"I do not dispute that the vehicles were used by the DCC but this letter of Mr Kapoor to the District Magistrate amounts to the implied authorization for the use of the vehicles in Mrs Gandhi's constituency. Therefore, the expenses on these vehicles must be included.

Justice Sinha: But how do we know the amount of the expenditure which was incurred on these vehicles?

Counsel: Chawla's case has laid down that if any expenditure is proved to have been evaded [in the return of election expenses], then it is the duty of the court to make a fair and reasonable estimate and add that to the amount shown in the return. It is unfortunate that the two persons who could have thrown much light on the expenditure on these vehicles were not produced in the court by the respondent. They are Mr Gaya Prasad Shukla who was keeping the accounts for Mrs Gandhi and Mr Dal Bahadur Singh, President of the DCC. The testimony of these persons would have been extremely valuable to the court. They were cited as witnesses of the respondent but later withdrawn. I submit that an adverse inference should be drawn against the respondent for this.

Counsel cited Chenna Reddy's case[6] in which the court had drawn an adverse inference against the respondent for the non-production of relevant witnesses. The judges had noted, "Inference can be drawn against a party who does not call evidence which should be available in support of the party."

Making an assessment of the expenditure which would have been incurred on these vehicles, Counsel said that the normal period during which they would have been used would be between 1 February (the date on which Yashpal Kapoor was appointed election agent) and 5 March, (the last date of the campaign) which came to 33 days. He went on, "At a reasonable rate of Rs 4,000 per vehicle, the total expenditure on these 23 vehicles works out to more than Rs 92,000. According to the return of Mrs Gandhi, about Rs 1,100 had been spent on petrol for one vehicle alone between 1 February and 5 March. Even if petrol expenses on other vehicles are estimated at Rs 1,000 each, the cost of petrol alone would be Rs 23,000.

Justice Sinha: But all these vehicles might not have been used in the Prime Minister's constituency.

Counsel: A reasonable estimate would be that 5/7 of these vehicles were used in Mrs Gandhi's constituency and 2/7 in the other constituencies. This is because Rae Bareli District consists of seven Assembly constituencies. Out of these, five are parts of Mrs Gandhi's parliamentary constituency. Therefore, 5/7 of Rae Bareli District was in Mrs Gandhi's constituency. Even if 5/7 of the total expenditure on

640 Election Law Reports, 390, *M. Chenna Reddy* v. *V.R. Rao.*

the vehicles was apportioned for Mrs Gandhi's constituency, it would be much more than Rs 35,000 and the corrupt practice would be proved.

DCC Bank Account

Counsel then produced the bank account of the DCC which was operated by the President of the DCC. According to this account, between 4 March and the end of April, about Rs 1,10,000 had been deposited by cheques mainly from the U.P. Congress Committee. Out of this, Rs 85,000 had been disbursed to various people by the end of April. Counsel contended that most of this expenditure must have been incurred by the DCC on Mrs Gandhi's election.

Justice Sinha: How do we know where this money went?

Counsel: It is not necessary to show exactly how much money was spent and where it was spent. If it can be shown that the expenditure of the campaign was such that at least Rs 35,000 must have been incurred, then the corrupt practice is proved.

Counsel then turned to the question of whether the money spent by the DCC on Mrs Gandhi's election had been authorized by Mr Kapoor. He stated, "These are the circumstances. Mr Kapoor was residing in the guest house of the DCC. All the work of the DCC and of Mr Kapoor was being carried on from the same office. The account of Mrs Gandhi's election were being maintained by Gaya Prasad Shukla who was also an active Congress Party worker. Moreover, it was Dal Bahadur Singh who got Mr Kapoor appointed as Mrs Gandhi's election agent. All these circumstances, I submit, overwhelmingly establish that this expenditure was incurred with the implied authorization of Mr Kapoor."

The Issue of Holding Out

Bhushan then addressed the court on the issue of when Mrs Gandhi became a candidate for the election. The issue was framed as follows : "Whether Respondent No. 1 held herself out as a candidate from any date prior to 1.2.71 and, if so, from what date."

This issue was relevant for the case because the R.P. Act defines a candidate as a person who has been or claims to have been duly nominated as a candidate, and in an election, any such person shall be deemed to have been a candidate from the time when, with the election in prospect, he began to hold himself out as a prospective candidate. Since all corrupt practices are defined in terms of a candi-

The Petitioner's Opening Arguments

date, therefore, the liability of corrupt practices would only be attracted after the person held himself out as a candidate.

Discussing the law on holding out, Counsel told the court that the Supreme Court in a case[7] had laid down what amounted to holding out of a person as a prospective candidate. They have laid down that a person holds himself out when he announces his intention to contest the elections or when by some act he leads people to believe that he would become a candidate in the election.

Bhushan contended that Mrs Gandhi had clearly held herself out as a candidate on 29 December 1970, just two days after the dissolution of Parliament. This, he said, was clear from Mrs Gandhi's reply to a question asked by a reporter in the Press Conference on that date. The reporter had said, "A few hours earlier there was a meeting of the Opposition leaders and they said that the Prime Minister was changing her constituency from Rae Bareli to Gurgaon." Mrs Gandhi had replied with an emphatic "No. I am not." The original tapes of this Press Conference had been obtained from the All India Radio and the Judge had himself heard them. Mrs Gandhi had explained that her statement meant that she would not be contesting from Gurgaon. She said that she did not mean that she would be contesting from Rae Bareli

Counsel claimed that the context in which the question was asked would also throw light on what she could have meant. He said, "This question had been asked in the context that since there was an Opposition Government in U.P. whether Mrs Gandhi would again be contesting from Rae Bareli which was in U.P. She was rightly annoyed with this question and replied indignantly, "No, I am not." This clearly meant that she intended to stick to her old constituency. If she had meant that she was not changing her constituency to Gurgaon than her reply would have been "No, I am not changing my constituency to Gurgaon."

Counsel cited four newspapers of 30 December 1970. They were, *The National Herald*, *The Statesman*, *The Indian Express* and *The Hindustan Times*. They all carried the news of Mrs Gandhi's Press Conference headlined: "Prime Minister not to change her constituency" and "Prime Minister sticks to Rae Bareli," etc.

Bhushan submitted that her reply to the question had given the whole world the impression that she would be contesting the election from Rae Bareli. He read out the depositions of many Opposition leaders who had come to give evidence on behalf of the

---

[7] AIR 1955, SC 775, *Khader Sharif* v. *Munnuswamy*.

petitioner. Among them were S. Nijilingappa (former President of the Congress Party), Karpoori Thakur (former Chief Minister of Bihar), Banarasi Das (former Minister of U.P.), L. K. Advani (President of the Jana Sangh). All of them had understood Mrs Gandhi's reply to mean that she would be contesting the election from Rae Bareli. Counsel charged that Mrs Gandhi's explanation was fabricated by her and could not be accepted by the court.

He then referred to a speech delivered by Mrs Gandhi in Coimbatore on 19 January 1971. In her speech, she had referred to the fact that the Opposition parties had chosen Raj Narain as their joint candidate for Rae Bareli to oppose her, and had lashed out against this choice saying that Raj Narain had been chosen because he was a well-known "Nehru baiter and hater." Counsel argued that this speech of Mrs Gandhi clearly showed that at that time at least she assumed that the people knew that she would be contesting from Rae Bareli.

Strongly contesting the truth of Mrs Gandhi's statement that she did not take any decision on her constituency before 1 February, Counsel also placed the tour programme of Mrs Gandhi for 1 February before the Court. This was for Rae Bareli and was issued on 25 January. On it were hand-written words, "file nomination papers" at 11 A.M. at the Collectorate. In her deposition, Mrs Gandhi had explained that this was only a provisional tour programme, and she could easily have changed her mind before that date and file her nomination paper from some other place.

Since this tour programme was secret and not a public document, Counsel said that he was not contending that this amounted to a holding out by Mrs Gandhi. "But I submit that this completely destroys her case that she did not take a final decision about her constituency before 1 February. I submit that one would have to stretch one's credulity too far to believe that even on 25 January she had not decided to fight the election from Rae Bareli. As far as changing her mind goes, she could change her mind even after filing her nomination paper. If this criterion is applied, then the whole concept of holding out will disappear because it is always possible for a candidate to change his mind and withdraw from the contest before the polling date."

Bhushan now played his trump card on this issue which completely demolished Mrs Gandhi's stand that she took a final decision only on 1 February. He read out a part of her additional written statement made in August 1972 where she had stated, "A final decision in regard to my constituency was announced by the

All India Congress Committee only on 29 January 1971." When confronted by this statement during the cross-examination she said, "The language contained in the additional written statement is legal language which I find difficult to understand."

"What is legal about that language, my Lord," Counsel explained. "It clearly states a plain simple fact that AICC announced a final decision about her constituency on 29 January. This is political language. Can anyone even for a moment believe that the Prime Minister of India is unable to understand this language." Bhushan became grave, and said, "I am extremely sorry to say that she has not been truthful to the court on this point, and henceforth, all her statements should be regarded by the court with utmost caution."

There was a stir in the court. The Prime Minister had been called a liar by a senior lawyer in the crowded court. The Judge listened passively and attentively. He did not say a word.

CREDIBILITY OF MRS GANDHI ASSAILED

Counsel argued that in the face of the mass of evidence adduced by the petitioner to support his contention that she held herself out much before 1 February, the only evidence in rebuttal before the court was Mrs Gandhi's statement. Impeaching the credibility of Mrs Gandhi, Counsel placed before the court a letter written to her in 1959 by the Lieutenant Governor of Himachal Pradesh. Mrs Gandhi at that time was the Congress President. The Governor in his letter informed Mrs Gandhi about the victory of the Congress candidate in a by-election in Himachal Pradesh. He said that he had thus successfully passed "the toughest test" that Mrs Gandhi had put him to. Counsel submitted that this clearly implied that Mrs Gandhi had asked the Lieutenant Governor[8] to somehow help the Congress candidate in winning the by-election. Mrs Gandhi's explanation was that "the test" mentioned in the letter could have been a "law and order" test. Ridiculing this explanation, Counsel said that one would have to really stretch one's imagination to read any suggestion of a "law and order" test in that letter. He charged, "It clearly demonstrates the unscrupulousness of Mrs Gandhi's character. She did not hesitate to procure the assistance of even the Governor of the State for party ends."

---

[8]Governor in India is only the constitutional head of a state Government. He does not belong to any party and is supposed to be politically neutral.

Maruti Land

Counsel then referred to another part of Mrs Gandhi's testimony where she had answered some questions about the Maruti car factory. She was asked whether the Air Force had raised any objection to the acquisition of land for Maruti on the ground that it constituted a security risk to the Explosives Depot at Gurgaon. Mrs Gandhi had replied that she did not know whether it was the Air Force or Parliamentarians who had raised this objection. Counsel said that it was strange that the Prime Minister, who is immediately concerned with the security of the country did not know who had raised the objection, particularly when the factory involved belonged to her own son.

Yet Another Lie

Bhushan then made another interesting revelation. He said that some of the secret documents released by the court on 2 April revealed that on 1 February, Mrs Gandhi did not go to the Circuit House at all before filing her nomination papers. Mrs Gandhi had sworn on oath that she had filed her nomination papers only after talking to Congress workers in the Circuit House. The documents revealed that her original tour programme which included going to the Circuit House before filing her nomination papers was changed at the last minute, and she had gone straight to the Collectorate without first going to the Circuit House.

Counsel submitted that in the light of all these untruths, her statement should not be accepted, and it must be held that she held herself out as a candidate from 29 December 1970.

THE ISSUE OF YASHPAL KAPOOR

Bhushan then turned to the issue of Yashpal Kapoor. It was framed as under: "Whether respondent No. 1 obtained and procured the assistance of Yashpal Kapoor in furtherance of the prospects of her election while he was still a Gazetted Officer in the service of the Government of India. If so, from what date."

Counsel first dealt with Yashpal Kapoor's resignation date. He submitted that the resignation became effective only on 25 January when an order accepting it was passed by the President. The respondent's case was that the resignation was submitted by Kapoor on 13 January and was orally accepted straightaway by P.N.

Haksar, the Principal Secretary of the Prime Minister. The recorded facts were that the resignation was officially accepted by an order dated 25 January. The order, however, said that the resignation was to be accepted with retrospective effect from 14 January.

Counsel first contended that it was not at all clear that the resignation was in fact submitted on 13 January. He said, "Firstly, it is dated 14 January. Why should Mr Kapoor put the date as 14 when he submitted it on the 13th? Mr Kapoor had said that he had post-dated it because of technical difficulties. What sort of technical difficulties can compel him to post-date his letter, I cannot imagine. Mr Haksar also deposed that the resignation was submitted on 13 January. It is, however, strange that Mr Haksar did not make any endorsement on the resignation letter before passing it on to his secretary. Moreover, your Lordship will see that Mr Haksar's testimony is also unreliable. He says that oral appointments and oral resignations take place every day in Government Offices. He says that he himself was appointed by an oral order of the Prime Minister and does not know yet whether there is any written order at all. I submit that it is monstrous to contemplate that work in Government offices can go on in such a fashion."

Counsel went on, "Apart from Mr Haksar, Mrs Gandhi also stated that she remembered the dates of Kapoor's resignation. Remembering the exact date of an event which took place four years ago requires a photographic memory, and it is evident that she does not even have a better than average memory, let alone a photographic memory. She does not even remember any event which took place exactly one month back. When such is the case, how can we rely on her memory about an event which took place four years ago? As far as Mr Kapoor's statement is concerned, I will show your Lordship how completely unreliable his word is."

Bhushan then took up the question of when Kapoor's resignation became effective in law. He stated, "The other side contends that Mr Haksar accepted Mr Kapoor's resignation orally on 13 January itself. Mr Haksar, however, did not know of any rule authorizing him to accept Mr Kapoor's resignation. He assumed that he was competent to accept it. This is something like Alice in Wonderland where each one thinks that he is competent to do things without citing any rule which authorizes him to do them. There is no rule which authorizes one Private Secretary to accept the resignation of another Private Secretary. Mr Haksar was not competent to accept Mr Kapoor's resignation."

"Moreover, even if Mr Haksar was the competent authority to

accept the resignation, it was impossible for him to do so orally. Even the Prime Minister cannot accept a resignation without passing a written order. Counsel further contended that a resignation could not be accepted with retrospective effect. He said, "In this case, the order accepting the resignation is dated 25 January, but it is given retrospective effect so as to apply from 14 January. This would raise the question of whether Mr Kapoor was a Government servant between 14 and 25 January, when his resignation letter was lying on the table and he could still have withdrawn it. I submit that he must be treated as having been a Government servant till the time an order was passed accepting his resignation."

Bhushan then dealt with the question of when Kapoor started working for Mrs Gandhi's election. He divided the issue into two parts: (1) The work done by Kapoor before 14 January, as before that date he was admittedly a Government servant, and (2) the work done by Kapoor between 14 January and 25 January.

Dealing with the work done by Kapoor before 14 January, Counsel told the court that there were two instances of Kapoor's working in Mrs Gandhi's election before this date. "The first instance was when Mr Kapoor accompanied the Railway Minister, Mr Gulzari Lal Nanda, to Munshiganj, near Rae Bareli on 7 January. Mr Kapoor has admitted that he made a speech at that meeting. He, however, said that he had only paid tributes to the martyrs in his speech and denied having said anything about the election of Mrs Gandhi.

Counsel produced an issue of a newspaper of January 1971, in which there was a news item to the effect that both Gulzari Lal Nanda and Kapoor had delivered election speeches for Mrs Gandhi at Munshiganj. Counsel argued that it was extremely improbable that Kapoor had gone with Nanda all the way to Munshiganj merely to pay homage to the martyrs, and that they did not utilize the opportunity to deliver election speeches particularly when elections were in the offing.

The only other evidence of Kapoor having worked for Mrs Gandhi before 14 January was the return of election expenses of Mrs Gandhi. In the return, there are two columns for dates. In one column is entered the date on which the expenditure is actually incurred and in the other, the date on which the expenditure was authorized. It was shown in the return that a voters' list had been purchased on 11 January. The date on which this expenditure was authorized was also shown to be 11 January. Since it was authorized by Kapoor, Counsel said that there was no reason why the court should not give

The Petitioner's Opening Arguments 49

full legal effect to the document and hold it as evidence of Kapoor's work for Mrs Gandhi's election before 14 January. Kapoor had explained that the voter's list was purchased by the District Congress Committee on 11 January for whosoever the Rae Bareli candidate would be. Kapoor had, therefore, included this item in the return later.

Counsel then dealt with the work done by Kapoor between 14 and 25 January. He produced another news item which appeared in the Swatantra Bharat on 22 January. The report said that Kapoor had arrived in Rae Bareli on 14 January with a convoy of 70 jeeps, thus giving a new boost to the election campaign of Mrs Gandhi. The paper also referred to Kapoor as the Chief Election Agent of Mrs Gandhi. Kapoor had denied this report. He had said that when he met Kamlapati Tripathi on 13 January, he was asked to make a general tour of eastern districts of U.P., which was how he had reached Rae Bareli (an eastern district of U.P.) on 14 January. He had no jeeps with him, he had stated.

Ridiculing Kapoor's deposition, Counsel said that it was an extremely strange quirk of fate that Tripathi had asked Kapoor to go to the eastern districts of U.P. and Kapoor going like a nomad chanced to reach Rae Bareli. "There is no reason at all to believe Mr Kapoor's deposition and disbelieve the report of *Swatantra Bharat*. The reporter of *Swatantra Bharat* must have been a remarkably good astrologer to have reported on 22 January itself that Mr Kapoor was the Chief Election Agent of Mrs Gandhi. This means that he must have been doing election work for Mrs Gandhi much before 22 January so as to give the impression that he was her Chief Election Agent."

Counsel further revealed that the return of expenses of Mrs Gandhi also showed that Kapoor paid a salary to the driver of his jeep from 15 January. Kapoor in his deposition had stated that the driver was working for the DCC from 15 January. When asked as to why he had included the salary paid to the driver from 15 January to 1 February in the return of expenses, Kapoor said that he had done so since there was a big margin available. Counsel charged that this also brought out the fact that the expenses shown in the return were cooked up at a later date and did not represent the actual expenses incurred in the election.

The next allegation relating to Kapoor's work was that he addressed several election meetings on the 16, 18 and 19 January along with important Congress leaders. A number of witnesses had deposed before the court that Kapoor had participated in an election meeting addressed by Chandrashekhar, (then a member of the Congress Working Committee) on 17 January. They had also deposed that he addressed further meetings on the 18 and 19 of January. These meetings were also addressed by Prof Sher Singh (Minister of Communications). Kapoor denied his participation in the meetings. He said that he had left Rae Bareli on 17 January and was not even present there on 18 and 19 January.

Counsel charged that the story about Kapoor leaving Rae Bareli on 17 January, and proceeding to Bara Banki and Sultanpur, was totally fabricated. He said, "In fact, earlier the other side had admitted Mr Kapoor's presence in Rae Bareli by suggesting to one of the petitioner's witnesses that Mr Kapoor in his speech on 19 January did not say 'Indira Gandhi *ko jitao*,' but merely said 'Indira Congress *ko jitao*.' Later when the Supreme Court judgment came, asking the High Court to reconsider the date of Mr Kapoor's resignation, the stand of the respondent changed. I find it incredible that Mr Kapoor should leave Rae Bareli and go to the remote districts of Bara Banki and Sultanpur just when important persons like Mr Chandrashekhar and Prof Sher Singh started arriving in Rae Bareli. Mr Kapoor could not even remember where he had spent the nights while at Bara Banki and Sultanpur. I submit that this completely nullifies the credibility of his statement."

Arguing on the reliability of Kapoor's deposition, Counsel said that there were many things which cast a grave doubt on his integrity. Bhushan charged, "His entire deposition is a tissue of lies. He says that he went to Rae Bareli in 1969 merely to cast his vote. It is unbelievable that he was so starved to cast his vote that he went all the way from Delhi to Rae Bareli merely for that."

Analyzing Mr Kapoor's answers about the purchase of a house by his wife in the Golf Links area, Counsel submitted that it was extremely interesting that the wife of a person whose life's savings were only Rs 20,000 wanted to purchase a house which costs more than Rs 4 lakhs. "In the financial position in which Mr Kapoor legitimately should have been, his wife could not have even dreamt of buying that house. He, however, stated that his wife had purchased the house by taking loans of slightly more than Rs 1 lakh each from a bank, her mother and a friend. Mr Kapoor professed that he did not even know the conditions on which the loans were obtained, which is fantastic. As for Kapoor's statement that he has seen this house only once, I wonder whether this is because the house evokes the memory of a shady transaction."

Counsel said that the next question was whether his assistance was "procured" by Mrs Gandhi. He contended that there was enormous circumstantial evidence to prove that Kapoor worked for her election entirely at her instance.

Counsel added, "Earlier too, during the 1967 elections, Mr Kapoor had resigned just before the elections to do election work for Mrs Gandhi. A few months after the elections he was re-appointed by Mrs Gandhi as an Officer on Special Duty. Mr Kapoor stated that he had resigned both in 1967 and 1971 to join public life. It is amusing that Mr Kapoor's appetite for public life is aroused only during election times, and his public life is confined merely to do election work for Mrs Gandhi. All this about his desire for public life is again a cock and bull story. Mr Kapoor admitted that before and after resigning in January 1971, he had several discussions with Mrs Gandhi. In those circumstances, with the election so close, the discussions must have ranged over the prospects of Mrs Gandhi's election. He must have got instructions from Mrs Gandhi regarding the election campaign. The fact that he was ultimately appointed the election agent of Mrs Gandhi also strongly indicates that she must have sent him to Rae Bareli on 14 January."

Counsel further said that the return of expenses filed on behalf of Mrs Gandhi showed Kapoor having authorized expenditure for the election right from 11 January onwards. "Since Mrs Gandhi has also signed the return, therefore, it must be concluded that she authorized him to keep the account right from 11 January. All these circumstances established beyond all reasonable doubt that Mr Kapoor did all this work at Mrs Gandhi's instance."

THE RELIGIOUS SYMBOL ISSUE

Bhushan lastly argued the symbol issue which was framed as follows: "Whether by using the symbol of the cow and calf which had been allotted to the party by the Election Commission, Respondent No. 1 was guilty of making an appeal to a religious symbol and committed a corrupt practice as defined in Section 123(3) of R.P. Act."

Section 123(3) of the R.P. Act provides that "the use of or appeal to National Symbol, such as, the National Flag, or the National Emblem, for the furtherance of the prospects of the election of that candidate or for prejudicially affecting the election of any candidate," would be a corrupt practice.

Counsel said that Mrs Gandhi had admittedly used the cow and calf symbol for her election. The only question was whether the symbol of the cow and calf was a religious symbol. He said that he would overwhelmingly establish this beyond any doubt.

Counsel submitted, "Your Lordship will see that a similar symbol had been asked for by the Akhil Bhartiya Ram Rajya Parishad in the 1952 elections but was refused by the Election Commission on the ground that it was a religious symbol. Further, a report on the First General Elections in India published by the Election Commission says that "no object having any religious or sentimental association, for example, a cow, a temple, a National Flag, a spinning wheel, and the like are found in the list of approved symbols." The Commission specifically mentions the cow as one of the objects having a religious association. The same Commission which had refused to allot the symbol of a cow to the Parishad in 1952 on the ground that it was a religious symbol had now allotted it to the Ruling Congress Party."

Counsel went on, "Just because the symbol has been allotted by the Election Commission, it cannot cease to be a religious symbol. Moreover, your Lordship will see that it has been allotted on the basis of a very suspicious piece of reasoning. The first preference of the Congress Party was "a mother with a child in her arms." The "cow and calf" was their second choice. The Election Commission did not allot the first preference though it was a completely harmless symbol, and allotted the second preference which is clearly a religious symbol. Their professed reason was that since the Congress (O) had been allotted their second preference, they were allotting the second preference to the Congress (R) too."

Counsel argued that just because the symbol had been allotted by the Commission, the party could not abdicate its responsibility. They had themselves asked for the symbol in the first place. So there was no reason why they should not be made to suffer.

Justice Sinha: Suppose the Election Commission allots a religious symbol on its own without the party asking for it.

Counsel: Even then the election would be void. The purpose behind this provision is that if a religious symbol is used by any one, then no matter whose fault it is, the election becomes unfair and it must be set aside. This is similar to the provision in the election law, that if a nomination paper is improperly rejected by the Returning Officer, the election is declared void even though it is no fault of the returned candidate.

Counsel then cited a judgment of the Supreme Court[9] in which it is observed that the cow in India has been raised to a status of divinity. He cited another recent decision of the Supreme Court in which it was

[9] AIR 1958, SC 731, *M.H Qureshi* v. *State of Bihar*.

The Petitioner's Opening Arguments 53

held that the candidate had committed a corrupt practice by proclaiming that a person voting for the Congress would be guilty of *go hatya* (cow slaughter). Placing strong reliance on these cases, Counsel submitted that they alone clinched the issue and proved that the cow was a religious symbol.

He also cited the Encyclopaedia Brittanica on Hinduism. The Brittanica, after explaining the concept of worship in Hindu mythology, says that while many animals are worshipped because of their associations with deities, the cow is "divine in her own right." Counsel submitted that something which was merely associated with a deity might not be a religious symbol, but the symbol of a deity itself must necessarily be a religious symbol.

Bhushan next analyzed the oral evidence which had come in from both sides on this issue. Both sides had examined one *pandit* (priest) each. While the *pandit* examined by the petitioner maintained that the cow was a deity, the respondent's *pandit* denied it. Bhushan humourously remarked, "Your Lordship will have to arbitrate between the two *pandits*, so you become a super *pandit*."

He then read out a few passages from Mahatma Gandhi's book *Go Sewa* (Service to the Cow) in which the Mahatma had said that he considers reverence for the cow one of the fundamental tenets of Hindu religion. Placing strong reliance on this, Counsel contended that if an authority like the Mahatma had said such a thing, there could be no dispute whatsoever about the cow being a religious symbol.

Bhushan ended his arguments on this issue with the plea that in the face of such overwhelming evidence, it was impossible to say that the symbol of "cow and calf" was not a religious symbol.

There were two other issues framed in the petition, one relating to the bribery of voters and the other relating to the conveyance of voters to the polling stations. Bhushan did not press these issues as the evidence on these was very flimsy. He ended his arguments by thanking the Judge for giving him a very patient hearing after arguing continuously for seven and a half days.

5

ATTORNEY GENERAL DEFENDS THE AMENDMENT

While Bhushan was arguing, it was announced that the Attorney-General,[1] Niren De, would appear in the High Court to defend the validity of the amendment of the R.P. Act. The validity of laws made by Parliament is often challenged in various High Courts. The court then serves notice to the Union to defend the law. Usually, the Union is represented by the Standing Counsel, but in this case, the Attorney-General had come in person to argue.

Commencing his arguments on 5 May, the Attorney-General launched a scathing attack on Justice Bhagwati's judgment in Chawla's case. He said, "The issue in Chawla's case was a simple matter of fact. Yet the learned Judges proceeded to lay down the law on election expenses, which they had no business to do. It is quite clear that the learned Judges were laying down their philosophy about elections and how in their opinion their could be electoral reforms in the country. It is easy for the Judges to say that there should be equality between candidates, but is it practical? How can there be equality between two candidates, one of whom earns only Rs 100 a month and another who earns Rs 50,000 a month. Even if the limit on election expenses was brought down to Rs 100, could a starving man afford to spend even that on an election?

"The fundamental fallacy of the learned Judges in Chawla's case was equating democracy with equality. No democracy has perfect equality. Women do not have the right to vote in Switzerland. But can

[1] In India the Attorney-General is the Government's Chief Legal Counsel.

any one say that it is not a democracy? Money still plays a very important role in the elections in the United States. Can it be said that democracy will be destroyed if absolute equality was not ensured among all the candidates?"

The Attorney-General argued that the distinction made in Chawla's case between expenditure on general party propaganda and the expenditure incurred by the party on individual candidates was illusory. "How can one distinguish between them? During elections, all expenditure of a party is impliedly for individual candidates. Does the dictum of Chawla's case mean that for general party propaganda you cannot even enter the constituency of the candidate?"

Justice Sinha: You can enter the constituency, but must speak about general party policies. Suppose a party sponsoring a candidate incurs all the expenses for a candidate, can it then be said that the candidate need not file any return of election expenses?

Counsel: Yes. No return need be filed.

"The Judges in Chawla's case have gone to the extent of saying that the expense on general party propaganda must be limited. If a small man's chance is the essence of the Indian democracy, why not abolish the political party. I wonder whether social, economic and political justice can be achieved by a ceiling on party expenses. That is crying for the moon."

Counsel further contended that money power did not make any difference to the prospects of a candidate in an election. "I fought the election for Parliament in 1951 against a Congress candidate. No one can say that I had less money power than him and yet I lost because of Nehru's posters all over my constituency. Kennedy was elected President of the United States despite the vast money power of the Republican Party against him, simply because women liked his face. Where does money power come into this?"

Counsel then proceeded to cite a number of cases on election expenses which were decided before Chawla's case. He argued that the law laid down in Chawla's case was a clear departure from all previous cases, although the Judges had disputed this in their judgment. "I submit that what the Supreme Court says about earlier cases is not relevant. The High Court will have to interpret the earlier decisions of the Supreme Court in their own way."

The Attorney-General then dealt with the validity of the Amendment. He argued that only two things had to be considered to determine its validity: (1) whether it was within the legislative competence of Parliament, and (2) whether it infringed any fundamental rights mentioned in the Constitution.

He submitted that it was open to the legislature to lay down any legislative policy which could not be questioned by the courts. "Even if the Amendment goes against any decision of the Supreme Court, it will have to be accepted by the courts. Changing the law following a judgment of the court is not disrespect to the court. Chawla's case had created considerable doubt as to what the law was, before the judgment was delivered, so the Amendment was made to clarify the law as it stood before Chawla's case."

Counsel then dealt with Bhushan's arguments that the Amendment was discriminatory because of its retrospective operation. He contended that before the petitioner could claim the protection of Article 14, he must first set up a case to show that the law had discriminated against him. "The petitioner has not done so. He has not even pleaded that he has understood the law to be that laid down in Chawla's case when he contested the election. All the arguments of Bhushan in this regard have been in the air. He has contended that there could be no retrospective laws. I find his contention fantastic."

Bhushan (interjecting): I never contended that the legislature has no authority to enact retrospective laws. All I said was that retrospective laws relating to corrupt practices were not permissible.

De: I thank Bhushan for clarifying his arguments. In any case he has not cited any authority to support his contention. I will cite many authorities to the contrary.

Counsel then cited a case in which the Supreme Court had declared the Cuttuck Municipal Elections invalid due to technical reasons. The Governor had retrospectively validated the elections by an ordinance. The Supreme Court had held this ordinance to be valid.

He also referred to the case cited by Bhushan in which the Bombay High Court struck down an appointment of the State Electricity Board on the ground that the Selection Committee had relaxed the qualifications prescribed in the advertisement. "The point in this case was that the advertisement had prevented others, we would have applied for that post had they known that the advertized qualifications were relaxable, from applying for it. There is no parity between this case and that case. No one had prevented Mr Narain from contesting the elections."

Counsel strongly rebutted Bhushan's contentions that Article 327 only empowered the Parliament to make prospective laws. "The power of the legislature includes power to make prospective as well as retrospective laws. If Parliament can make a law prospectively, it can also do retrospectively."

He also contested Bhushan's contention that this amendment was made to protect a single individual and was thus a colourable piece of legislation. "There is nothing at all in this amendment to suggest that it was done only for Mrs Gandhi's election. It would apply equally to several other cases pending before the courts. However, even assuming that it was done to protect Mrs Gandhi, it does not affect the legislature's powers to pass such a law. The intention of the legislature cannot be questioned."

Counsel finally made his submissions on Bhushan's contention that the amendment destroyed a basic feature of the Constitution. "All that Keshvanand Bharati's case lays down is that basic features of the Constitution cannot be destroyed. It does not say that democracy is a basic feature of the Constitution. The basic features of the Constitution regarding elections are adult suffrage and that no person can be deprived of his right to vote on the ground of race, caste, sex or religion. All other laws about elections are made by Parliament, so they can always change these laws. The corrupt practices are defined by Parliament. If they change the definitions, how can one contend that democracy is destroyed? To say that you can have a better form of Government is not the same as to say that you have altered the basic form of democracy. Suppose Parliament had not fixed any ceiling on election expenses, could one say that there was no democracy in the country? Can anyone say that there was no democracy in India before the decision in Chawla's case?"

The Attorney-General ended with a vigorous plea that the amendment could not be challenged as being destructive of democracy, or on any other vague ground. His arguments ended on the afternoon of 7 May after two and a half days.

6

THE PM's COUNSEL

When the Attorney-General ended his argument, Khare was not present in court, as he had gone home only a few minutes earlier complaining of a headache. J.N. Tewari, his junior, requested the court that the rejoinder of the petitioner on the validity of the amendment be heard before the respondent's reply. Bhushan was willing to accommodate him but the Judge did not agree. He told Tewari that Khare's absence did not matter, and since Tewari was fully acquainted with the case, he could start the arguments.

Tewari: My Lord, I do not have the paper books (records of the evidence) with me at this time.

Bhushan: You can use my paper books.

Tewari grimmaced. He had tried his best to get Bhushan to argue first but his attempts had been thwarted. So with the help of the paper books supplied by Bhushan, he began his arguments on the Air Force Plane issue.

Meanwhile, an SOS was sent to Khare, who forgot his headache and rushed back to court. Tewari had been at his feet for only twenty minutes when Khare came back and took over from him.

Starting dramatically, he said, "Your Lordship will notice that this is not a usual election petition at all."

Justice Sinha: Not at all.

Counsel: This petition has been filed to provide a platform for the leaders of the grand alliance to malign the Prime Minister. It was filed for the same purpose for which Mr Raj Narain was set up as a candidate against the Prime Minister, for mud-slinging. The scheme of propaganda is much the same as that of Goebbles, which was to go on throwing mud so that something might stick. Even the arguments of the petitioner have been directed at throwing as much mud as possible. I am surprised at the irresponsibility with which the petitioner's counsel has argued the case. He has maintained no sense of propriety at all, making wild and unsubstantiated allegations against the Prime Minister.

Counsel charged that all sorts of preposterous, irresponsible and concocted allegations were made in the election petition, most of which were given up during the trial. "Even though some of the allegations were sworn on personal knowledge by Mr Raj Narain, he did not bring himself to the witness box. The court has only to see the array of witnesses examined by the petitioner to reach the conclusion that the petition is frivolous and filed solely for political reasons. Mr Nijlingappa, the President of Congress (O) had come to give evidence in this case all the way from Mysore. All that he had done was to produce a newspaper. He had no personal knowledge of anything connected with the petition. Similarly, Mr Banarasi Das (a Congress[O] Leader), Mr L.K. Advani (President of the Jana Sangh) and some other leaders had come all the way from Delhi for the same purpose."

Counsel charged that all these leaders of the grand alliance were produced only from the point of view of publicity; to create an impression that there was some serious issue involved in the election petition. "Moreover, when the Prime Minister testified before the court, many leaders of the grand alliance, like Mr Jyotirmoy Bosu, Mr Piloo Mody, Mr Rabi Ray and Mr Madhu Limaye, were present as *pairokars* (special attorneys) of the petitioner in the court. This itself shows the frivolousness of the petition."

Counsel further said that this was one case where every adjournment had been sought by the petitioner. This was done so that this platform for political propaganda could continue for as long as possible.

Justice Sinha: Proceedings have been adjourned on the joint request of both parties too.

Bhushan (interjecting): In fact it was they who mostly went to the Supreme Court.

Justice Sinha: You also went to the Supreme Court.

Bhushan: Yes, we went once. They went twice and once on such a frivolous issue that it was given up even before the arguments were completed in the Supreme Court.

Khare told the court that most of the issues originally framed in the petition had been given up by the petitioner during the course of the petition. "Initially, an issue was framed to the effect that

Yashpal Kapoor gave a bribe of Rs 50,000 to Swami Adwaitanand. This was given up by the petitioner's counsel on 16.12.71. Another issue framed was that a large number of quilts, blankets, *dhotis* and liquor were distributed amongst the voters of the constituency. The only evidence produced on this issue was the oral testimony of one witness named Buddu. The Buddu summoned by the petitioner was the son of Rubal. But the Buddu produced in the court was the son of Babu. This only shows how lightly they have treated such a grave issue. For all practical purposes this allegation of bribery was also given up.

"Another issue that some voters were conveyed to the polling stations in vehicles arranged by Mr Kapoor has also been given up for all practical purposes. Yet another allegation in the petition was that the ballot box had been tampered with. A simple inspection was done by Justice Broome and it was found that this allegation was also absolutely false and baseless. So three-fourths of the petition has already been given up and what remains could not be treated with any seriousness either."

Counsel further stated, "The facts of the issues which are left are known to everyone. Nothing was done secretly or clandestinely by the Prime Minister. The fact that she travelled by an Air Force plane on 1 February, 1971 is no secret. All the Prime Ministers in the past 25 years have done so. The election meetings addressed by Mrs Gandhi were no secret either. The symbol of the cow and calf was allotted by the Election Commission openly. Mr Yashpal Kapoor was publicly appointed Election Agent from 1 February 1971. Thus whatever was done was done openly."

Counsel submitted that the arguments raised by the petitioner seemed to suggest that the burden of proof in election petitions was not on the petitioner. He said that the petitioner had tried to show that it was the respondent who had to prove herself innocent of corrupt practices as if allegations based on conjectures were proof of corrupt practices. Khare also charged that a mass of irrelevant evidence had been collected by the petitioner in the hope that something might come out of it. It was an attempt to fish out a floating straw in order to build up a case.

The Validity of the Amendment

Khare first made his submissions on the validity of election law amendment. He said, "The petitioner's contention of the amendment being a colourable piece of legislation is absolutely untenable. Firstly, it does not confer any benefit on the Prime Minister in this case. Even if all the expenses incurred by the party for the Prime Minister were added to her return, the maximum limit would still not be reached. Secondly, the Supreme Court has unambiguously stated in many cases that the courts could not examine the motives of Parliament in enacting a particular law. All that the court can do is to enquire whether Parliament was competent to pass such a law."

He then referred to Bhushan's arguments that the amendment affected a basic feature of the Constitution. He said that this attack could have been sustainable if the validity of a constitutional amendment was at issue. "However, even assuming that the limitation applies equally to ordinary legislation, I submit that it does not affect the basic structure at all. The basic structure of democracy has to be found from the Constitution itself."

Counsel said that according to him the provisions laid down in the Constitution itself about elections established the basic features of democracy. None of these, he said, had been affected by the impugned amendment.

He also rebutted the contention that the Amending Act was discriminatory. He said that all the people who had contested the election in 1971 acted on the assumption that party expenses were not to be included in the candidate's return. "Chawla's case came in 1974 and had altered this position, placing some candidates at a disadvantage. It was because of this that the Parliament had stepped in to clarify the law."

Counsel contended that even Chawla's case did not apply to the present case because here the expenses were incurred for the security arrangements of the Prime Minister. "These were like personal expenses. Suppose a Minister fell ill during his election campaign and medicines worth Rs 40,000 were imported for his treatment. Could this be treated as his election expenses? Take the case of a lady candidate who gets a face lift at the cost of Rs 20,000 during the elections. This increases her appeal to the voter. But can it be said that this expense has to be included in the return? Further, suppose the candidate buys a new suit costing Rs 10,000 for every day of his campaign, would that be an election expense? In England too, personal expenses are not added to the election expenses.

"Retrospective Amendments Earlier Too"

Counsel claimed that there had been many other cases of retrospective changes in election law. He cited the Bihar Legislature (Removal of Disqualification) Act, which read: "Removal of disqualification for membership—a person shall not be and shall be deemed never to have been disqualified for being chosen as for being a member of the Bihar Legislature or the Bihar Legislative Council by reason only of the fact that he holds any of the offices being offices of the profit mentioned in the Schedule."

He also cited similar acts passed by other State legislatures. He said that even the First, Fourth and Twentieth Amendments to the Constitution were given retrospective effect. "If the Constitution can be amended with retrospective effect, why not ordinary laws?"

THE ISSUE OF THE AIR FORCE PLANE

Counsel then took up the issue of the Air Force plane. He said that firstly, Mrs Gandhi did not obtain or procure the services of Air Force personnel, and secondly, it did not further the prospects of her election. Elaborating on his point, he said that obtaining or procuring would mean direct action on the part of the candidate, whereas "Mrs Gandhi was provided an Air Force plane not because she asked for it but because of the standing instructions which were already there for the tours of the Prime Minister. Way back in 1951-52, a high-powered committee recommended this facility for specified VIPs after studying the question carefully. The other side argues that since these instructions were reviewed in 1968 by a committee headed by Mrs Gandhi, therefore, it amounted to her obtaining or procuring the Air Force plane. This argument is fallacious because the 1968 instructions were merely a re-editing of the earlier instructions. Moreover, this was a decision of the Government and not of Mrs Gandhi alone. She was a party to that decision not as a candidate but as the Prime Minister of the country. That decision was taken to ensure the safety of the Prime Minister which is the primary duty of each State."

Counsel argued that the facility of Air Force planes was necessary even for election tours because the Prime Minister continued to function even during the elections. "The other side has argued that if the rival candidates could not use Air Force planes, then why should the Prime Minister be allowed to use them? Consider, my Lord, what would happen if the Prime Minister was going to her constituency in a bullock cart, and suddenly a neighbouring country declared war on our country? How would anybody contact the Prime Minister in such a situation? It is for these peculiar situations that the Prime Minister is provided this facility. The advantage which accrues to the Prime Minister because of this facility is a compromise in accordance with international practice."

Counsel pleaded that the court should give a realistic rather than a literal interpretation of the election law. He said that it was difficult to understand the petitioner's grouse in this regard when chartered planes were available on hire to any one. He gave the examples of Biju Patnaik, the Rajmata of Gwalior and Maharani Gayatri Devi of Jaipur, all of whom used their own planes for electioneering.

Counsel further argued that if any assistance rendered by any Government servant to a candidate was a corrupt practice, then if a person travelled in a railway train during the elections he would also stand disqualified. "He is procuring the services of the railway driver, the station master, the signal inspector, etc., all of whom are Government servants specified within Section 123(7). But this is not a corrupt practice because these are commercial services provided to every person. Similarly, the facility of Air Force planes is also a commercial service created for the Prime Minister. She paid for her flight in the Air Force plane."

Justice Sinha: Would paying for the services of Government servants make any difference? What is prohibited in the R.P. Act is the obtaining and procuring of any assistance.

Counsel: My Lord, this is like a commercial service for the Prime Minister. The special privilege is given to her for security reasons.

Counsel then contended that the Prime Minister's trip from Delhi to Lucknow did not in any way further the prospects of her election. He quoted from the observations made by the Judges of the Allahabad High Court where it was held that if a candidate's car broke down on his way to the railway station and he took a lift in the car of a Government servant, it would not amount to a corrupt practice. Relying strongly on this case, Counsel said that the position here was exactly similar. "The Air Force officers had done nothing more than to carry the Prime Minister from Delhi to Lucknow which was not even in her constituency but only near it."

He further contended that the dominant purpose of Mrs Gandhi's trip to Lucknow was to address election meetings on her way to Rae Bareli. All these meetings were addressed outside her constituency. "Moreover, when she landed at Lucknow on 1 February, she was not even a candidate, because her nomination papers were filled subsequently. So how can it be said that the assistance was obtained by her as a candidate."

THE ISSUE OF ROSTRUMS

Khare next took up the issue of rostrums and loudspeakers. He placed before the court the original Blue Book instructions issued by the Comptroller and Auditor General to various State Governments in 1958. The Blue Book gave instructions to the State Governments regarding security precautions for the Prime Minister's public meetings. The rationale for the security arrangements is also given. It says:

> It is the desire of all these persons who collect, to have an un-interrupted glimpse of the Prime Minister and to hear him, and it is for the State authorities to see that this desire is fulfilled. Unless order is maintained at the meeting place, there will be terrific uproar and people who have walked 20 to 30 miles will return disappointed and criminals will have a field day. For this purpose, therefore the place of meeting is broken up into two segments by setting up barricades, and proper loudspeaker arrangements are made so that every one can hear the Prime Minister's speech. The Prime Minister has to stand on a prominent and raised platform so that he can be seen by the congregation from every angle, and proper police arrangements are to be made at all approaches to the place of meeting.

Counsel also read out the amendment which was made to these instructions in 1969 to which Mrs Gandhi was a party. This amendment, he said, was merely a re-edition of the earlier instructions. The amendment says:

> It has been noticed that the rostrum arrangements were not always properly made because the hosts are sometimes unable to bear the cost. As the security of the Prime Minister is a concern of the State, all arrangements for putting up rostrums, barricades, etc., at the meeting place including that of an election meeting will have to be made by the State Government concerned.

Counsel submitted that it was quite clear from the initial instructions that all these arrangements were security arrangements for the Prime Minister. He argued that since the amendment merely re-edited these instructions, it would be wrong to say that they were issued at the instance of Mrs Gandhi. The original instructions, he said, where issued by the Comptroller and Auditor General, who was an independent constitutional authority just like a High Court Judge.

Counsel then referred to the letter written by T.N. Singh, then Chief Minister of U.P., to the Central Government which said that the costs on the Prime Minister's visits were an extremely heavy financial burden on the State. Khare said that T.N. Singh only wanted a reallocation of the expenditure. He did not dispute the propriety, necessity or advisability of the security arrangements for the Prime Minister.

Arrangements for Opposition Leaders Too

Counsel also claimed that similar arrangements were also made for all Opposition leaders. He said that only three things were done for the Prime Minister: (1) provision of Police officers for law and order, (2) provision of barricades for crowd control, and (3) provision of rostrums for security purposes. What was done for Raj Narain in his meeting? "Everything except for the damn rostrum." Counsel showed a number of documents to prove that Raj Narain directly solicited the help of police and other officers of the Government. "Two full truckloads of policemen were provided for Mr Narain. Some distinction in the quantum of arrangements made for the Prime Minister and Mr Narain is only natural because it is assumed that the Prime Minister will draw larger crowds. If the Government felt that there was need for security of Mr Narain too, they would have also insisted on the construction of rostrums in his meetings."

Counsel submitted that the allegation of corrupt practice here was malicious, politically motivated, and irresponsible. "How could Mr Narain say that what was legal, justified, and democratic for him was illegal, unjustified and undemocratic when it was done for the Prime Minister?"

Counsel next contended that this assistance was not for the furtherance of the prospects of her election. "The first important component of an election meeting is the audience. The Government officials did not collect the audience for her speeches. The second important component is the speaker who gives the speech which was given by the Prime Minister herself. The third component is the decorations which were done by the party. The party even paid one-fourth of the cost of the rostrums. They did not pay the full cost because the rostrums have to be of specified dimensions for security considerations."

Counsel urged that the court should give a realistic interpretation of the statute rather than a literal one. He said that the Prime Minister had to submit to these arrangements made by the State Governments. "It is incumbent on the Prime Minister to obey all the security arrangements made for her. These security arrangements are made wherever the Prime Minister goes. Security arrangements were made when she came to give evidence in this court. There were special arrangements for her inside the court. She was provided with a chair on a raised platform unlike any other witness. Did it further the function of giving evidence in this case?"

Justice Sinha: It did. I could hear her better.

R.C. Srivastava (interjecting): We could see her better.

Counsel ended his submissions on this issue with a plea that this frivolous and malicious charge of corrupt practice be thrown out by the court.

THE ISSUE OF YASHPAL KAPOOR

Khare then dealt with the issue about the date of resignation of Yashpal Kapoor. Referring to the nature of office held by Kapoor, he claimed that the post of Officer on Special Duty was a purely temporary post, and that no rules governing his service conditions existed. He said that three points arose about the date of resignation: (1) Can a resignation be accepted orally? (2) Who was the competent authority to accept the resignation?, and (3) Did Kapoor cease to be a Government servant by not working in his office from the afternoon of 14 January.

He contended that in the absence of statutory provision for the resignation of a Government servant, the resignation could be accepted orally by the competent authority. He cited a number of cases to establish this proposition. He also read out a passage from an American Journal *Corpus Juris Secondum* which says:

> In order to be effective, the resignation must be made with the intention to relinquish office accompanied by the act of relinquishment. In the absence of a constitutional or statutory provision, no particular formalities are required.

Turning to the facts of this case, Counsel submitted that Kapoor tendered his resignation to Haksar on 13 January which was accepted orally by Haksar on the same date. This, he said, was conclusively established by the oral depositions of Haksar, Kapoor and Mrs Gandhi. There was no reason, Counsel said, to doubt the testimony of Haksar on this point, as he was an honourable man who had held important positions and was then the Deputy Chairman of the Planning Commission. "In fact," Khare said, "when Mr Kapoor approached the Prime Minister and told her of his intention to resign, the Prime Minister's consent implied that she herself had accepted the resignation."

Justice Sinha: She did not accept the resignation but only consented to it.

Counsel: By implication it follows that she accepted it.

Justice Sinha: How can it follow by implication? She only permitted him to see Mr Haksar in this connection. How does she know whether he actually went to Mr Haksar or not? Whether he actually tendered his resignation or not?

Counsel: In the first place, she herself asked him to see Mr Haksar and secondly, the following day Mr Haksar told her that he had accepted the resignation.

Justice Sinha: That is exactly the point here. Mrs Gandhi had no personal knowledge about the acceptance of the resignation. She was only briefed by Mr Haksar on this point. Do you mean to say that if Mr Kapoor goes to her and expresses his desire to be relieved, it follows that the resignation stands accepted?

Counsel: Yes.

Justice Sinha: But at that moment the resignation does not even exist. Where is the question of it being accepted, even orally?

Counsel said that the fact that Kapoor had worked for Mrs Gandhi in the 1967 election after resigning from his post would show that he knew that he had to resign before doing any election work for Mrs Gandhi. "There was no reason why he should not have tendered the resignation before starting work for Mrs Gandhi. There is evidence to show that Mr Kapoor did not work in his office after 14 January, as he had only drawn salary up to 13 January. In these circumstances, I submit that the court must accept that the resignation was tendered on 13 January."

On the question of whether Haksar was competent to accept the resignation, Counsel cited the Transaction of Business Rules, 1961. Rule 11 of this reads as follows:

Responsibility of Department's Secretaries: In the Department, the Secretary shall be the administrative head thereof and shall be responsible for the proper transaction of business and the careful observations of these rules in that Department.

This, he said, left no doubt that Haksar as the Principal Secretary was competent to carry on the entire business of the Department which included accepting resignations.

"Moreover, even the notification in the Gazette shows that the President accepted the resignation with effect from 14 January. All these facts cumulatively leave no doubt that Mr Kapoor ceased to be a Government servant on 14 January."

Work done by Yashpal Kapoor

Taking up the issue of Yashpal Kapoor's work for Mrs Gandhi, Counsel said that he would divide it into two parts: (1) work done before 14 January, and (2) work done between 14 January and 25 January.

Dealing with the work done before 14 January, Counsel stated that the only evidence to substantiate the petitioner's claim that Kapoor spoke about Mrs Gandhi's election in Munshiganj on 7 January was the oral evidence of a few witnesses of the petitioner. Seeking to destroy the credibility of the witnesses, Counsel said that all the witnesses had stated that Gulzari Lal Nanda in his speech at Munshiganj had spoken only about Mrs Gandhi's candidature and had not said a word about the martyrs in whose memory the function was organized. "I do not feel shy to admit that even in a function in the memory of martyrs, Mr Nanda might have spoken about politics, but is it not possible that he did not speak a word about the martyrs in whose memory the function was organized." Dealing at length with the oral evidence of the petitioner's witnesses, Counsel claimed that all these witnesses were partisan and could not be relied upon by the court.

Coming to the oral evidence of Kapoor at this point, Counsel said, that there was no reason to disbelieve his testimony. Kapoor had deposed that he had merely paid tributes to martyrs in his speech and not said a word about Mrs Gandhi's candidature. Counsel argued, "On 7 January, the Congress Party had not even taken a preliminary decision about the constituencies of candidates. How could Mr Kapoor say that Mrs Gandhi was contesting the election from Rae Bareli at that time? Why should Mr Kapoor have spoken at that meeting? Nobody has said that Mr Kapoor is a great speaker or a great leader. There are some leaders who are great and some who are merely attendants of great leaders."

Counsel then referred to the other evidence which existed to show that Kapoor had started working in the election even before 14 January. This was the return of election expenses in which it was stated that the purchase of a voters' list had been authorized by Kapoor on 11 January. Kapoor had explained that the list wsa.

purchased by the District Congress Committee of Rae Bareli for the candidate who was ultimately chosen to contest from Rae Bareli. Since this list was later handed over to Kapoor, he had decided to include the expenditure on this in the return of expenses. Khare said that there was no reason to disbelieve Kapoor on this point as he could not have been in Rae Bareli on 11 January.

Coming to the question of whether Kapoor had done any work between 14 and 25 January, Counsel referred to the newspaper report which said that Kapoor had arrived in Rae Bareli on 14 January with a convoy of 70 jeeps to launch the election campaign of Mrs Gandhi. He contended that since the correspondent of the newspaper who had filed this report was not produced before the court, the value of the report became nil, and the other side could not rely on it.

Another piece of evidence relied on by Bhushan was the fact that Kapoor's driver was paid from 15 January. Kapoor had explained that the driver was engaged by the District Congress Committee from 15 January. So when he was provided with the driver and the jeep on 1 February, he had decided to pay him for the period between 15 January and 1 February. Khare claimed that this explanation of Kapoor was extremely logical and reasonable and there was no reason why it should not be accepted by the court.

The next piece of evidence submitted by the petitioner on this issue was the oral deposition of a number of witnesses that Kapoor had delivered election speeches for Mrs Gandhi in the election meetings organized for Chandrashekhar and Prof Sher Singh on 17, 18 and 19 January. Khare argued that the allegation of Kapoor's participation in Prof Sher Singh's meeting on 19 January was made by only one witness, who was a worker of the Opposition parties.

Counsel then referred to the deposition of another witness of the petitioner who had stated that he attended a meeting of Prof Sher Singh on 19 January at which Kapoor also spoke. The witness had produced a printed invitation card which was allegedly distributed for that meeting. Counsel found it strange that the witness had preserved this unimportant card for more than three years. He asserted that no such meeting was held, because Prof Sher Singh, being a Minister, would not go to an unscheduled meeting. He urged that the court disbelieve this witness as he too was an Opposition party worker and had worked as a polling and counting agent for the petitioner.

Counsel further contended that even if Kapoor did deliver speeches as contended by the petitioner, he would still have to prove that they were for Mrs Gandhi's benefit. "The witnesses only say that

Mr Kapoor raised the slogan of *Indira Jitao*. Just as the slogan *Indira Hatao* did not mean the removal of Mrs Gandhi from her office but the removal of her Government, similarly, the slogan *Indira Jitao* merely meant victory for the Congress. This slogan indicates that Mr Kapoor was engaged in general party propaganda and not in furthering the prospects of Mrs Gandhi."

Not with Mrs Gandhi's Consent

Counsel then dealt with the second part of the issue: "whether the services of Mr Kapoor were 'obtained' or 'procured' by Mrs Gandhi." He argued that even if Kapoor worked for Mrs Gandhi's election, it was not with her consent. "Mrs Gandhi had decided to contest from Rae Bareli only on 1 February as I will presently establish. Therefore, the question of her asking Mr Kapoor to do election work for her before that date does not even arise. They want, your Lordship, to infer Mrs Gandhi's consent only through circumstantial evidence. The circumstantial evidence is that Mr Kapoor resigned from her Secretariat on the eve of the 1967 election, and worked in Mrs Gandhi's constituency. He rejoined the Secretariat soon after the elections, and again resigned before the 1971 elections. Does this lead to the unescapable conclusion that Mrs Gandhi must have consented to Mr Kapoor working for her before 1 February?

"Even if Mrs Gandhi reposed the greatest confidence in Mr Kapoor, it was not at all necessary for her to confide in him her decision to contest from Rae Bareli. Confidence is in relation to the work assigned to a person. Your Lordship may have a lot of confidence in your Reader,[1] but that does not mean that he can dictate your judgments. Mrs Gandhi had at least 10 Secretaries who were close to her. That, however, did not make any of them her confidante."

Counsel submitted that even if Kapoor worked for Mrs Gandhi before 1 February, he must have done so on his own. "He has admitted before your Lordship that he was an ambitious man and was looking for a public office. Is it unnatural for him to go out of his way to help Mrs Gandhi on his own so that he may be suitably rewarded later?"

THE ISSUE OF HOLDING OUT

Khare next took up the issue of Mrs Gandhi's holding out as a

---

[1] A Reader is a Court Assistant.

candidate. As a preliminary point, he drew the attention of the Judge to that fact that this issue was not there in the original petition. It was only included later by the Supreme Court. "Though I dare not question the wisdom of the Supreme Court, your Lordship may bear in mind that it is an afterthought."

Khare said that neither of the petitioner's claims of evidence —the Press Conference and the CPB decision—amounted to holding out. "The Opposition parties' sponsoring a joint candidate to oppose her is not holding out. They can shout at the top of their voice, but unless Mrs Gandhi herself declared categorically that she would be contesting from Rae Bareli, she had not held herself out as a candidate." Citing a number of cases to support his contention, Counsel submitted that a case of holding out could only be made out if the candidate made a categorical and unambiguous declaration that he would contest the election from a particular constituency.

He further contended that a person could only hold himself out as a candidate after the election was in prospect. "The election became in prospect only after the presidential notification calling for the elections was issued on 27.1.71. The other side contends that the election came into prospect on 27 December 1970 as soon as the Lok Sabha was dissolved. If the mere fact that the election would be held presently is enough to make the election 'in prospect,' then the next election is 'in prospect' as soon as one election is over, because people know that another election would take place five years later. If this is correct, then a person holds himself out as a prospective candidate when he goes to his constituency to nurse it."

Counsel said that even if the election came into prospect with the dissolution of the Lok Sabha, he would establish that Mrs Gandhi did not hold herself out before 1 February. Khare referred to Mrs Gandhi's statement in her Press Conference on 29 December 1970. The petitioner had produced a number of Opposition leaders who had deposed that they understood her statement to mean that she would contest the election from Rae Bareli. Khare charged that all these political witnesses were summoned merely for political propaganda and their testimony had no relevance to the case. "What they interpreted her statement to mean does not throw any light on what she really meant, which is what is really relevant in the case of holding out. Mr Nijilingappa had come from Mysore but the newspaper copy which he brought with him belonged to the Moti Mahal Library, Lucknow. So, he did not even have the newspaper with him in Mysore. He is a frustrated man having political animosity against Mr Gandhi."

Justice Sinha: Has he not tried to show how he understood the news item about Mrs Gandhi's Press Conference?

Khare: What he understood from the newspaper is not relevant for Mrs Gandhi's holding out. In any case, Mr Nijilingappa is not an expert on the English language. Mrs Gandhi has clarified that she meant that she was not changing her constituency to Gurgaon, and her statement must be accepted.

The next piece of evidence relied upon by the petitioner was Mrs Gandhi's speech in Coimbatore on 19 January, in which she denounced the opposition parties' decision to jointly sponsor Raj Narain from Rae Bareli. Counsel explained that this speech of Mrs Gandhi did not mean that she would be contesting the election from Rae Bareli. She was merely attacking the Opposition for the reasons for which they had chosen Raj Narain to oppose her.

LT. GOVERNOR ACTED ON HIS OWN

Khare then launched a strong rebuttal of Bhushan's argument that Mrs Gandhi had asked the Lt Governor to help the Congress candidate in winning the by-election. Khare argued that there was no evidence to prove it. "Mrs Gandhi was not only the Congress President at that time but also the daughter of the Prime Minister. Therefore, the Lt Governor must have been naturally anxious to please her. So he must have helped the Congress candidate on his own to oblige Mrs Gandhi."

YASHPAL KAPOOR'S INTEGRITY

Khare also defended Kapoor's integrity. Bhushan had referred to the purchase of a house by Kapoor's wife as a shady transaction and had alleged that Kapoor had lied to the court on several occasions. Khare said that he was proud of a man like Kapoor who had started on a monthly salary of Rs 99 and had reached such a height that he could afford a house of Rs 4 lakhs. "If there was anything wrong with the transaction, the income-tax authorities would have examined it."

TOUR PROGRAMME WAS TENTATIVE

Another piece of evidence relied upon by Bhushan was Mrs Gandhi's tour programme for Rae Bareli issued on 25 January, which included the words "file nominatian paper." Counsel argued that this tour programme was a secret communication between the Prime

Minister's Secretariat and the U.P. Government and could not be exploited for a case of holding out. "A person can only hold out by a public announcement. Suppose a man tells his wife or writes a secret letter to his friend saying that he proposes to file his nomination papers from a particular constituency on a given date, does it amount to holding out? It only means that at a later stage he might become a candidate. Mrs Gandhi's tour programme meant that she was going to Rae Bareli to consult her constituency before taking a final decision. The words 'file nomination paper' mentioned in it were only tentative."

Justice Sinha: One way of looking at it is that the Prime Minister secretly decided about contesting from Rae Bareli. This decision was secretly communicated by her Personal Secretary to the U.P. Government, who in turn secretly communicated it to the District Magistrate, the whole chain being engulfed in secrecy. There was no question of holding out. Looking at it from another angle, a rather natural inference can be drawn that the constituency had been previously consulted and a final decision to contest from Rae Bareli was being made known by the tour programme.

Counsel: This is not the natural inference because she had not yet made up her mind to contest from Rae Bareli and there were several offers to her to contest from various parts of the country.

Justice Sinha: What was the last date of nomination?

Counsel: 3 February.

Justice Sinha: For which period was the Prime Minister's tour programme issued?

Counsel: 1 February to 7 February.

Justice Sinha: Assuming that the mention of filing of nomination papers in the tour programme was only tentative, did the tour programme mention any other similar tentative place from where she could file her nomination papers? If she was thinking of contesting from some other place, a separate tentative tour programme should have been issued, or a mention made in the above programme.

Counsel: This programme related to only eastern India and there was no suggestion of her contesting from any other place here. The alternative places were Rajasthan etc.

Justice Sinha: Was there any other tour programme for those places?

Counsel: No.

Justice Sinha: That means she must have made up her mind about contesting from Rae Bareli.

Counsel: Gradually the alternatives were being eliminated. She had practically made up her mind but the decision was not final.

Justice Sinha: You mean to say that if even after reaching Rae Bareli on 1 February, she decided to contest from some other place, she could have reached this new place in time without a previously chalked out programme.

Counsel: Yes. A new programme can be chalked out in a few minutes, and the Prime Minister can be flown in a few hours.

Justice Sinha: In that case, even after a categorical statement, you can still say that there was some reservation.

Counsel: No. A final categorical announcement would amount to holding out.

ADDITIONAL WRITTEN STATEMENT DRAFTED BY GOKHALE AND RAY

Khare then came to the most controversial part of this issue, the Prime Minister's additional written statement in which she had stated that a final decision about her constituency was announced by the AICC only on 29 January 1971. Bhushan had charged that this gave a lie to Mrs Gandhi's statement that she took a final decision only on 1 February.

Khare, however, argued that there was no incongruity between the additional written statement and Mrs Gandhi's oral deposition. "The additional written statement merely says that a final decision in regard to her constituency was announced by the AICC on 29 January. This only means that on 29 January the AICC finally decided to leave the decision about her constituency to the Prime Minister herself."

Justice Sinha: That means the AICC did not take any decision?

Counsel: No, the AICC decided to leave the decision to Mrs Gandhi.

Justice Sinha: Normally, if the Board says that it has finally decided about the constituency, what does it mean?

Counsel: The Board decides either normally or abnormally about the candidate.

Justice Sinha: Let us first confine ourselves to normally, which means that on 29 January the Board finally announced its decision as to who would be the candidate from Rae Bareli.

Counsel: Your Lordship should not try to read what is not written.

Justice Sinha (angrily): I have to decide the petition. I will read it in the normal manner.

Counsel: The verdict given in favour of the returned candidate by a majority of over one lakh votes cannot be set aside merely on the ground that there are some minor contradictions in the statement.

Justice Sinha: Admitted that there was some slip in the additional written statement, but when the respondent came to the court accompanied by a galaxy of lawyers, she could have made the position clear.

Counsel: I was ill when the additional written statement was drafted and it was drafted by Mr Gokhale (the Law Minister) and Mr S.S. Ray (Chief Minister of West Bengal). It is not surprising that a person as busy as the Prime Minister will not be able to exactly remember her written statement filed four years ago. She may not be able to tally her oral evidence with her written statement word by word. But the fact need not be stretched beyond all proportions.

Counsel contended that while evaluating the oral evidence of Mrs Gandhi, the court must remember that the person holding the office of the Prime Minister of this country was unlikely to say anything false.

Justice Sinha: Her evidence will be treated like the evidence of any other person.

Khare argued that the integrity of a person flows from his or her status. He quoted some observations from the Judgment of Supreme Court in V.V. Giri's Election case;[2] the court had said that while evaluating the evidence, the integrity, ability and the status of the witness must be kept in view. Khare contended that when the Prime Minister chose the Chief Ministers of various States and candidates from various constituencies, she must surely have had the choice of her own constituency.

THE ISSUE OF EXPENSES

Turning to the issue of election expenses, Khare contended that since the expenses alleged in the petition were not specific, but merely general allegations on wild conjectures, the court could not estimate or add any expenses to the return filed by the respondent. He cited a number of cases to support his contention. Counsel said that the petitioner had only made wild claims that Rs 2 lakhs were spent on barricading, Rs 1.8 lakhs on some 23 vehicles, etc., but had produced no evidence to prove these expenses.

"Even if we condone the lacuna of non-specific pleadings, it will still be found that most of the expenses alleged were incurred by the

[2] AIR 1970, SC 2097, *Shri Kirpal Singh and others* v. *V.V. Giri.*

State Government. Even Chawla's case does not lay down that expenditure incurred by a Government for a candidate could be included in the candidate's election expenses. Chawla's case only lays down that expenditure incurred by the party or friends and supporters of the candidate has to be included if authorized by the candidate. A Government is neither a party nor a friend and supporter of the candidate. And in this case, the U.P. Government which incurred this expenditure was headed by the Opposition parties, and was thus an enemy of Mrs Gandhi. How could expenditure incurred by an enemy be included in the candidate's election expenses?

"The other expenditure alleged in the petition was incurred by the Congress Party. Even Chawla's case does not specify any limit on the money spent by a party for general party propaganda. No evidence has been led to show that the expenditure of the party was for Mrs Gandhi and not on general party propaganda. With such serious defects in the petition, the charge cannot be upheld even if the amendment was neglected."

Counsel's next submission was that even if expenditure incurred by the Government could be included, the expenditure here was for Mrs Gandhi's security. "This was like expenditure incurred by a candidate on bodyguards. The expenditure on bodyguards who do no election work for a candidate cannot be treated as an election expense. The State Government when it arranged for barricades and rostrums did not participate directly or indirectly in the electioneering of Mrs Gandhi. It had merely acted as a bodyguard. However, even if expenditure on the rostrums is to be treated as Mrs Gandhi's election expense, it would only be one-fourth of the total expenditure. This is because the Blue Book provides that the rostrums have to be of certain specifications due to security considerations. In fact, the security requirements made it mandatory for Mrs Gandhi to address the meetings from those rostrums. She could not ask her political party to provide them. Left to themselves, the political party could have made a suitable dias with hardly any expense."

'Propriety of Kapoor's Action not the Issue'

Coming to the most crucial part of this issue, i.e., expenditure which was allegedly incurred on 23 vehicles used by the DCC, Counsel pointed out that the petitioner had agreed that the vehicles were used by the DCC in three constituencies. The petitioner had contended that since these vehicles were released from the District Magistrate by Kapoor, they must be deemed to have been used in Mrs Gandhi's

The PM's Counsel

election. Counsel placed before the court a letter written by Dal Bahadur Singh, President, DCC, to Yashpal Kapoor. Singh in his letter had asked Kapoor to get the vehicles released since he was unable to locate the candidates of the other two constituencies. This was because during election time requisitioned vehicles could only be released by a candidate or his election agent by stating that they were being used in his election. "At present, the question before the court is not the propriety of Mr Kapoor in getting the vehicles released for other candidates, while under the law he was only permitted to get them released for himself. The real question is whether they were actually used in Mrs Gandhi's constituency. In fact, there is no evidence even to show that these vehicles were hired or even used at all by the DCC. They might have been supplied without payment by friends and sympathizers of the Congress. Moreover, there is no evidence to show the amount of expenditure incurred on them. In such circumstances, I submit that the court cannot estimate and add any expenditure on these vehicles to Mrs Gandhi's election expenses."

Regarding Bhushan's argument that an adverse inference should be drawn against the respondent for the non-production of two relevant witnesses, Dal Bahadur Singh and Daya Prasad Shukla, Khare argued that if they were all that relevant, the petitioner should have summoned them himself. "Initially, Mr Shukla was cited as a petitioner's witness but later given up. How can an adverse inference be drawn in these circumstances?"

THE RELIGIOUS SYMBOL ISSUE

Khare lastly took up the symbol issue. He argued that the petitioner had missed one vital point on this corrupt practice. "He has argued on the assumption that the use of a religious symbol alone was enough to set aside the election. But your Lordship will see that the petitioner must also show that the use of that symbol had materially affected the results of the elections." Counsel was relying on Section 100(c)(2) of the R.P. Act which provides that the election of a returned candidate could be set aside if the High Court was of the opinion that the result of the election had been materially affected by a corrupt practice committed in the interest of the candidate (by an agent other than his election agent). Counsel submitted that the entire arguments of the petitioner were of no avail because of this defect in his pleadings.

He further argued that the symbol had been allotted to the Congress Party by the Election Commision, and Mrs Gandhi being a

Congress candidate had no choice but to use it. "The decision of the Election Commission allotting the symbol cannot be challenged in an election petition. The only way it could have been challenged was by a direct suit filed at the time the symbol was allotted. He cited Rule 10(5) of the Conduct of Election Rules, 1961. It reads: "The allotment by the Returning Officer of any symbol to a candidate shall be final except where it is inconsistent with any directions issued by the Election Commission in this behalf."

Counsel argued that this rule made it clear that the allotment was final except when it was inconsistent with the directions of the Commission. "The question then arises: 'final against whom?' I submit that it is final against everybody. Finality to something is granted in law to avoid litigation. It is the duty of the court to provide a harmonious construction of the law; the construction which would preserve order instead of creating chaos. If this symbol is held to be a religious symbol now, the election of all Congress candidates who had contested the 1971 election would be set aside, causing total chaos."

Counsel then quoted from the report of the Election Commission on the General Elections of 1971 (Lok Sabha) and 1972 (State Assemblies). The Chief Election Commissioner in his report said, "The Cow may be a religious object held in reverence by the Hindus, but it is difficult to accept the view that a cow represents Hindu religion. Hinduism saw God in everything and in that view whatever was used could be regarded as a religious symbol." Counsel argued that the fact that the Election Commission had refused this symbol to the Ram Rajya Parishad in 1951 did not make it a religious symbol. The Commission at that time had mentioned the cow as one of the objects having religious or sentimental appeal. Counsel argued that all that was sanctified or sacred was not religious.

Counsel went on to quote from a mass of religious texts which he had brought with him. He cited the Encyclopaedia of Religion and Ethics by Hastings which lists the religious symbols of Hindus. The cow is not mentioned in it. Counsel also dug out, from a Vedic Scripture the prescription of the sacrifice of a cow as penance for the sin of killing a Brahmin.

Justice Sinha (amidst laughter): Is it also vice-versa?

Dealing with the oral testimony of the *pandits* summoned by both sides, Counsel charged that the petitioner's *pandit*, Raghbar Lal Shastri, had not been fair in maintaining that the cow was regarded as a God. Shri Shastri in his depositions had said that according to Hindu *Shastras* (scriptures), *Namaskar* was offered to a cow because it was a God. Counsel drew the attention of the court to a *mantra* (hymn) of the Vedas to show that the *namaskar* mentioned in it was not only offered to cows but to human-beings and also other animals. Counsel, therefore, contended that it was wrong to interpret the word *namaskar* to mean worship.

Referring to Shri Shastri's depositions that the cow had been called the mother of Rudra (a God), Counsel said that it was just an allegory. "Moreover, motherhood does not bestow Godliness. Kaushalya was the mother of Rama who was regarded as God, but thereupon Kaushalya did not become a Goddess." He also referred to the deposition of the respondent's *pandit*, Pattabhiram Shastri, who had deposed that the cow, although revered by the Hindus was not regarded as a God.

After summing up his arguments, Khare ended thus: "In the end, I appeal to your Lordship not for any favour, but for justice according to law for my client. I also appeal to your Lordship to decide the case like a statesman."

He ended his arguments on 20 May, after arguing continuously for about 34 hours over a period of nine days.

7

THE PETITIONER'S REJOINDER

Opening his arguments in his rejoinder, Bhushan first referred generally to the arguments advanced by Khare and the Attorney General. "During the last 13 days, your Lordship has heard at length the Attorney-General and my learned friend, Mr Khare. I must confess that while both of them have drawn heavily for their submissions on their personal experience of fighting elections, I am under a handicap in this respect. I have not fought any election.

"Mr Khare from his experience was able to enlighten your Lordship about heavy expenses on facelifts and make-up amounting to Rs 20,000. He also told your Lordship about the expenses on Scotch whisky presumably for keeping up the morale of the candidate, and then he mentioned the huge expenditure on several suits so that the candidate could wear a new one at each election meeting.

"The Attorney-General, on the other hand, told your Lordship about his unhappy experience in the general elections of 1951 which he contested as an independent candidate, and in which, despite the use of his money-power which he said was not too little, he lost on account of the attractive posters of Jawaharlal Nehru pasted throughout his constituency. The Attorney-General concluded from his personal experience that money could not play any significant part in the elections. I was, however, wondering as to whether my learned friend would really have used his enormous money-power during the elections. The ceiling on election expenses in 1951 was fairly low, and I am sure that he must have taken good care to keep himself within the prescribed ceiling. In that event, the Congress candidate opposing him could not have suffered any handicap of money-power and with the other advantages available to him as a party candidate, particularly the high image of the Congress in 1951, it is not surprising that the Attorney-General lost.

"Before going into the various points which have been raised by the other side, I would like to refer to certain submissions of a general nature which have been made by them and which appear very startling to me.

"The Attorney-General so strongly commented on the judgment of Justice Bhagwati in Chawla's case that the Delhi newspapers almost gave a full-page headline, 'Attorney-General questions the wisdom of the Supreme Court.' I would, on my part, like to cite the judgment of Justice Bhagwati as a very learned judgment by a great judge. It was indeed my misfortune that I was not able to appreciate the significance of the Attorney-General's criticism of the Supreme Court judgment which is binding under Article 141 on this court.

"What was more astounding was the manner in which the *de jure* leader of the Indian Bar referred to the judgment of the Supreme Court in Keshvananda Bharati's case. He frankly conceded that the majority in that case had laid down an important principle about inviolability of the basic features of the Constitution, but proceeded to tell your Lordship that he was not attaching any importance to that judgment. He did not tell us why. But if his reasons could be surmized, it appears that he treated this decision in a cavalier manner, because three of the Judges who were parties to the majority decision have been superseded by the Government in the matter of appointment to the office of the Chief Justice. If I may say so, with respect to my learned friend, his attitude towards this historic judgment of the Supreme Court was unworthy of the High Office which he holds.

"So long as the decision of the majority continues to be binding under Article 141, what can possibly be the relevance of the Attorney-General's ceasing to attach importance to that decision. One has heard of judgments being marked AFR meaning 'approved for reporting.' Was the Attorney-General trying to evolve a new concept of the Supreme Court judgments being marked 'DAG,' that is to say, 'disapproved by the Attorney-General,' in which event the judgment would cease to be binding on the High Court. Fortunately, no such proviso has yet been added to Article 141.

"My learned friend Mr Khare propounded the doctrine that the credibility of the witness is directly related to his status. If that be so, perhaps the evidence of witnesses should be assessed with the aid of the order of official precedence. I submit that the high office which the witness might be holding is quite irrelevant to the assessment of evidence particularly in a case in which he is a party and has personal stakes. The evidence has to be assessed in the same way as any other witness. On the other hand, it is a matter of common experience that the people of so-called status would sooner resort to false statements as they have much more to lose than a poor man.

"Mr Khare at some stage asked your Lordship to decide the case as a 'statesman' although not as a politician. On my part it would be presumptuous to tell your Lordship how to decide the case, because I know that your Lordship will decide it like a Judge and only as a Judge. Though a rich businessman has the glamour of money and a politician or a statesman has the glamour of office, a Judge is the highest of them all. A great Judge lives in the hearts and minds of men. He lives in their hearts on account of his moral stature and in their minds on account of his intellectual stature.

"Mr Khare also desired that the consequences of the decision should be taken into consideration as well. May I, in this connection, be permitted to draw attention to the speech of William Wilberforce in the House of Commons in 1789. He said, 'Sir, when we think of eternity and of the future consequences of all human conduct, what is there in this life that should make any man contradict the dictates of his conscience, the principles of justice, the laws of religion and of God.'

"A country is great when it worships principles and not men. The glory of justice lies in being based upon principles than on any other trivial considerations."

VALIDITY OF AMENDMENT

Coming to the points raised by the other side in the writ petition, Bhushan said that the whole premise of the respondent's argument was that the amendment only restored the law as it stood declared by the Supreme Court prior to Chawla's case. He contended, "Even if there was any controversy about the legal position prior to Chawla's case, it was only on the question of whether express authority was necessary or whether implied authority by consent, acquiescence, etc., would have the effect of making a candidate liable for the expenditure. The explanation added by the amendment does not deal with the matter of express or implied authority but says that all expenses incurred by a political party or any other person shall not be deemed to be incurred or authorized by the candidate. If my interpretation is rejected, the explanation even provides that all expenditure incurred by the candidate himself, as long as it was authorized by a third person, would not be treated as a candidate's election expenses. I can say with great confidence that not a single court has ever pronounced this to be the law."

Counsel cited the last decision of the Supreme Court prior to the 1971 election to rebut the Attorney-General's theory that the candidate in the 1971 election understood the law to be that which is declared by the amendment. In this case, Justice Shah had observed, "expenditure incurred by a person other than the candidate for election purposes will not be taken into account, (unless incurred by such a third person as the candidate's agent) and when any expenditure is incurred by another person with the express or implied consent of the candidate, the person incurring the expenditure becomes an agent of the candidate." Counsel argued that this case clearly laid down the principles of express or implied authority.

Counsel strongly contested the Attorney-General's contention that money-power did not play any part in the election. He said that this was in direct conflict with the observations of the Supreme Court in Chawla's case. Their Lordships had observed, "It can hardly be disputed that the way in which the elections are held in our country, money is bound to play an important part in the successful prosecution of an election campaign."

Counsel then referred to the Attorney-General's contention that the Legislature normally had the power to legislate prospectively as well as retrospectively. The Attorney-General had cited a number of cases to support this. Counsel said that the cases cited by the Attorney-General in this connection were useless, as none of them dealt with retrospective legislation which created a situation in which one person was discriminated against. "This discrimination was bound to occur in retrospective laws about the rules of contest. Consider the case of retrospective legislation by which a requirement to appear in an interview with ties was introduced after the interview had already been held, and entailed the disqualification of the best candidate on this basis. Could this law be said to be non-discriminatory?"

Counsel wondered whether the Parliament by making retrospective changes in the rules of an election contest thought that the country was like the world of Alice in Wonderland where executions took place first and trials came later. "If we do not want this country to be the Wonderland of Alice, laws will have to come first and elections later."

Counsel further said, "A strange argument has been raised by the Attorney-General, that Mr Narain has neither pleaded nor given evidence to prove that he had not similarly violated the law on election expenses as it originally stood. He has argued that unless it was shown that Mr Narain had not violated the law there could be no case of discrimination against him. The fallacy in the Attorney-General's arguments is his assumption that the person is required to plead or prove that he has not acted contrary to law. The law always presumes that a man is innocent until proved guilty. Consider the following illustration. If a law was made that only those who had been stealing property or indulging in copying in examinations would be granted licences for establishing industries, would it be necessary for the petitioner who was challenging the law as discriminatory, to plead and prove that he had not been stealing property or copying in the examination himself?"

Referring to the other cases of retrospective laws relating to elections cited by Khare, Counsel said that all these related to removal of disqualifications. "In these cases, the elections of some candidates were held invalid because they held some offices of profit and were thus not qualified to contest the election. The Legislature in these cases had retrospectively removed the disqualification of the elected candidates and thus validated their election. The retrospective removal of this disqualification does not discriminate against the opposing candidate. The election was fought under equal laws. Thus, there is no analogy between this and the retrospective change in the laws relating to corrupt practices."

Coming to the argument that the Amending Act was against the basic features of the Constitution, Counsel said that it was a matter of deep regret that the Attorney-General had said that although the majority in Keshavananda Bharati's case had laid down the principle of inviolability of the basic features of the Constitution, they had not laid down that democracy is a basic feature of the Constitution.

Counsel quoted from the judgments of the seven majority Judges in Keshavananda's case to show that all of them had held democracy to be a basic feature of the Constitution. He said, "It does not even require a reading of the judgment to conclude that democracy is a basic feature. If democracy is not a basic feature, then what is?"

Holding a book on the Constitution in his hand, Bhushan said that perhaps the Attorney-General understood that book only and not the principles enshrined in it, to be the Constitution of India. "Perhaps he feels that the basic features of our Constitution are the binding and the printing of this book; and not the principles laid **down in it."**

# The Petitioner's Rejoinder

THE EXPENSES ISSUE

Submitting his rejoinder on the issue of election expenses, Bhushan referred to Khare's contention that the expenditure on Air Force planes was not an election expenditure as it did not further the election prospects of Mrs Gandhi. Bhushan contended that the Supreme Court had interpreted election expenses to mean any expense having to do with the election and which would not have been incurred in the absence of the election. He cited a Supreme Court case in which the money paid by a candidate to his party as application fee for nomination was treated as an election expense of the candidate, although ultimately the candidate did not get a ticket from that party and he fought as an independent candidate. So the money was actually used by that party against his interest, but was still treated as election expenses.

He also referred to Khare's argument that since the petitioner had not been specific about the expenses incurred, they could not be taken into consideration. Counsel cited a number of Supreme Court cases to show that even if specific expenses were not pleaded, they would still be taken into account if no prejudice was caused to the respondent's case.

He then dealt with Khare's argument regarding the expenditure on the 23 vehicles. Khare had argued that the petitioner had not led any evidence to show that these vehicles were used at all. He had argued that they could have been used in other constituencies or only for general party propaganda. Bhushan submitted that the fact that Kapoor obtained the release of those vehicles was evidence enough to hold that they were used for Mrs Gandhi's election. "A vehicle can only be released by a candidate or his election agent if it is used in his constituency. Once we have shown that the expense on these vehicles has been suppressed by the respondent, the burden shifts on them to show that these vehicles were not used in their constituency. Otherwise, the court must estimate the expenditure which should have been incurred on these vehicles and, at best, apportion it equally among the three constituencies."

About the expense on rostrums, Khare had contended that since they were for security, no expenditure on them could be treated as an election expense. Bhushan strongly contested this claim. He said, "The Blue Book says, 'It is the desire of all persons who come, to have an uninterrupted glimpse of the Prime Minister and to hear her, and it is duty of the State authority to see that this desire is fulfilled.' It is clear from the Blue Book that the rostrums have to be of specific dimensions so that the people can have an uninterrupted glimpse of the Prime Minister. There is no question of security involved here. Moreover, even if security is involved, the fact remains that the expenditure was occasioned by the election, and this, not whether it furthered the prospects of the election, is the material point."

Counsel further argued, "A very peculiar argument has been raised by Mr Khare on this issue. He says that Chawla's case lays down that only the expenditure incurred by a political party or friends or supporters of the candidates has to be included. He says that here the rostrums were constructed by the State Government and the State Government being run by the Opposition party was not a friend or supporter but an enemy of the Prime Minister. Suppose the candidate with a gun in his hand, tells his enemy to get petrol filled in his car, then can the candidate claim exemption for this expenditure? The case is exactly the same here. The Central Government at the point of a gun tells the State Government to construct the rostrums for the Prime Minister."

Justice Sinha: Where is the gun?

Counsel: Article 356 of the Constitution is the gun. It is a provision for the failure of constitutional machinery in States. It says, 'If the President on receipt of a report from the Governor of a State or otherwise, is satisfied that a situation has arisen in which the Government of the State cannot be carried on in accordance with the provisions of the Constitution, the President may, by Proclamation, assume to himself all or any of the functions of the Government of the State and all or any of the powers vested in or exercisable by the Governor or any body of authority in the State other than the Legislature of the State."

Counsel argued that if a State Government did not obey the directions of the Blue Book, it could be said that there had been a failure of the constitutional machinery and the State Government could be suspended.

Counsel also disputed Khare's contention that the Prime Minister was bound to deliver speeches from the rostrums constructed for her by the State Government. "There are no statutory provisions that the Prime Minister has to submit to her security arrangements. If she had used other rostrums, she would not contravene any law. Who can force any Minister, let alone the Prime Minister, to submit to any security arrangements."

AIR FORCE PLANES

Giving his rejoinder on the issue of the Air Force Plane, Bhushan strongly refuted Khare's contention that since the Air Force plane was not used in Rae Bareli, therefore, there could be no corrupt practice on this account. "The R. P. Act does not say that the corrupt practice has to be committed in the constituency of a candidate. All that it says is that a corrupt practice must be committed by a candidate for the furtherance of his election prospects.

"Another strange argument raised by Mr Khare is that Air Force planes have been used by Prime Ministers right from the beginning. Can a corrupt practice cease to become so merely because it has been committed from time immemorial? An official taking a bribe cannot justify it on the ground that his predecessor also did so. If this corrupt practice has been committed by all our Prime Ministers, it is time that it was stopped and it can only be stopped if it is held to be a corrupt practice."

Referring to Khare's argument that the facility of Air Force planes was like a commercial service established solely for the Prime Minister, Counsel said that a commercial service should be available to all people. "One cannot say that it is a commercial service and yet make it available to only one person."

DO THEY WANT A COMPROMISE

In his rejoinder on the issue of rostrums, Bhushan said, "It has been contended by the other side that the petitioner is prevented from complaining against the respondent for obtaining assistance from Government officers because he also asked for and obtained the same assistance. I wonder whether the other side wants a compromise, that is, if the respondent is disqualified for the corrupt practice, then the petitioner should also suffer the same disqualification."

Khare was not present in court, so Justice Sinha jokingly asked Khare's junior, Mukerji, whether he was willing to make that compromise. Mukerji immediately protested: "Not at all. Khare never made any suggestion of a compromise. He only pointed out the peculiar stand taken by Mr Narain that although he could commit any corrupt practice, Mrs Gandhi could not."

Referring to Khare's argument that the rostrums were for security purposes and did not in any way further the prospects of Mrs Gandhi's election, Counsel said that another look at the Blue Book would clearly refute this contention. Reading out the relevant passages, he argued that the real purpose of providing a rostrum of specified dimensions was to fulfil the desire of the people to have an uniterrupted glimpse of the Prime Minister and also so that she could be seen from every angle. "My Lord, look at the specious reasoning given in the Blue Book. It says, 'unless order is maintained at the meeting place, there will be a terrific uproar and people who have to come from 20 to 30 miles will return disappointed and criminals will have a field day.' I suppose that the criminals forget their business when they hear the sweet voice of the Prime Minister. I submit that the whole purpose of this arrangement was to make these meetings successful. Since the whole purpose of an election meeting is to further the election prospects of the candidate, these arrangements clearly did so."

Rounding off his submissions on the issue, Bhushan submitted that the decision on this issue would have far-reaching consequences on elections in India. He said that by delivering election speeches from rostrums constructed by the State Government, Mrs Gandhi had not only placed her election in jeopardy but also the elections of her party candidates in whose constituencies she had delivered speeches in the Gujarat elections (which were about to be held). This, Counsel explained, was because the candidates in these constituencies must have consented to Mrs Gandhi making use of these arrangements made by officers of the State Government. "Since a candidate's election is liable to be set aside if a corrupt practice is committed with his consent, the election of all Congress candidates whose constituencies Mrs Gandhi visited in the Gujarat elections could be set aside."

THE ISSUE OF HOLDING OUT

In his rejoinder on the issue of holding out, Bhushan rebutted Khare's contention that the election would be deemed to be in prospect only after the Presidential notification was issued. "Your Lordship will notice that the period for nomination starts as soon as a Notification has been issued by the President. Since nominations are part of the election, it is clear that the election process begins on the date the Presidential Notification is issued. The election has to be in prospect at least some time before this date."

Counsel then cited the meaning of the word "prospect" as given in the Webster Dictionary. It says, "anticipation, foresight, something that is awaited or expected." This, he said, made out quite clearly that the election came into prospect when it was in sight. "When the Houses of Legislatures are dissolved, a fresh House has to be consti-

The Petitioner's Rejoinder

tuted within six months. Thus elections become imminent and are, therefore, in prospect at that time."

Counsel further submitted that a person held himself out as a candidate when by some act or statement, he led people to believe that he would be contesting the coming election. Khare had contended that only a final decision taken by a candidate and communicated to his constituents would amount to holding out. "If he is correct, then any person can start a campaign of character assassination of his rival candidates, bribe all the voters in the constituency, use undue influence, etc.,till the time he gets himself nominated as a candidate. He cannot be held guilty of a corrupt practice till then. Even after filing his nomination papers, he can still say that his nomination is tentative, and he may possibly withdraw before the last date of withdrawal. Thus the whole concept of a prospective candidate would be abolished."

Justice Sinha: Suppose a person commits a corrupt practice before he holds himself out as a candidate, can he be held guilty of a corrupt practice?

Counsel: If the corrupt practice is like a bribery, then the act would itself provide definite proof of holding out. If a person is bribing the people in a constituency to vote for him, then he is clearly announcing his intention to contest the election.

Counsel further submitted that in Khader Sharif's case, a person was deemed to hold himself out as a prospective candidate when he applied for a party's ticket. "The application for a party ticket is certainly not an unconditional declaration by the candidate that he would stand as a candidate."

At this point, Justice Sinha read out a passage from a 1955 Judgment of the Supreme Court. He said that the Supreme Court in that case had ruled that for holding out a candidate must make an unambiguous declaration of his intention to contest.

Bhushan: When I say that I am likely to contest the election, it is a clear and unambiguous but not a definite or firm declaration.

Coming to the facts of this issue, Counsel argued that Mrs Gandhi's reply to a question in the Press Conference clearly amounted to a holding out. "What is really relevent here is what other people, particularly her constituents, understood the statement to mean. From the newspaper reports and the statements of various leaders it is quite clear that everybody understood her statement to mean that she would contest from Rae Bareli. Whether she had any reservations at that time is not material."

Yashpal Kapoor's Resignation

On the question of the date of Kapoor's resignation, Bhushan referred to *Corpus juris Secundum* cited by Khare. In this, it was said that in the absence of a particular mode of resignation provided by any statutory regulation, a resignation could be oral and also implied. Bhushan said that in this case however the position was quite different because of Articles 77 and 166 of the Constitution. "The Constitution itself lays down the specific mode in which the business of the Government has to be conducted and, therefore, excludes any other mode. Appointment of Government servants and termination of their services are all parts of the executive actions of the Government, and have, therefore, to be in writing."

The Religious Symbol Issue

Coming to the symbol issue, Bhushan rebutted Khare's argument that since the petitioner did not object to the symbol at the time when it was allotted, he could not complain now. He said that in Ponnuswamy's case, it has been held by the Supreme Court that once the election process had begun, nobody could go to court to challenge an order of the Election Commission till the election process was over. It could only be challenged by an election petition. "The symbol of a cow and calf was allotted to the Congress Party on 25 January, just two days before the Presidential Notification was issued. In fact, as soon as the symbol was allotted, I received a telegram from Mr C. Rajagopalachari complaining about it, but as the election process had already begun, nothing could be done about it at that time."

Counsel then turned to Khare's argument that the petitioner had failed to fulfil an important requirement on this issue by not giving evidence to the effect that the election result had been materially affected by the allotment of the symbol. Khare had relied on section 101(d) of the R.P. Act which reads: "An election can be declared void if it is found that the result of the election insofar as it concerns the returned candidate has been materially affected by corrupt practices committed in the interest of the returned candidate (by an agent other than the election agent). Mr Bhushan said that this provision was only to cover instances of corrupt practices committed by agents other than the election agent. "But if a corrupt practice was committed by the candidate himself, then the election would clearly become void whether or not the result of the election was materially affected. The allegation here is that the symbol has been used by Mrs Gandhi herself.

"Another very peculiar argument raised by Mr Khare was that the symbol in this case has not been used by Mrs Gandhi but by the Election Commission. He said that since there was no evidence to show that Mrs Gandhi ever displayed that symbol, it cannot be said that she had used it. This is totally fallacious. The very fact that the symbol of the 'cow and calf' was her election symbol proves that she used it."

Counsel referred again to the Supreme Court decision which held that a cow in India has been raised to the status of divinity, and to the Encyclopaedia Britannica which says that the cow is divine in her own origin. He submitted that these facts alone were enough to establish that the symbol of the respondent was a religious symbol.

Bhushan concluded his rejoinder on 22 May after arguing for three and a half days.

DR DWIVEDI'S ARGUMENTS

The last arguments in the case were advanced by Dr R. S. Dwivedi, who was a Sanskrit scholar assisting Bhushan on the symbol issue.

He quoted extensively from Hindu scriptures to show that the cow had always been regarded as a deity in the Hindu religion. He cited Chapter XVIII of the *Mahabharata* to show that it contained *mantras* for worship of the cow. As the cow had been treated as an object of worship, it became a deity and a God, he argued.

Justice Sinha: Do we sell our Gods?

Counsel: It is prohibited by religion. Religious people do not sell their cows. They may give it to a *gaushala* (cow protection home).

Justice Sinha: Still, people sell cows, otherwise how could common people like you and me get cows? Is there any other deity among the Hindus which is treated in the same manner?

Counsel: What about temples?

Justice Sinha: No Hindu has ever desecrated a temple. Let us see the common man's point of view. When we try to find out what a religious symbol is, we must see how a common man thinks. Is this our deity which we sell, starve and treat so shabbily?

Counsel: Still it is respected by everyone.

Justice Sinha: Everything we respect is not treated as a deity.

Counsel then cited a case where an Adivasi candidate had held out the threat of divine displeasure of an Adivasi deity Cock if a voter did not vote on the symbol of the cow. This was held to be a corrupt practice.

Justice Sinha: That was a different case. In this case, if the respondent had said that the voters would invite divine displeasure if they did not vote for the cow, then it would have been different. If we accept a cow to be a deity, then every cow is a deity. Every cow is a God and we must touch the feet of every cow and worship it.

Counsel: There are some persons who do that.

Justice Sinha: What is the percentage of such people?

Counsel: It is difficult to specify the exact percentage, but a substantial number of Hindus do so.

Dr Dwivedi said the problem of the cow being a religious symbol could not be analyzed logically as religion was not logical. He said that religion begins where logic ends and the scriptures as they were religious texts had to be believed even though they were illogical.

Dr Dwivedi ended his arguments on 23 May, which was the last working day in the High Court before it recessed for the summer vacations.

A UNI reporter present there asked the Judge when the judgment would be delivered.

Smiling, Justice Sinha said, "Counsels have quoted many authorities but none on when the judgment will be delivered." More seriously, however, he said that he would try to deliver the judgment during the vacations in June.

8

THE VERDICT

With the conclusion of the arguments, the long wait for the judgentm began. Both sides were equally hopeful of winning the case. hnhusaB believed that he had better than even chances of winning. Khare, on the other hand, ridiculed the idea of the case being decided against his client, the Prime Minister.

Elsewhere too there was a lot of speculation on what the judgment would be. A number of bets were made by enthusiasts of the case and it would be fair to assume that on the date of the judgment a lot of money changed hands. The noticeable fact was the difference in attitude between those who had witnessed the court proceedings and those who had not. Among people who had heard the arguments, odds offered were even. The people who had not heard the arguments, however, were extremely sceptical about the "boldness" of Justice Sinha. The general opinion outside Allahabad High Court was that the Judge would not have enough courage to declare the election void. The fact of the Prime Minister being the respondent over-awed the people, who made their speculations independent of the merits of the case.

Justice Sinha had constantly been taking notes of the arguments. Thus, as soon as the court closed, he was ready to write the judgment. Before beginning to dictate it, he asked his Private Secretary gravely' "I don't want the judgment to leak out to any one, not even to your wife. It is a big responsibility. Can you undertake it?" The Secretary had been with the Judge for a long time and was a trusted man. He swore not to disclose the judgment even to his own wife.

Manoeuvrings behind the Court

The Judge wanted to write his judgment in peace. But as soon as the court closed, he started receiving daily visits from a Congress MP from Allahabad, which annoyed him immensely. He requested the person not to visit him. When he persisted, the Judge had to ask his neighbour, Justice Parekh, to request the MP to stop bothering him. When even this did not succeed, he decided to disappear. He "disappeared" inside his house, not showing his face even in his own verandah. All visitors calling on him were told that he had gone to Ujjain, where his brother resided. He did not receive any phone calls either. So from 28 May till 7 June, no one was able to meet him, not even his closest friends.

Before he went into seclusion, however, the Judge had another distinguished visitor. In the course of their conversation the distinguished visitor mentioned that he had been to Delhi recently and that he had heard Justice Sinha's name being mentioned in high political circles there, for elevation to the Supreme Court. Justice Sinha was shrewd enough to understand the implications. He said that he was too small a man for that big chair.

The judgment was almost completed by 7 June. Around that date, Justice Sinha got a phone call from Dehra Dun. It was the Chief Justice of Allahabad calling. Justice Sinha had to talk to him. The Chief Justice said that the Additional Secretary of the Home Ministry, P.P. Nayar had met him and he wanted the judgment to be postponed till July. This was probably because of Mrs Gandhi's planned visit to Mexico for the International Women's Year Conference. She probably wanted to be in India when the judgment came. Justice Sinha was angry at this request. After telling the Chief Justice that this was not possible, he immediately drove down to the High Court, to order the Registrar to inform the parties and the Press that the judgment would be delivered on 12 June.

The parties were informed. Bhushan was in Bombay when the news reached him. Commenting on the date chosen by the Judge, he said, "It is a singularly appropriate date for the judgment. I think the Judge had chosen this date because of the Gujarat elections. The polling will be over on 11 June; the counting starts on 12 June. So the judgment will come after the polling is completed, and before any result is declared. Whichever way the judgment goes, nobody can now accuse him of influencing the polling or being influenced by the results." This analysis was penetrating. As I found out later, this was indeed the real reason why Justice Sinha had chosen that date.

Bhushan met Morarji Desai on 11 June, the day he returned

from his election tour of Gujarat. Desai asked him what he thought the judgment would be. This was his reply. "Strictly on the merit the case is almost impregnable. However, because of the high stakes involved, any normal judge would be subconsciously affected, so I would say that the chances are 75 per cent in our favour."

Khare was in Srinagar on 9 June. His address was not known. A senior Police Officer of Srinagar was charged with the duty of locating him. He was finally located and summoned to Allahabad. He managed to reach Allahabad in time for the judgment.

Meanwhile, things were warming up in Allahabad. A special task force of the CID was employed to find out the contents of the judgment. They went to the house of Justice Sinha's secretary, Manna Lal, late on the night of 11 June. He was asked to disclose the judgment. He said that he did not know it, (which had an element of truth in it, because the crucial parts of the Judgment were added of the last moment by Justice Sinha). When he stayed mum even after much coaxing, they left with a veiled threat. "We will come back in half an hour. You better tell us the judgment then, if you know what is good for you."

Manna Lal was frightened, and did not waste any time. Packing off his wife to the house of some relatives, he quickly went to seek refuge in Justice Sinha's house. For that night, he was saved. In the morning he went back to his house to get ready. Just before 8.00 A.M., a fleet of cars arrived at his house. The CID was back. With them this time were two of Khare's juniors. They again enquired about the judgment and told Manna Lal that Mrs Gandhi herself was on the hot line. He could tell her the judgment personally. He said that he was getting late and left for Justice Sinha's house.

Manna Lal's harassment did not end there. After the judgment, for many days the CID kept coming to him to find out about Justice Sinha's visitors during June. They also wanted to find out whether the Judge's life style had changed lately. It was indeed strange that the CID should ask such questions as Justice Sinha was known to be a Judge of unimpeachable integrity. But this is not so strange in the light of Khare's outbursts after the judgment, when in fits of rage he stated on occasions that the CIA had spent a lot of money to procure this judgment.

Here one might also wonder whether any attempt was made to presurize Bhushan to drop the case. There was actually one extremely naive attempt to lure him away. It was on 7 May, the day the Attorney-General ended his arguments of the validity of the amendment. B.N. Sapru had thrown a dinner party in his honour. Sapru (now a High Court Judge at Allahabad) was the Government Advocate who was assisting De in this case. He had been Bhushan's class-fellow, so Bhushan was also invited. During the course of the party, the Attorney-General took Bhushan aside and dropped a subtle hint. He told Bhushan that everybody had formed a very high opinion of him when he had argued the privilege issue before the Supreme Court and that a new post like that of an Additional Attorney General could be created for him. The Attorney-General, however, added that his (Bhushan's) invoment in politics came in the way, and he wanted Bhushan to sever his connections with it. (Bhushan was at that time the Treasurer of the All India Congress (O)). Bhushan responded by saying that he attached more importance to any contribution he could make in the political life of the country. The Attorney-General tried to reason with him saying that he did not believe that any such effective contribution was possible or practical. The talk ended there. It is interesting to note that after the Janata Party victory in 1977, the Attorney-General in a congratulatory letter wrote to Bhushan that he now saw his point and agreed that it was possible for right thinking people to contribute to politics.

It was finally 12 June. The High Court compound was swarming with policemen. Justice Sinha's court room was packed by 9.30 A.M. Bhushan was not present as he was in Bombay and did not judge it necessary to go to Allahabad for the judgment. This was a tactical error as he later realized. It is indeed strange how this small error of judgment cost the country such a great deal. Bhushan's juniors in the case, R.C. Srivastava and M.C. Gupta were, however, present in the court. On the other hand, Khare was present with his juniors. The excited and restive crowd in the court room waited for the Judge to arrive.

Justice Sinha was greeted by the glare of flash bulbs as he drove into the court compound at 9.50 A.M. True to his characteristic punctuality, he entered the court room exactly at 10 A.M. Everyone got up for the Judge, who bowed and sat down. A hush fell in the court room. The Judge looked at the crowd and started reading out the operative order. (In the High Court unlike in the Supreme Court, only the operative part of the judgment is read out by the Judge.) He began: "In view of my findings on issue No. 3 and issue No. 1 read with additional issue No. 1, additional issue No. 2 and additional issue No. 3, the petition is allowed and the election of Smt. Indira Nehru Gandhi, respondent No. 1, to the Lok Sabha is declared void." The rest of the order was lost in the roar which reverberated in the court room. The Judge read the rest of the order quickly and left the court room. Nobody heard him. The

The Verdict

crowd was raising loud cheers of "Raj Narain *Ki Jai*," "Shanti Bhushan *Ki Jai*." They had gone beserk with joy. They lifted Ramesh Srivastava and M.C. Gupta on their shoulders and carried them outside the court room and down the corridor in a boisterous mood. Never had such a scene been witnessed in the court.

While there were boisterous cheers in the petitioner's camp, there was despondency and gloom among Mrs Gandhi's lawyers. Khare was dumbstruck. It wase vident that he never expected this judgment. Someone brought him water. Slowly recovering his wits, he proceeded to draft an application for a stay order.

The application was drafted in 15 minutes and at 10.20 A.M. a junior of S.C. Khare, went to Justice Sinha's chamber to present the application. The application listed two grounds for the stay of operation of the order:—(1) That Mrs Gandhi was the leader of the Congress Party and in that capacity working as the Prime Minister; and (2) That unless a leader of the Congress Party is elected and appointed the Prime Minister, the work of the Government will come to a standstill and many complications would arise thereupon. It was, therefore, pleaded that in the interest of justice the operation of the order be stayed.

The Judge looked at the application and asked Khare's junior to call the lawyers of the other side. It was perhaps because of the stakes involved in the case at that time that the junior counsel did something highly unethical which he might not have done in other circumstances. He said that he had already informed the lawyers of the other side. This according to R.C. Srivastava, junior counsel for Raj Narain was an incorrect statement. Raj Narain's lawyers were totally oblivious of the stay application. It was here that Bhushan paid for his absence. Had he been present, he would have been on the lookout for such a move to get a stay order.

The Judge, thinking that Narain's lawyers were not interested, then passed an ex-parte (after hearing only one party) stay order, staying the operation of the judgment unconditionally for 20 days. This was at 10.30 A.M. As soon as Ramesh Srivastava learnt about the stay order, he rushed to the Judge's chamber. He asked Justice Sinha why he was not informed of the stay application. The Judge told him what Khare's junior had said. Srivastava told the Judge that he would be filing an application for the review of the stay order on the ground that it had been procured by professional misconduct by one of Mrs Gandhi's lawyers. Srivastava was told that this review application could only be filed before the Vacation Judge and not before Justice Sinha. So although the review application was filed before the Vacation Judge, it was of no avail as it did not come up for hearing for a few days. After that it was given up by Srivastava.

The judgment of Justice Jag Mohanlal Sinha ran into 258 pages. These are the highlights of the judgment.

Issue of the Air Force Plane

The Judge first dealt with the issue of Air Force planes. Accepting the petitioner's argument that the plane was obtained at the instance of Mrs Gandhi, he said, "Since the tour programme is sent from the Secretariat of Respondent No. 1 after her approval is obtained, and since Respondent No. 1 as Prime Minister knew fully well that thereafter it was the duty of the Air Headquarters to place the plane at her disposal, there is no escape from the conclusion that by sending the tour programme to the Air Headquarters, the respondent No. 1 required an IAF plane being placed at her disposal."

He rejected the respondent's argument that since the aircraft was provided on the basis of the Pillai Committee Report on travel arrangements for VIPs, therefore the use of that could not be held to be a corrupt practice. The judge observed, "The aircraft being manned by the armed forces of the Union, the use thereof under such circumstances can fall within the mischief of Section 123(7) of the Act. Neither the interim Pillai Committee Report nor the Office Memorandum referred to by Respondent No. 1 can under such circumstances salvage the position."

The Judge also rejected the respondents argument that this facility of Air Force planes was like a commercial service established exclusively for the Prime Minister.

He, however, accepted the respondent's argument that the flight from Delhi to Lucknow was part of a general election tour of the country. He said that since the halt at Lucknow was only an incidental halt on an extensive tour of the country, it could not be held that the dominant purpose of her flight was to go to Rae Bareli to file her nomination paper. It is, therefore, on this ground that the Judge acquitted her of a corrupt practice.

The Issue of Rostrums

The Judge then took up the issue of rostrums. He held that the rostrums constructed by officers of the State Government enabled Mrs Gandhi to address her meetings from a dominating position. He observed, "I do not think it was indispensable for the State Government for the maintenance of law and order or security that its officers should have taken upon themselves to get rostrums constructed for the meetings of respondent No. 1 and to make arrangements for the supply of power for the functioning of the loudspeaker at the meetings. Both these things could have been left to be arranged by the political party concerned."

Coming to the question of whether the services of the State Government officers were obtained or procured, the Judge observed, "As already stated earlier the word 'obtained' occurring in Section 123(7) only applied to some effort or initiative on the part of the returned candidate. Since the programme was sent from the office of Respondent No. 1 with her approval and contained an implied direction that the State Government may, *inter alia*, arrange for the construction of rostrums and for loudspeakers for her meetings, the needed initiative had thereby emanated from her."

For these reasons, the Judge held Mrs Gandhi guilty of a corrupt practice on this issue.

THE SYMBOL ISSUE

Taking up the issue of the symbol, the Judge made it clear that in deciding whether the symbol was a religious one or not, he would not take into account the fact that it was refused by the Election Commission to the Ram Rajya Parishad in 1952 or the fact that it was allotted to the Congress party in 1971.

The Judge said that the oral testimony of the *pandits* did not lead to the conclusion that the cow was regarded as a God in Hindu religion. He also did not accept Bhushan's argument that Mahatma Gandhi in his book *Go Seva* (service of the cow) said that the cow was regarded as a God in Hindu religion. He observed, "To my mind that does not mean anything beyond this: that to carry love for the cow is one of the tenets of Hindu religion. That obviously is based on the fact that since a long time the cow has been treated as sacred in Hindu religion. Everything that is sacred does not become God."

He then referred to Encyclopaedia Britannica where in the chapter on Hinduism it is stated, "Many animals, plants and natural objects are sacred in varying degrees, the most noteworthy being the cow. The bull is especially sacred because of his connection with God Shiva, but the cow is divine in her own right and is generally revered as the representative of Mother Earth." The Judge commented that, the sense conveyed is that while bulls and other animals are held sacred because of their association with some God, the cow is sacred without any such association." This he says did not mean that the cow was regarded as God.

The Judge then stated his conclusions on this issue. He said, "whether the cow is a religious symbol should, in fact, be understood in the sense a common man understands it. The common man in our country does not delve deep into the *Vedas*, *Purans* and *Smritis* in order to know the identity and status of a deity in Hindu mythology. No one can deny that cows, like other cattle, are brought and sold all over the world since time immemorial. It also cannot be denied that cows are treated shabbily by an ordinary man.... Again if the cow is a deity, the entire race thereof in this universe should be held deities, which is not very much understandable. The rational view therefore, is that in view of her high utility, the cow is treated with great reverence. It however cannot be equated with God or a deity."

The Judge then committed what was the most serious error in his judgment. He said, "according to *Corpus Juris Secundum* 'symbol' means an object chosen to typify or represent some idea or quality in something else because of a resemblance in one or more of their characteristics or association." He says that according to this meaning of the word 'symbol' the picture of a cow and calf cannot be held to be a symbol of a cow herself.

With great respect it is submitted that if a picture of a cow is not a symbol of it then nothing can be a symbol of a cow.

For these reasons the Judge held that the symbol of a cow and calf was not a religious symbol.

The Expenses Issue

Taking up the issue of expenses, the Judge said that we would first consider the petitioner's case assuming that the Amending Act did not exist and accept the law as laid down in Chawla's case. He added that unless the petitioner showed that the expenses of the respondent exceeded Rs 35,000, on the law declared in Chawla's case there would be no need to go into the validity of the Amending Act.

As regards the expenses on the 23 vehicles used by the District Congress Committee, the Judge observed, "The petitioner has not established that these vehicles were obtained on hire and not been provided free of change by some friends and supporter of the respondent."

He did not accept the petitioner's contention that since Kapoor

The Verdict

had got those vehicles released, they should be deemed to have been used in Mrs Gandhi's constituency. For these reasons, the Judge did not add any expenditure on these vehicles to the respondent's election expenses.

Coming to the expenditure on the construction of rostrums, the Judge agreed that on the basis of law declared in Chawla's case this expenditure could be included in Mrs Gandhi's election expenses. He, therefore, added a sum of Rs 16,000 which was incurred on the rostrums to the election expenses of Mrs Gandhi. He added another sum of Rs 800 for loudspeakers and Rs 1151 for the electricity for the loudspeakers. He did not add the expenses on the Air Force plane on which Mrs Gandhi travelled from Delhi to Lucknow. It was part of a general election tour of the country, and, therefore, did not further her election prospects.

The Judge further held that the telephone expenses alleged by the petitioner also could not be added as they were not pleaded in the petition.

Lastly, the Judge added an amount of Rs 232.50 as cost of motor transport from Lucknow to Rae Bareli. According to the return of election expenses of respondent No. 1, an amount of Rs 12,892.97 was incurred over her election expenses. Adding the aforesaid amount of Rs 18,183.50 to this figure, the total comes to Rs 31,076.47, sufficiently below the prescribed limit of Rs 35,000.

For this reason he held her not guilty of corrupt practice on this issue too.

The Judge did not find it necessary to go into the validity of the election Law Amendment as the validity of that would not have affected his findings on this Issue.

THE ISSUE OF HOLDING OUT

The Judge then dealt with the issue of the date from which Mrs Gandhi held herself out as a candidate. Observing that the tour programme of Mrs Gandhi for February 1 was issued on 25 January with her approval, and that it contained the words "file nomination papers," the Judge said that "there appears to be no escape from the conclusion that respondent No. 1 held herself out as a candidate from Rae Bareli at least some time before 25 January 1971."

Office Not Relevant

On the question of Mrs Gandhi's credibility as a witness, the Judge did not agree with Khare's suggestion that while assessing the veracity of the evidence of Mrs Gandhi, the fact of the high office held by her should be taken into account. He observed, "it should be conceded that when a person appears in court as a witness and his evidence appears to be natural and probable, the status and respectability attached to him is also taken into consideration to lend further assurance to his testimony. The status and respectability of the witness alone cannot however induce the court to accept his testimony, more so when he is himself a party to the proceedings and interested in the result of the case. In such cases, the evidence of that person has to be assessed without in any manner being obsessed by the high office which he may hold."

Mrs Gandhi's Statements Inconsistent

The Judge noted that Mrs Gandhi's stand during her oral deposition that she only decided to contest the election from Rae Bareli on 1 February was inconsistent with her earlier written statement filed in 1972. Mrs Gandhi had explained the inconsistency by saying that her written statement was drafted in legal language which she found difficult to understand. The Judge observed, "the statement made by Mrs Gandhi to explain the inconsistency failed to satisfactorily explain the same."

Justice Sinha rejected outright the respondent's argument that the final decision of the All-India Congress Committee mentioned in the written statement was to leave the choice of her constituency to Mrs Gandhi herself.

Regarding Mrs Gandhi's Press Conference of 29 December in which in reply to the question whether she was changing her constituency from Rae Bareli to Gurgaon, she said, "No I am not," the Judge observed: "The answer given by respondent No. 1, to my mind does not mean anything except that she was not changing her contituency and that she would contest the election from Rae Bareli."

Justice Sinha also did not agree with the respondent's contention that the election was in prospect only after the Presidential Notification calling for the election was issued on 27 January. He held that the election became in prospect on 27 December 1970, with the dissolution of the Lok Sabha.

In view of all this, the Judge concluded that Mrs Gandhi had held herself out as a prospective candidate from 29 December 1970.

Yashpal Kapoor

On the question of Kapoor's resignation, Justice Sinha found

Haksar's claim fantastic that the resignation of a Government servant could be accepted by word of mouth alone. He said,"The appointment of persons in Government offices, more so to gazetted posts, as well as termination of their services, is now governed by statutory rules, and the appointing authority has to act under those rules. It is the implied intention of the rules that there should be an order in writing terminating his services." He also noted that the plea of oral acceptance of resignation was for the first time set up in the additional written statement which was filed a year after the original written statement. He said that, it, therefore, was an afterthought. He further said, "It is true that according to the Gazette Notification, the resignation of Shri Yashpal Kapoor has been accepted with effect from 14 January 1971. It cannot, however, be ignored that the order accepting the resignation was passed on 25 January 1971. Till that order was passed the status of Yashpal Kapoor continued to remain that of a Government servant despite the fact that the order was given retrospective effect so as to be valid from 14 January 1971."

The Judge therefore held that Kapoor's resignation became effective only from 25 January 1971.

Justice Sinha then took up the aspect of Mrs Gandhi's obtaining the assistance of Kapoor for the furtherance of her election prospects before 25 January.

As the preliminary point Justice Sinha considered the relationship of Kapoor with Mrs Gandhi. He noted that Kapoor had been working in the Prime Minister's Secretariat and therefore in effect with Mrs Gandhi's since 1951. During the 1967 elections, he had resigned from his job in order to work for Mrs Gandhi's election, rejoining the Prime Minister's Secretariat immediately after the elections. In the 1971 elections too he was Mrs Gandhi's election agent. All these facts, the Judge noted, indicate that Kapoor had become extremely useful and almost indispensable to Mrs Gandhi.

Taking up the question of when Kapoor had started doing election work for Mrs Gandhi, the Judge agreed with the petitioner's contention that Mr Kapoor had delivered an election speech in Munshiganj on 7 January.

Regarding the fact that the return of election expenses showed Kapoor having authorized the purchase of voters list on 11 January, the Judge held that since there was no evidence to prove that Kapoor was in Rae Bareli at that time he would not hold that against the respondent.

On the period of 14 January to 25 January, the Judge after examining all the evidence available on this, held that Kapoor reached Rae Bareli on 14 January to launch Mrs Gandhi's campaign. He did not believe Kapoor's statement that he had reached Rae Bareli on 14 January on Kamlapati Tripathi's directions to go on a tour of Eastern UP. He found it extremely improbable that of all the places in Eastern UP, Kapoor chose Rae Bareli without having any prior intention of going there. He held that Mr Kapoor had been in Rae Bareli all those days and had participated in election meetings addressed by Shri Chandrashekhar and Prof. Sher Singh.

Kapoor had stated that he had resigned in 1967 and again in 1971 to do public service. Kapoor had also stated that he had an ambition to get into Parliament. "That being so," the Judge observed, "it is obvious that Shri Yashpal Kapoor did not resign in 1967 nor in 1971 for the sake of any public service but only to work for respondent No. 1 in her constituency and thereby obtained her help in the fulfilment of his ambition."

Commenting on the reliability of Kapoor's deposition, the Judge observed that the statement of Kapoor "is not a statement of a straightforward nature and on several points it is an admixture of half-truths and untruths."

The Judge further held that all the surrounding circumstances made it almost doubtless that Kapoor must have worked for Mrs Gandhi's election at her instance. The circumstances were that Mrs Gandhi reposed great trust in Kapoor, that Kapoor had submitted his letter of resignation on 13 January after consulting Mrs Gandhi, that he again met her between 21 and 26 January.

Because of these findings, Justice Sinha concluded that the respondent had obtained and procured the assistance of Yashpal Kapoor for the furtherance of her election prospects while he was still a gazetted officer and, therefore, held her guilty of a corrupt practice on this issue.

Justice Sinha made this final order.

"In view of my findings on Issue No. 1, Issue No. 3 and additional issue No. 3, the petition is allowed and the election of Smt Indira Nehru Gandhi, respondent No. 1, to the Lok Sabha is declared void."

The Judge accordingly also disqualified her from holding any public office for a period of six years from that date, as provided by the R.P. Act. The election petition was allowed with costs. The writ petition filed for challenging the validity of the election law amendment was, however, dismissed, because the Judge held that the petitioner had not been able to lay any foundation on facts to compel an inquiry into its validity.

3

The Repercussions

9

RUMBLINGS AFTER THE JUDGMENT

Mrs Gandhi got news of the judgment at 10.10 A.M. She reportedly stayed calm and asked her Secretary to get the details. Meanwhile her main legal advisers, H.R. Gokhale, the Union Law Minister and S.S. Ray, the Chief Minister of West Bengal rushed to her house as soon as they heard of the judgment. Palkhivala, who happened to be in Delhi, also rushed to Mrs Gandhi's house.

By the time Palkhivala reached her house, Justice Sinha had granted a 20 day absolute stay. So in the closed door consultations which Mrs Gandhi had with her legal advisers, she was told that it was not legally imperative for her to resign because of the stay order. They waited for further details of the judgment to come in.

Bhushan was in his hotel suite in Bombay when he first got the news. He was having a conference with some lawyers, when, at 10.15 A.M. he received a phone call from his brother Vijay Kumar from Delhi. He was elated. His hard labour had paid off.

When reporters reached him, Bhushan was asked whether he thought Mrs Gandhi could continue as Prime Minister. He said that legally perhaps she could, but morally he had no doubt that she was under an obligation to resign. "Apart from holding her guilty of corrupt practices, the Judge has also held her guilty of giving false evidence. Consider what would happen if she went to an International Conference and the Pakistani delegate got up and said: 'Why are you listening to her? Her word has not been believed even in her own court.' That would be very embarrassing for the country."

Raj Narain got news of the judgment at 10.20 when a friend of his phoned him from Allahabad. He was overjoyed. Sweets were offered to all who came to his house that day. Commenting on the judgment, he said that Justice Sinha had raised the prestige of the judiciary. He asked Mrs Gandhi to resign at once and warned that no power on earth could save her now.

The Opposition as a whole was overjoyed by the news of the judgment. For them it was a God-sent opportunity to remove Mrs Gandhi. They were quick to capitalize on it. The reactions of almost all Opposition leaders were similar: high praise for Justice Sinha and a demand for Mrs Gandhi's resignation. They said that a person against whom the court had recorded findings of corrupt practices had no right to remain Prime Minister. The Swatantra Party leader, Piloo Mody, went further. He said that as of 10.00 A.M. that day, India had ceased to have a lawful Prime Minister. "Now we have to see how to deal with this imposter," he added.

THE CONGRESS REACTION

At 6.00 P.M. that evening, there was a meeting of the Congress Parliamentary Board. It was attended by the Party President Barooah, Jagjivan Ram, Chavan and about a hundred other Members of Parliament. The notable absentes in the meeting were, Mohan Dharia, Chandrashekhar, Krishna Kant and Ram Dhan. Mohan Dharia, who had been dropped from Mrs Gandhi's Cabinet for suggesting a dialogue with JP, was perhaps the only prominent Congress leader who publicly announced that Mrs Gandhi should resign after the judgment. Chandrashekhar, Krishna Kant and Ram Dhan were also known to hold the same view, though they did not announce it.

The Parliamentary Board meeting turned out to be merely an exercise of expressing confidence in Mrs Gandhi's leadership. All those who spoke in that meeting spoke of Mrs Gandhi's leadership as indispensable for the country and urged her not to quit. Jagjivan Ram's speech, however, struck a slightly different note. He said that the judgment had at least shown that the judiciary in India functioned without fear or favour. Pointedly avoiding the use of the word "indispensable," Ram, however, stated that whether in or out of office, Mrs Gandhi would contiuue to lead the nation.

Meanwhile, various Congress stalwarts and Chief Ministers of States were rushing to Delhi, trying to out do each other in expressing their allegiance to Mrs Gandhi. Her house was surrounded by people chanting slogans in her praise. Some of them also raised slogans against Justice Sinha.

That evening Mrs Gandhi addressed the few thousand people who had gathered outside her house. Leaving the resignation issue deliberately vague, she said that she had always served the people in the past and with their support she would continue to do so in the future.

Thus it seems that she had probably not yet made up her mind on whether she ought to resign. The factors which must have been weighing in her decision were obvious. It was clear that a resignation at that time would give the lie to the opposition charges that she was a dictator, and give a much needed boost to her slumping popularity ratings. Then, if she was exonerated by the Supreme Court, she could stage a triumphant come-back. But there was the other side of the coin too. If she left now, someone else would replace here. She could be left stranded if that person refused to make way for her even in her event of a favourable Supreme Court judgment. In politics, particularly that of India, power accrues mainly on the basis of the office which one holds. There is no easy come-back in politics—at least in the short term.

Mrs Gandhi to Appeal

By the evening, details of the judgment had come in and had been studied broadly by Mrs Gandhi's legal advisers. Palkhivala thought that there were very good chances of the judgment being reversed by the Supreme Court. So it was decided that an appeal be preferred to the Supreme Court, and Mr Palkhivala was selected to argue the appeal. Most people found it rather surprising that Palkhivala, the famed lawyer who had been a rather vocal critic of Mrs Gandhi, should deem it fit to accept her brief. One might say that a lawyer's is a professional job, and it is his duty to argue the cases of all those who approach him. But this was not an ordinary case; it was a case with immediate and far-reaching political consequences. If Palkhivala was a political opponent of Mrs Gandhi, he was perhaps obliged not to accept the brief in this case. He was supposed to write an article in the *Illustrated Weekly of India* wherein he was to set out his reasons for accepting the brief, but unfortunately no such article appeared, perhaps because the circumstances changed. However, his public image was considerably tarnished by his acceptance of Mrs Gandhi's brief.

PRESS REACTIONS TO THE VERDICT

The next day's papers were full of the judgment: "Court unseats Indira.

Disqualified for 6 years," screamed the banner headlines. *The Hindustan Times* in their editorial commented, "While the stay order was absolute, the judicial pronouncement was not politically obliterated although an appeal was pending in the Supreme Court, and it is to this reality rather than the technical legality of the stay to which the country must address itself. ... The proper course in these circumstances would be for the Prime Minister to resign her office pending disposal of the appeal which she legitimately intends to prefer before the Supreme Court. In doing so, she would not only uphold the judicial process but uphold Indian democracy and the value on which it is found."

The Statesman, in an article entitled, "A Time to Resign" commented that after this judgment, Mrs Gandhi would not be able to command confidence of the party or of the nation. Advising her to resign they warned, "By not resigning, she will be guilty of far more than any violation of an electoral law."

By and large, the Press felt that the judgment would undermine her moral authority, and most newspapers urged her to resign. The world press also reacted fast to the High Court judgment. Their main reaction was surprise at the decision. After the supersession of the Supreme Court Judges in 1973, the prestige of the Indian Judiciary had been considerably devalued in the eyes of the world, and such a "bold" decision was thus not expected. The western world, however, was pleasantly surprised at the decision, which was in their eyes an indication of a healthy democracy. They waited expectantly for further news.

The day following the judgment, Mrs Gandhi addressed another rally organized outside her house. The crowd was in a boisterous mood. They performed the "Bhangra" for Mrs Gandhi. An effigy of Justice Sinha was also burnt. Mrs Gandhi in her speech made her first comment on the judgment. Obviously referring to the issue of rostrums on which the Judge had found her guilty of obtaining the assistance of Government servants, Mrs Gandhi said that the rostrums had been constructed by officers of the State Government. The State Government was headed by the Opposition parties at that time, she said.

On 14 June, there was a news item in some newspapers which said that Justice Jagmohan Lal of the Allahabad High Court had died. Although this Justice Jagmohan Lal was an old retired judge, the people, who were ready to believe anything at that time, inferred that Justice Jag Mohan Lal Sinha had been murdered. The speed with which this rumour gained currency reveals the extent of the erosion of Mrs Gandhi's credibility that had taken place since 1971.

As the days progressed, it became routine for Mrs Gandhi to address five to six meetings outside her house each day. She became increasingly hysterical and critical of the Opposition. All her speeches had the same theme. Lashing out at the Opposition, she said that the Opposition was out to destroy the country. "They have a single point programme, 'Indira Hatao.' They are not bothered with 'Desh Bachao.' One of the Opposition leaders even wears a badge saying 'I am a CIA agent'." On 16 June, at a public meeting, she made it clear that she did not intend to resign, and that she intended to fight it out with the Opposition.

PRIME MINISTER OR NOT?

Bhushan saw that Mrs Gandhi did not intend to resign. The Congress party too, instead of choosing a new leader, was rushing to express confidence in her leadership. So he made another move. Addressing some newsmen, he said that moral considerations aside, legally too, Mrs Gandhi was not the Prime Minister.

Explaining, he said, "At 10.00 A.M. when the judgment was pronounced, Mrs Gandhi immediately ceased to be a Member of Parliament, and consequently also the Prime Minister. A person can remain a Minister for six months without being a Member of Parliament. But in this case, Mrs Gandhi's election has been set aside, so she ceased to be a Member of Parliament with effect from December 1970 when the last Parliament was dissolved. Her six months having expired, she automatically ceased to be the Prime Minister from 10.00 A:M. on 12 June. The stay order being given at 10.30, could only revive her membership of Parliament. Her Prime Ministership cannot be revived by a stay order given under the Representation of People Act. That is governed by constitutional provisions. That can only be revived by a fresh appointment and by taking a fresh oath as provided by the Constitution."

Siddhartha Shankar Ray was enraged by Bhushan's statement. He said that he did not understand how a lawyer like Bhushan could say such a thing. He pointed out that Section 116§ of the R.P. Act, when dealing with the effect of a stay order says that in the event of a stay order, the High Court order shall be deemed never to have taken effect.

Bhushan commented on Ray's reply in a public meeting organized

---

1 This Opposition leader was Piloo Mody, who once went to Parliament wearing this badge.

by the Uptown Jaycees of Bombay. He said that Ray did not understand the difference between statutory and constitutional provisions. "Suppose the stay order had been obtained 20 days after the judgment. For those 20 days at least, she would not have been the Prime Minister, and a new Prime Minister would have been sworn in. Does Ray mean to say that even if a stay was given after 20 days, she would have automatically become the Prime Minister? What would be the status of the new Prime Minister then? Therefore, it is clear that with a stay order she would not automatically become the Prime Minister."

'India is Indira'

The Congress Parliamentary Party meeting was scheduled for 18 June. Many people expected the Congress Party to choose a new leader at the meeting. But their hopes were belied. The meeting turned out to be no more than a repetition of their earlier exercise of firmly expressing supreme confidence in Mrs Gandhi's leadership. At the meeting attended by Mrs Gandhi and more than 300 Congress Ministers and Legislators, speaker after speaker got up to shower torrents of praise upon Mrs Gandhi. Urging her to continue, they said that her leadership had become indispensable for the country and she had become inseparable from the people. Swaran Singh went to the extent of saying, "What happens to her happens to India and what happens to India happens to her." The Congress President, Barooah, improved upon this and coined the slogan, "India is Indira and Indira is India."

There were, however, five notable absentees at the Parliamentary Party meeting. Knowing what the agenda of the meeting was, Chandrashekhar, Krishna Kant, Mohan Dharia, Ram Dhan and Mrs Lakshmi Kanthamma had chosen to disassociate themselves from it.

The Congress Parliamentary Party Resolution was greeted by voices of protests from the Opposition party. Jayaprakash Narayan, commenting on the resolution, said that it was yet another instance of unabashed political immorality of the Congress leadership. "Here is a clear notice given that no matter what the law of the land might be, Mrs Gandhi will remain the Prime Minister as long as she or the Congress party has the say in it." In response to the resolution, Piloo Mody composed a poem, which went like this:

Humpty Dumpty sat on a throne,

Rumblings After the Judgment 113

> Humpty Dumpty out was thrown.
> All the Queen's asses and all the
> Queen's yesmen, could not put
> Humpty on the throne again.

Bhushan was hoping that the Congress Parliamentary Party would nominate a successor to Mrs Gandhi. The outcome of the meeting angered him. Commenting on the meeting he said that the stay was obtained by Mrs Gandhi on the ground that the Congress party would need some time to elect a new leader. The Congress party had met and no new leader was elected. Therefore, the stay was being clearly misused by Mrs Gandhi. He rang up his junior, Ramesh Srivastava, in Allahabad, and asked him to file an application for the vacation of the stay order on the ground that it was being misused. Nothing, however, came of it, as a few days later the matter of the stay came up before the Supreme Court.

The Press was sharply critical of the Congress Parliamentary Party meeting. *The Statesman* said that the meeting "was a ritual, and like all rituals followed a predictable course. The purpose was to do reverence to Mrs Gandhi and this was done with the slogans, chants ecomiums and verbal extravagance usual to such stage managed occasions of which there has been a surfiet since the Allahabad judgment." B.G. Verghese writing in the *Hindustan Times* said, "The resolution drafted by the party managers carefully obfuscated the real issues confronting the country after the Allahabad judgment to propound what is no less than Fuehrer principle of the indispensability of Mrs Gandhi's leadership as Prime Minister."

Meanwhile Mrs Gandhi's legal advisers were busy preparing for her appeal in the Supreme Court and the application for the extension of the 20 day stay granted by the High Court. Since the Supreme Court was on vacation, the appeal was to be preferred before the Vacation Judge, Justice Krishna Iyer. The Vacation Judge normally sits only on Tuesdays and Fridays. On Friday, 20 June, Mrs Gandhi's Advocate-on-Record, J.B. Dadachandji, appeared before the Vacation Judge at 10.30 A.M. and made an oral plea that an early date be fixed for the hearing of Mrs Gandhi's stay application. He also requested the Judge to permit an unusual procedure by which he could file the appeal in the Supreme Court on the same day on which the application for the stay was to be heard. Normally, an appeal is formally filed, and then only is the date for the hearing of the stay application fixed. The law is that as soon as the application is filed in the Supreme Court, the stay given by the High Court stands automatically vacated. Dadachanji made this request so that there was no legal hindrance in Mrs Gandhi's continuance as Prime Minister, in the interim period between the time an appeal was filed and the time when an extension of the stay was granted. J.P. Goyal, Advocate-on-Record for Raj Narain did not object to this procedure and so the Judge allowed it.

Justice Krishna Iyer fixed Monday, 23 June, as the date of hearing of the stay application, observing that Monday would be a virgin day as he had no other work on that day. He told both parties to exchange relevant papers before that date.

THE 'LARGEST EVER' RALLY

As this was going on in the Supreme Court, a massive rally was being addressed by Mrs Gandhi on the Boat Club grounds. Preparations for this rally had been made several days in advance. It is said that Sanjay Gandhi himself was personally in charge of the arrangements of the rally. Special, free trains were run from all over the country to bring in people to attend this meeting. All the buses of Delhi had vanished from the city as they had been sent to neighbouring States to collect people for the meeting. There were elaborate police arrangements and barricading for miles around the Boat Club. Mrs Gandhi claimed this to be the largest ever rally in the history of this country. It is estimated that about 5 lakh people attended this meeting.

In her speech, Mrs Gandhi launched a scathing attack on the Opposition parties. Explaining why this rally was held, she said, "It is not to show strength or to seek support for myself, it is being held essentially to demonstrate the will and unity of the people."

Apart from Mrs Gandhi, the meeting was also addressed by others. It was once again Barooah who stole the show, further substantiating J.P's statement that he was the court jester of the Congress party. Giving vent to his scholarly bent of mind, he recited a poem, specially written by him for this occasion. He chanted:

Indira tere subah ki jai
Indira tere sham ki jai
Indira tere kaam ki jai
Indira tere naam ki jai.

He capped it by shouting the new slogan which he had invented—"Indira is India and India is Indira."

Rumblings After the Judgment

This rally, as expected, evoked an angry response from the Opposition. They charged that the entire Government machinery was being misused by the Congress party to show their muscle. The response of the Press was also unfavourable. The London Economist in a penetrating comment said that the blatant misuse of the Government machinery by Mrs Gandhi for her Boat Club rally was a move "ironically reminiscent of the very offences for which she was convicted."

THE OPPOSITION RALLY

The opposition was not sitting quiet either. Seeing that Mrs Gandhi had no intention of resigning, they were preparing for a countrywide agitation to force her out of office. They organized a massive rally at the Ramlila Grounds on 22 June. Jayaprakash Narayan was also expected to address that meeting, but could not do so as his flight from Patna was cancelled under rather suspicious circumstances. The meeting was nonetheless addressed by most of the top opposition e aders which included Morarji Desai and Raj Narain. Thousands of people braved the rain and repeatedly cheered them as they spoke. Their strategy was to mobilize public opinion against Mrs Gandhi's continuing in office, so the theme of their speeches was similar. They asked the people to organize themselves and prepare for a non-violent agitation to force Mrs Gandhi out of office. They, however, did not give a final call for the agitation on this day. They were waiting for the outcome of the Supreme Court hearing on Mrs Gandhi's stay application.

10

THE STAY ORDER

By the evening of 22 June, the relevant papers regarding the appeal and the stay application had been exchanged by both sides. A copy of the appeal and the stay application was also sent to Justice Krishna Iyer, even though the formal appeal was only to be filed the next morning. Mrs Gandhi in her stay application had asked for an extension of the absolute and unconditional stay granted by the High Court. This would stay the operation of the High Court order till the appeal was decided by the Supreme Court.

Raj Narain, in his affidavit, had vehemently opposed the extension of the stay to Mrs Gandhi. Alternatively, he had pleaded that if a stay was to be granted at all, it should only be a conditional stay, the sort which is granted normally by the Supreme Court in cases where charges of corrupt practices were upheld against an elected candidate. A conditional stay has the effect of allowing the person to keep alive his membership of Parliament, but deprives him of all other rights as a member, including his right to vote or participate in the proceedings of Parliament.

It was Monday, 23 June, the day that had been fixed for the hearing of Mrs Gandhi's stay petition in the Supreme Court. Justice Krishna Iyer had chosen the Chief Justice's court-room for the stay hearing. Although it was the largest court room in the Supreme Court, it could accommodate only 150 people. Thousands of people wanted to witness the drama that was to determine the future of Mrs Gandhi and of the country. The eyes of the entire country were focused on the Supreme Court that day.

Out of the 150 odd people who got entry into the court room that

The Stay Order

day, there were about 100 lawyers, about 30 visitors and about 25 newsmen. Hundreds of people jammed the corridors outside the court room in the hope that someone from inside might come out, giving them a chance to go in. There were hundreds of others who could not even get entry inside the court premises as the gates were closed to prevent more people from coming in. The Supreme Court was surrounded by helmeted policemen wearing brick-bat guards.

When Bhushan and Palkhivala arrived, they had to push their way to the court room because of the fantastic crowds jamming the corridors. They somehow managed to get inside by 11.30 A.M. The Judge arrived punctually at 11.30 A.M. and the stage was set for the arguments to begin. Palkhivala, being the applicant's counsel, was called upon to open his arguments.

PALKHIVALA'S ARGUMENTS

As a preliminary issue, Palkhivala requested that the decision on the stay application be given retrospective effect so that the decision would be deemed to have been given from the moment the appeal was filed. This, he said, was to circumvent a technical difficulty which was arising. This was that the stay of the Allahabad High Court would stand vacated as soon as the appeal was filed which had been filed at that very time. So the question would arise as to whether Mrs Gandhi could remain the Prime Minister till the time the judgment on the stay petition was delivered. Justice Iyer turned to Bhushan who said that he had no objection to it.

'Trial Judge Made Manifest Errors'

Opening his arguments, Palkhivala first contended that the Trial Judge of the Allahabad High Court had made manifest errors in holding Mrs Gandhi guilty of two corrupt practices. He said that on the issue of whether Mrs Gandhi obtained the assistance of Government servants by getting rostrums constructed for her, the learned Judge had made a manifest error in not observing the distinction between the Government and Government servants. Counsel went on: "The Representation of People Act prohibits the procuring or attempting to procure the assistance of a Government servant. But if a Government, the State Government in this case, itself provides some assistance to a candidate, it could not be regarded as a corrupt practice. In the present case, it is clear that the assistance was provided by Government servants acting in their official capacity so that in effect it was provided by the State Government and not by Government servants acting in their private capacity."

Counsel further argued that for a corrupt practice there must be a conscious attempt to obtain or procure the assistance, whereas here it was part of the routine security drill undertaken for the Prime Minister. "If the election was set aside on this ground, it would have alarming consequences. Today it might be set aside for the construction of rostrums, but tomorrow it would be set aside for barricading, and then for police arrangements. There can be no elections in these circumstances."

Counsel further contended that the Trial Judge had erred in finding that the appellant held herself as a candidate on 29 December. He said that the first art of politics was to confound the opponent, and Mrs Gandhi was no novice to politics. Therefore, there was no reason why she should have declared herself to be a candidate from ae Bareli till she filed her nomination paper.

Counsel went on to argue at length the issue of the date of Yashpal Kapoor's resignation, and contended that on the facts of the case there was absolutely no doubt that Haksar had orally accepted Kapoor's resignation on 14 January. Further there could be no doubt of Haksar's competence to accept his resignation orally.

At this point the Judge asked Palkhivala not to go into the merits of the case as that would take a long time. Justice Iyer said that the matter before him was only the stay application and not the appeal. Palkhivala said that he was only trying to show how weak the case of the petitioner was, and that it was bound to fail in the appeal.

Offences are Technical

Leaving the merits and going on to the question of why an absolute stay should be granted, Palkhivala submitted that the offences on which the appellant was found guilty were technical in nature and did not involve any moral turpitude. He said that since the appeal would be disposed of expeditiously by the Supreme Court, therefore in the interest of convenience and justice the status quo should not be disturbed for these few days. He said that continuity in the politics of the country would be disturbed if Mrs Gandhi was prevented from remaining the Prime Minister. He also claimed that the nation was solidly behind Mrs Gandhi as could be seen from the massive rallies which were held in her support.

Counsel next submitted that there were some precedents in which an absolute stay had been granted by the Supreme Court, even in cases where the candidate was found guilty of corrupt practices.

Justice Iyer: Are you referring to the cases of 1953 and 1954?

Counsel: Yes.

Justice Iyer: But those are vintage cases. At that time the Election Tribunal was the trial court for election petitions. I do not think there has been any case of absolute stay after the High Courts have been constituted as the trial courts.

Counsel: My Lord, such a case has never arisen before. An election petition has never succeeded against a Prime Minister. So we cannot search for a precedent in a case where there can be no precedent. Your lordship in this case will be laying down a precedent.

Counsel next contended that public and private justice were clearly in Mrs Gandhi's favour for the grant of an absolute stay.

Justice Iyer: I am mystified by the expression 'private justice.' You mean justice as between two citizens?

Counsel: Yes, justice as between the appellant and the respondent. If an absolute stay is not granted to the appellant, it would cause irreparable damage to her political career. It is easy for my learned friend on the other side to say that there could possibly be no damage to her career if she resigns now and resumes office after she is exonerated by the Supreme Court. But there is no easy come-back in politics. On the other hand, an absolute stay would do no harm at all to Raj Narain. It is also in the public interest that an absolute stay be granted. My Lord, it would be very embarrassing for the country to have a Prime Minister whose hands were fettered by a conditional stay."

Palkhivala said that the aim of the respondent was to inflict maximum damage on the appellant and in such a case where considerations of national security and other international considerations were involved, the respondent should not be allowed to succeed in his plea.

Justice Krishna Iyer at this point asked the counsels of both sides to look up the effect of a conditional stay. He wondered whether both the sides were not shadow-boxing on the issue of absolute versus conditional stay. He said that functioning of the Prime Minister in Parliament would not be affected by a conditional stay as this was governed by other rules. He said: "The only difference between the two types of stay is perhaps that the voting rights in Parliament are affected. Would it cause irreparable injury to public justice if one member is prevented from voting?"

Counsel: It would be extremely embarrassing for the country to have a Prime Minister who is not allowed to vote in Parliament.

Repeating his vehement request for an absolute stay Palkhivala concluded his opening arguments.

Palkhivala's arguments concluded at 2.30 P.M. At 1.00 P.M. when it was time for lunch, Justice Iyer had asked the Counsel whether they would mind skipping lunch and continuing the arguments. Nobody objected, so it was probably for the first time in the protocol observing Supreme Court that arguments continued even during the lunch hour.

BHUSHAN'S REPLY

Opening his reply Bhushan said that he could not understand the argument hat the offences on which the appellant was found guilty were technical in nature. He said, "When the law provides that certain acts are corrupt practices, it is the duty of each candidate to see that he does not commit these acts. Transgressing the law is itself a major offence. Moreover, in this case no one could say that the offences are technical. The learned High Court Judge has found her guilty of being untruthful before the court. That is not a technical offence."

Going into the merits of the case, Counsel strongly rebutted Palkhivala's contention that the petitioner's case was flimsy and was bound to fail in the appeal. Bhushan said that the petitioner's case was so strong that it was almost impregnable. He said, "The learned Trial Judge has only found her guilty on two counts and has given her the benefit of doubt on the other five issues. I have full confidence that the Supreme Court will find her guilty on more than two issues."

Referring to Palkhivala's argument that there was a fine distinction between a Government servant and the Government, Counsel said that the whole purpose of the law on this was to prevent misuse of Government machinery by influential candidates. There would be no purpose, he said, in prohibiting the procuring of assistance from Government servants in their private capacity.

At this stage again Justice Iyer remarked that he would not be going into the merits of the case, so he urged Bhushan to refrain from arguing on the merits. Bhushan said that he was only referring to the merits because Palkhivala had done so and because Palkhivala was relying on his submission that this petition was bound to fail in the Supreme Court.

Answering a question by Justice Iyer, hushan made it clear that he was totally opposed to the grant of any stay by the Supreme

The Stay Order

Court and it was only as an alternative submission that he was arguing for a conditional stay. Counsel said that he was arguing that a stay should not be granted at all because Mrs Gandhi should not be allowed to remain the Prime Minister. "Political and moral propriety demand that a person who has been placed under a cloud by being found guilty of corrupt practices should not be allowed to remain the Prime Minister. The court while exercising its discretion should consider the value of these healthy, moral and political conventions."

Justice Iyer: Moral or political conventions have nothing to do with legal conventions.

Counsel said that *till* then there had been no precedent of an absolute stay being granted by the Supreme Court when an election had been set aside on corrupt practices. He explained, "The reason for this practice is that a conditional stay prevents a person from functioning as a Member of Parliament. It merely allows him to attend Parliament to sign the attendance register so that in the event of the reversal of the High Court judgment he would be able to retain his membership. The court should go by the principle which lies behind the convention of granting a conditional stay. The principle is that the person against whom charges of corrupt practice had been recorded should not be allowed to function in Parliament. "This principle applies with greater force to the Prime Minister. The Prime Minister is the leader of the nation and, being so, should be above all suspicion. In this case she can only be prevented from functioning if no stay was granted by the Supreme Court, not even a conditional stay."

Alternatively, Counsel submitted that if the court did not accept his plea, then he would argue that the appellant be granted only a conditional stay. He said that the only time when absolute stays were granted was prior to 1954 when Election Tribunals were the trial courts. He said that since this power had been delegated to the High Court, there had not been a single case of absolute stay in cases where charges of corrupt practices were upheld against the candidate. He said that the court should not make a departure from the established convention merely because the appellant in this case happened to be the Prime Minister of the country.

Referring to Palkhivala's contention that the present case was unique because the Prime Minister was involved, Counsel said that he could cite any number of instances where Ministers and Chief Ministers had to quit offices on their being found guilty of corrupt practices. He cited the example of D.P. Mishra, former Chief Minister of Madhya Pradesh and Dr Chenna Reddy, former Union Minister, who were both made to resign by Mrs Gandhi herself, because charges of corrupt practices had been established against them. Counsel also cited the recent instance of the West German Chancellor Willy Brandt who had quit office merely because his Secretary was found to be an East German spy, although Mr Brandt had no knowledge of it. He said that the rationale behind this was that the conduct of a person holding a high office must not only be above board, but must also be seen to be above board.

Bhushan said that no country professing democratic ideals could afford a state of affairs where any individual was considered indispensable for the nation. "The past history of our country shows that whenever there has been a sudden exit of the Prime Minister due to any reason, the work of the Government has gone on smoothly and there has been no difficulty in finding a successor to that person. That is exactly the difference between a democracy and a dictatorship. In a dictatorship, the death of a leader plunges the country into a war of succession, but in a democracy, succession is always a smooth affair having no serious repercussions. This is because democracy envisages a Government of laws and not of men."

Justice Iyer: I am unable to understand this expression. I think we are a Government of laws and also of men.

Consel: That is true, but the importance lies not in the individual but in the institutions of the conntry. If Mrs Gandhi has to go, I am sure that the Congress Party can find some capable person to step into her shoes. If they cannot find anyone capable enough, then I must say that such a bankrupt party has no right to rule the country.

Stay Misused

Counsel next contended that the stay obtained by Mrs Gandhi from the High Court had been misued by her and, therefore, this court should not respond to her plea. "The Hig Court had given a stay on a particular representation made by the appellant. The representation was that a sudden exit of the Prime Minister would create a void in the country which would bring the work of the Government to a standstill. The stay was given because of the plea that some time was required by the Congress Party to elect a new leader. But we find that the Congress Parliamentary party met on 18 June and all that they did was to express full confidence in Mrs Gandhi's leadership. Was it not

The Stay Order

incumbent on Mrs Gandhi to ask her party to elect a new leader in her place? It is no argument to say that the party only wanted her and no one else as the leader. I submit that it is impossible for the party to force her to remain the Prime Minister."

Bhushan's last submission was that the stay order granted now could produce technical and legal complications if the judgment of the High Court was affirmed in the appeal. He referred to Section 107(2) of the R.P. Act, which says:

> Where by any order under Section 98, the election of a returned candidate is declared to be void, the acts and proceedings in which that returned candidate has before the date thereof participated as a Member of Parliament or as a Member of the Legislature of a State, shall not be invalidated by reason of that order, nor shall such a candidate be subjected to any liability or penalty on the ground of such participation.

Bhushan argued that it was this section alone which legalized all the acts done in his official capacity during the pendency of a petition by a person whose election had been set aside. Therefore, although the election is deemed to be void from the very beginning, yet the acts done by such a person till the time the High Court judgment is rendered shall be treated to be legal. He further said, "But this legality is conferred only to things done by the person till the High Court judgment is pronounced. This does not legalize the acts done by the person after the High Court judgment is pronounced. Therefore, if the stay is granted now, and later on the High Court judgment is affirmed by the Supreme Court, then it would raise the question as to whether Mrs Gandhi was legally the Prime Minister between the date of the High Court judgment and the date of the Supreme Court's affirmation of that judgment."

Bhushan ended his arguments with an impassioned plea that the court should not grant any further stay to Mrs Gandhi.

PALKHIVALA'S REJOINDE

After Bhushan concluded his arguments, Palkhivala briefly replied to them. He rebutted Bhushan's contention that Mrs Gandhi's continuance as the Prime Minister would be embarrassing for the country. He said that this was only Bhushan's personal viewpoint. According to him, it would be embarrassing for the country if a conditional stay and not an absolute stay was granted. He said that it would be embarrassing for the country to have a Prime Minister who was not able to vote in Parliament. "The institution of Prime Ministership is involved here. A conditional stay will greatly damage this institution."

'Stay was Only to Elect a Leader'

In reply to Bhushan's arguments that the appellant had not abided by the representation made in the stay application in the Allahabad High Court, Palkhivala said that the application presented to the Trial Judge was drafted hurriedly by the Counsel present there and therefore was not properly framed. "Moreover, the application asked for time to elect a leader of the Congress Party. The Congress Parliamentary Party met on 18 June and passed a thunderous resolution affirming support for the appellant and recognizing her as the only leader. The representation does not say that the Congress Party will elect a *new* leader."

Palkhivala ended with a plea that an absolute stay be granted because a conditional stay would have disastrous consequences for the country. The arguments finally ended at 5.05 P.M., which was one hour beyond the normal sitting time of the Supreme Court.

When asked about when the judgment would be delivered, Justice Iyer said that he would deliver his judgment at 3.45 P.M. the next day.

CONDITIONAL STAY

After the arguments ended in the Supreme Court, Bhushan met some Opposition leaders. Ashok Mehta, the President of the Congress (O), asked him what he thought the judgment would be. Bhushan said that he expected it to be a conditional stay. Mehta was pleased. He said that they would throw her out if it was a conditional stay.

The whole country had followed the arguments in the Supreme Court through the newspapers with great interest. Now all awaited the judgment of the Supreme Court. A huge crowd began to gather around the Supreme Court on 24 June as the time of the judgment approached. The judgment was delivered exactly at 3.45 P.M. The Judge had granted a conditional stay. He had however, clarified in his order that there was no legal embargo on Mrs Gandhi's continuing as the Prime Minister.

Going on to the actual arguments advanced, Justice Iyer rejected

The Stay Order

Bhushan's argument that Mrs Gandhi had misused the stay granted by the Allahabad High Court. He accepted Palkhivala's contention that "since her party so full-bloodedly plumbed in favour of her remaining in office as Prime Minister, she could do nothing else but remain the Prime Minister."

He also rejected Bhushan's contention that the High Court had found her guilty of being untruthful before the court and agreed with Palkhivala's argument that the offences on which Mrs Gandhi was held guilty were not the "graver electoral vices."

Regarding Palkhivala's argument that the High Court's findings were based on flimsy grounds, the Judge observed that he could not take the *prima facie* view that the justice of the case justifies indifference to those findings.

The Judge then noted that in such cases it is the usual practice of the court to grant a conditional stay. He further noted that since 1956, when the High Court was made the Election Tribunal, the Supreme Court had always granted only conditional stays.

He then proceeded to analyze the implication of a conditional stay for the Prime Minister. He said:

> This appeal, it is plain, relates solely to the Lok Sabha Membership of the appellant and the subject matter of her office *qua* Prime Minister is not directly before this Court in this litigation. Indeed, that office and its functions are regulated carefully by a separate fasciculus of Articles in the Constitution. There is some link between Membership of one of the two Houses of Parliament and Ministership (Art. 75) but once the stay order is made, as has been indicated above, the disqualification regarding appellant's membership of the Lok Sabha remains in force so long as the stay lasts. However, there will be a limitation regarding the appellant's participation in the proceedings of the *Lok Sabha* in her *capacity as Member thereof*, but, independently of the Membership, a Minister and a *fortiori*, the Prime Minister, has the right to address both Houses of Parliament, (without right to vote though) and has other functions to fulfil. (Arts. 74, 75, 78 and 88 are illustrative.) In short, the restrictions set out in the usual stay order cannot and will not detract from the appellant being entitled to exercise such rights as she has, including addressing Parliament and drawing salary, *in her capacity as Prime Minister*. There will thus be no legal embargo on her holding the office of Prime Minister. However, this legal sequitur of the situation arising from the stay of the judgment

and order of the High Court, including the suspension of the disqualification under section 8A has nothing to do with extra-legal considerations. Legality is within the Court's province to pronounce upon, but canons of political propriety and democratic *dharma* are polemical issues on which judicial silence is the golden rule.

After summing up, the Judge concluded his order by adding that either party could apply to the Division Bench of the Court for a review of the order if fresh considerations arose, justifying a change in the order.

Reaction to the 'Stay'

The news of the judgment on the stay order was broadcast by the All India Radio at 4.00 PM. It spread like wild fire across the country.

On the political scene, the Congress as well as the Opposition interpreted the stay as having vindicated their stand. Barooah truimphantly pointed out that the Judge had clearly said that there was no legal impediment to Mrs Gandhi's continuance as the Prime Minister. Commenting on the stay, Gokhale said that there was no resignation issue now. Most of the other Congress leaders also reacted on the same lines and appealed to the Opposition leaders to end their *satyagraha*. Mrs Gandhi, however, made no comment on the stay.

The Opposition, on the other hand, interpreted the conditional stay as having vindicated their stand. They all demanded Mrs Gandhi's immediate resignation. "Has anyone heard of a Prime Minister who cannot vote in Parliament?", they asked

M.C. Chagla, the former Chief Justice of Bombay High Court commenting on the stay said, "Legally she may be entitled to continue as the Prime Minister, I have no views on it. But on grounds of political morality and propriety she should not hold that high office of Prime Minister with a cloud over her head."

Reacting to the conditional stay, Bhushan said that it had brought into existence a "crippled" Prime Minister, because she was deprived of the right to vote in Parliament. He said that even Palkhivala had argued before the Supreme Court that a conditional stay would do irreparable damage to her. Bhushan said that it was still possible for Mrs Gandhi to resign gracefully. He pointed out that even in the Supreme Court order, there was a hint that considerations of healthy political conventions might cast an obligation on a person in these circumstances to resign from the office of Prime Minister.

The Press reacted to the conditional stay by calling for Mrs Gandhi's resignation. All the four major newspapers in their editorials next day asked Mrs Gandhi to resign.

The National Executive of the Opposition Party met that evening at Desai's house to decide their line of action. Jayaprakash Narayan was also present at that meeting. It was decided at that meeting that if she did not resign, a country wide *satyagraha* would be launched to protest against her continuance as the Prime Minister.

The Opposition parties were also going ahead with their plans of holding a massivive rally at the Ramlila grounds on 25 June. The rally which was attended by about two lakh people was to be addressed by Jayaprakash Narayan.

In his speech, Jayaprakash Narayan appealed to the Chief Justice of the Supreme Court A.N. Ray not to be a member of the Bench which heard Mrs Gandhi's appeal. Making it clear that he was not advancing this plea due to any lack of faith in Ray's impartiality, Jayaprakash Narayan said that since Mrs Gandhi appointed Ray the Chief Justice by superseding three Judges, even an honest verdict given by him in Mrs Gandhi's favour would not be accepted by the people. Jayaprakash Narayan also appealed to Mrs Gandhi to resign gracefully. He praised the stand taken by the five dissenting M.Ps. who had asked Mrs Gandhi to resign, and expressed surprise at the quietude shown by senior Congress leaders like Jagjivan Ram and Y.B. Chavan. He also deliberately reiterated his appeal to the police and armed forces not to obey illegal orders of the Government. He challenged the Home Minister Brahmananda Reddy to try him in court for high treason for this statement.

Reddy, however, had other plans for JP. Within eight hours of the speech, JP found himself in detention, though without a trial.

11

LAW? WHAT LAW?

It was just past midnight of 25 June 1975. The city of Delhi was resting after witnessing another day of intense political activity. But this night the streets of Delhi were witnessing another strange kind of activity. Police cars in hundreds were moving purposively in search of their prey. A plan which had been hatched by Mrs Gandhi to hold on to her power was being put into effect. About 28 years ago while the world slept, India had awakened to freedom. This fateful night, free India was sleeping in oblivion as the country was being transformed from a working democracy into a police state.

JP was asleep at the Gandhi Peace Foundation after an exhausting day when the midnight callers came. He was shaken from his sleep and told that the Government found his freedom prejudicial to the security of the State and that he was being detained under MISA.[1] Before he was taken away, JP made one last comment. Obviously referring to Mrs Gandhi, he said *"Vinash Kale Vipreet Budhi"* (in the face of destruction reason deserts).

Meanwhile other Opposition leaders were also being roused from their sleep to be surprised in the same way. The midnight operation was not confined to Delhi. In a superbly coordinated and executed plan, the police swooped down on almost all the Opposition leaders all over the country. While Morarji Desai, Charan Singh, Raj Narain,

---

[1]The Maintenance of Internal Security Act was enacted in 1971, mainly to nab smugglers and foreign exchange racketeers. It gave Government power to arrest people without trial for a limited period, if any act prejudicial to the security of the State was apprehended from them.

Piloo Modi and Ashok Mehta etc., were "picked up" in Delhi, L.K. Advani, Atal Behari Vajpayee, Shyam Nandan Mishra, Madhu Dandawate etc., were picked up in Bangalore. Others were arrested in cities where they happened to be that night.

The next morning Mrs Gandhi came on the air to inform the people that the President had declared an Emergency to thwart the Opposition move to imperil the country's security. The news of the Emergency and the arrests stunned the nation but there were no signs of public protest. What had happened was so unexpected that fear of the unknown had gripped the hearts of the people.

There were, however, some isolated signs of protest. At about 10 A.M. the same day Palkhivala issued a press note saying that he was withdrawing from Mrs Gandhi's case, because he was horrified by the arrests of JP and other Opposition leaders.

THE STING OF THE CENSOR

Meanwhile the arrests of other Opposition leaders was continuing, and the news of that was coming on the ticker tapes of all the news networks. At 1.00 P.M. came the order of the Press Censorship and with that the teleprinters stopped. All newspapers and news networks were ordered to have their material examined by the Censor before publication.

However, even under these conditions some newspapers managed to show their resentment. The Delhi edition of the *Hindustan Times* and the Bombay edition of the *Indian Express* carried blank editorials which perhaps because of their conspicuousness, spoke volumes. The Bombay edition of the *Times of India* managed to insert a small, subtle news item in the obituary column to evade the eyes of the censor. The obituary said, "Died, D.E.M. OCRACY, mother of Freedom, and daughter of L.I. Berty, on 26 June 1975."

The international press, however, which was not subject to any censorship reacted very sharply to the events in India. The *Times*, London, labelled the clamp-down as a *coup de etat* by Mrs Gandhi and said that the "coup seems to have been planned when Mrs Gandhi's own power seems to be threatened and its first objective was to defend that power, whatever measures were necessary." *The Economist* in an article entitled "Empress turns Imperious" commented that with the Emergency, Mrs Gandhi had "broken all the rules which India remarkably has adhered to in 28 years of democracy."

Commenting on the events in India, *Newsweek* magazine said, "By her actions, Mrs Gandhi had served harsh notice that if it came to a choice between the rule of law and the rule of Indira Gandhi, the law quite likely would lose."

However, it was not all criticism for Mrs Gandhi. The Soviet Government Organ, Izvestia, called Mrs Gandhi's action "a blow to the rightist plot."

Plugging the Loopholes

The next day, the President issued an order suspending the right of citizens to move to courts to enforce the fundamental rights given by Articles 14, 19 and 22. Article 14 grants the right of equality. Article 19 grants the rights of speech, movement, trade, etc. Article 21 deals with the rights of life and liberty, while Article 22 provides the right of being communicated the grounds of detention. The rights were suspended under Article 359 of the Constitution which is the main power which accrues to the Government during the Emergency. Article 19 was already under automatic suspension because of the Emergency (due to external aggression) already in force since the Bangladesh War of 1971. (Article 358 provides that Article 19 will come under automatic suspension, as soon as a proclamation of emergency is issued.)

It is interesting to note here that the proclamation of Emergency of 25 June was an exercise in futility. This is because the earlier proclamation (due to external aggression) had not been revoked. Thus from 25 June 1975 there were two Emergencies in operation. The only difference between these was a matter of words. While the first was due to a threat of external aggression, the second was due to a threat of internal disturbances. Thus, no further powers accrued to the Government by virtue of the proclamation of 25 June. All that had been done could very well have been done without a second proclamation of Emergency. The proclamation of 25 June seems to have been a part of the shock tactics employed by Mrs Gandhi to overawe and subdue any opposition in one stroke.

The Case is Adjourned

The Supreme Court reopened after its vacation on 14 July. Mrs Gandhi's appeal was listed before the Chief Justice's Court that day. Appearing on behalf of Narain, Bhushan sought an adjournment of the case for four weeks on the ground that he was busy in the Back Bay reclamation case in Bombay which was likely to last for another month. Although this was indeed true, the real reason why he sought an adjournment was that he did not want to argue this case in the atmosphere of crippling fear which was prevailing in the country at that time. Bhushan reasoned that the Judges would not be unaffected by it. He believed that the fear would decrease after some time when the situation crystallized further. Meanwhile, due to Palkhivala's exit from the case, Mrs Gandhi had decided to engage the Advocate General of Haryana, Jagannath Kaushal to argue he case in the Supreme Court. Kaushal vehemently opposed Bhushan's plea for adjournment. He said that the extraordinary nature of the case demanded that it be disposed of as expeditiously as possible. The Chief Justice, however, accepted Bhushan's plea, and the case was adjourned for four weeks.

The Monsoon Session of Parliament was scheduled to begin from 21 July. As some petitions challenging the proclamation of Emergency on the ground that it was malafide were about to be filed in some High Courts, the Union Cabinet met on 20 July and decided to make an amendment in Article 352. In this article, the satisfaction of the President regarding the proclamation of Emergency was sought to be made non-justiciable. This meant that the judiciary could no longer go into the question of whether the President was really satisfied about the need for the Emergency.

In the Monsoon Session of Parliament, the question hour was suspended. Although Parliament is competent to regulate its own procedure, the suspension of the question hour is highly unusual. Now, for the first time since the proclamation of Emergency, Jagjivan Ram came out openly in support of it. Speaking at the debate on it, Ram said, "The Opposition wanted to subvert democracy. Mrs Gandhi is known for taking the right action at the right time."

The Opposition MPs who had not been detained spoke out courageously against the Emergency. They exhorted the Congress MPs to stand up against the tyranny of Mrs Gandhi. But their exhortations were of no avail as the fear was too strong. When the Emergency proclamation came up for voting, there was thunderous approval by the Congress MPs. It was approved by the Rajya Sabha on 22 July by a vote of 136 to 33. The Lok Sabha put its stamp of approval the next day by a vote of 336 to 59.

The Opposition saw that their participation in Parliament was unlikely to achieve much as the rubber-stamp Congress majority was going to steamroll any legislation that Mrs Gandhi thought fit to introduce. So they decided to boycott the session. They walked out before the constitutional amendment making the Emergency non-justiciable was introduced and did not participate during the remaining session.

Thus the 38th Constitution Amendment, making the Emergency non-justiciable, was passed almost unanimously by both ouses. It got the Presidential assent on 1 August.

The Supreme Court's refusal to expedite the appeal on the plea of Kaushal had clearly worried Mrs Gandhi. The consequences of an adverse decision by the Supreme Court could have been disastrous. According to Bhushan, the only way in which she could have remained in office in the event of an adverse Supreme Court decision was by getting her disqualification removed by the Election Commission, which had the power to do so under the election law; and then getting the President to nominate her to the Rajya Sabha. She, however, would have had to resign the moment the Supreme Court announced its verdict and then there was no reason why the Election Commission should have accommodated her. It was probably this sombre thought that prompted the ensuring spate of panicky legislation.

The Bombshell

On 4 August the Law Minister, Gokhale, exploded a bombshell in Parliament. He introduced an Election Laws (Amendment) Bill which sought to amend retrospectively all the corrupt practices on which Mrs Gandhi's election had been challenged. The amendment not only took care of the issues on which she was convicted by the Allahabad High Court, but also most of the issues on which she was exonerated by the Court and on which a cross-appeal had been filed by Raj Narain.

Mrs Gandhi had been convicted on two charges: (1) that she had procured the assistance of the District Magistrate and Superintendent of Police by getting rostrums constructed and loudspeakers installed for her election meetings and (2) that she had procured the assistance of Yashpal Kapoor while he was still a gazetted officer in the service of the Government. The amendment[1] now provided that "any assistance, rendered to any candidate, by a Government officer, in the discharge or purported discharge of his official duty, would not be deemed to be assistance for the furtherance of the prospects of that candidate's election." This took care of the issue of rostrums, and

---

[1]See Appendix 7 for text of amendment.

also the issue of Air Force helicopters and planes, which was the subject matter of the cross-appeal.

The amendment also provided that the date of appointment or resignation of a Government servant would be taken to be the date mentioned in the official gazette. This took care of the issue of Yashpal Kapoor. An amendment was also made in the definition of a candidate in the Act. It was now provided that a "candidate" means, "a person, who has been, or claims to have been duly nominated as a candidate in any election." The result of this amendment was that since Mrs Gandhi had only been nominated as a candidate from 1 February, she could not have committed any corrupt practice before this date. Yashpal Kapoor's resignation in any case became effe tive on 25 January. So this issue was doubly covered. The amendment also provided that no symbol allotted by the Election Commission to a candidate would be deemed to be a religious symbol, thus taking care of the issue of symbols. The only remaining issue, that of expenses, was already covered by the 1974 amendment which provided that any expenses incurred or authorized by a political party etc. would not be treated as the candidate's election expenses. This Bill, however, also provided that expenditure incurred by Government officers on a candidate's election in the performance of their "official duties" would not be treated as the candidate's election expense.

The amendment did not stop at this. It also made a change regarding the Election Commission's power of removing the disqualification incurred by a candidate for the commission of a corrupt practice. Instead of the Election Commission, which till then had the power to reduce or remove any such disqualification, the power was now vested with the President. The disqualification now did not flow as a direct consequence of being found guilty by the courts. It was now provided that the case of each person found guilty would be referred to the President who could impose whatever period of disqualification he deemed fit.

Thus all loopholes were plugged. And it was not as if these amendments made in the R.P. Act were part of the general overhauling of the Act, which could arguably be said to have become out-dated. Even this subtlety could not be granted to Gokhale. The amendments made were only of those corrupt practices which were in issue in Mrs Gandhi's case. No one could argue that these amendments were not being made to influence the decision in Mrs Gandhi's case. Gokhale, in his speech in Parliament, did not even attempt to do so. Addressing his colleagues in the Congress, he told them not to be apologetic about these amendments. He said that this was being done to protect an institution which was pivotal to the very functioning of democracy.

As members of the Opposition Parties were not present in the House, the Bill was passed in the Lok Sabha on 5 August by an overwhelming majority. The next day it was approved by the Rajya Sabha and received the Presidential assent.

Since this amendment left no loopholes, one should have thought that this would satisfy Mrs Gandhi. But it appears that she is not easily satisfied.

'Overkill'

On 7 August, another bombshell was exploded by Gokhale by introducing a constitutional amendment Bill in Parliament. The constitutional amendment was slightly more general than the Election Laws Amendment as it also related to the elections of the President, Vice-President and the Speaker, apart from the election of the Prime Minister. In the amendment[2] it was provided,

> any dispute, arising out of the election of the President, Vice-President, Speaker and the Prime Minister, would only be gone into by a forum constituted by a special law made by Parliament. Parliament could also make special laws relating to the elections of these dignitaries and those laws could not be challenged in any court of the country.

These provisions, however, only related to future elections. There was a special provision for elections which had already taken place, and in which an order had already been pronounced by a court. This section provided,

> no law made by Parliament, before the commencement of the Constitution (Thirty-ninth Amendment) Act, 1975, insofar as it relates to election petitions, and matters connected therewith, shall apply, or shall be deemed ever to have applied to, or in relation to the election of any such person, as is referred to in Clause (1) (Prime Minister or Speaker), to either House of Parliament, and such election shall not be deemed to be void, or ever to have become void, on the ground on which such election could be declared to be void, or has before such commencement been declared

[2] Text of the amendment is given in Appendix 8.

to be void under any such law, and notwithstanding any order made by any court before such commencement declaring such election to be void, such election shall continue to be valid in all respects, and any such order or any finding on which such order is based shall be and shall be deemed always to have been void and of no effect.

The election of Mrs Gandhi which came under this section was thus declared to be valid and the High Court judgment was declared to be void.

Piloting the Bill, Gokhale sought justification for it on the ground that "since the Prime Minister had not only been elected by a vast majority but is also recognized throughout the length and breadth of the country as the undisputed leader, she should not be subjected to a process of judicial scrutiny where the election could be set aside even on the flimsiest ground." The only opposition to this amendment came from Mohan Dharia, who said, "This amendment is a surrender of parliamentary democracy to the coming dictatorship." Dharia, however, abstained from voting, and the amendment was passed unanimously by the Lok Sabha. The next day, the Congress members in the Rajya Sabha too gave unanimous approval to the amendment. The amendment was ratified by 17 States[3] on 9 August and received the Presidential assent on the night of 10 August. This incidentally is the record time for the passing of any constitutional amendment in India. Only three days had elapsed between the introduction of the amendment in Parliament and the Presidential assent.

The Indian Press, which was under strict censorship, could hardly carry the details of the amendments and their effect on Mrs Gandhi's case, let alone comment on them. Comment was, however, forthcoming from the international news media. *Newsweek*, in an article titled "Law? What Law?," painted a ridiculous picture of Mrs Gandhi. The article said, "What to do if convicted of breaking the law? Simple. Just change the law, retrospectively. That at least was Indira Gandhi's handy solution last week as she had her rubber-stamp Congress Party majority in Parliament retrospectively legalize the electioneering acts for which she had been convicted." *Newsweek* also ridiculed the Congress legislators, who, it said, "laughed and shouted and thumped their desks as India slid further towards

[3]A constitutional amendment, after being passed by a two-thirds majority of both Houses of Parliament, has to be ratified by half the State legislatures.

totalitarian rule." *Time* called the amendments, "The harshest step towards authoritarianism since original clamp down," and labelled the constitutional amendment, "A ludicrous case of overkill."

August 9 was the last date for the sitting of Parliament. Even this day was not to pass without its surprises. Gokhale on this date introduced yet another constitutional amendment Bill in the Rajya Sabha. This amendment gave life-long criminal immunity to the President, Governors and the Prime Minister for all acts done before assumption of office and during their tenure of office. This meant that a person committing the most heinous crime could escape the rigours of the Penal Code by becoming a Governor even for a day. The Constitution did provide certain immunity to the President and Governors but this was only during their term of office and applied only to acts done in the discharge of their official duties. This constitutional amendment is without parallel in the history of civilized jurisprudence. One had to strain one's credulity to the limit in order to believe it. One could believe such a thing happening in Idi Amin's country but not in India.

The unanimous approval of this amendment by the Rajya Sabha is indeed an index of the fear which dominated the rank and file of the Congress Party. The Congress legislators had lost their voices. They had become dummies, who could be used and manipulated by Mrs Gandhi in any way she chose. They would give their stamp of approval to anything which Mrs Gandhi placed before them.

Since Parliament adjourned the same day, this amendment could not be tabled before the Lok Sabha and, therefore, remained an unpassed Bill. It was, subsequently, never brought before the Lok Sabha, perhaps because of the widespread criticism it generated and the political capital which the Opposition made from it.

Bhushan made his comment on this amendment while speaking in a symposium on constitutional amendments a few months later. He said that for his part he could not see how this amendment could benefit the common people in any way, "Unless, of course, these dignitaries become modern-day Robinhoods, who will steal money from the rich and distribute it to the poor. In that case, certainly, the criminal immunity given to these people would be justified. But then I must warn you, my friends, to keep your hands in your pockets, whenever any of these people pass your way."

The Supreme Court was scheduled to assemble to hear Mrs Gandhi's appeal on 11 August. The Chief Justice, A.N. Ray, had announced the constitution of the Bench which would hear this case.

They would be the five seniormost Judges of the Supreme Court. Apart from the Chief Justice, they were Justices Khanna, Mathew, Beg and Chandrachud. The amendments though, had thrown the future of the case into serious doubt. When the newspapers announced on the appointed day that the Court would be sitting to hear Mrs Gandhi's appeal, the people wondered why this was at all necessary. In their eyes, the constitutional amendment had disposed of the case, and the Supreme Court's sitting seemed to be an exercise in futility.

On the evening of 10 August, Raj Narain's lawyers held a conference to decide what was to be done. There were some suggestions that they withdraw from the case in protest. Bhushan, however, could see no purpose being served by this. It was clear that all that could be done now was to attack the validity of the amendments. It appeared that unless the validity of the constitutional amendments was successfully impugned, the Supreme Court could not proceed with the case. Although Bhushan was clear about the grounds on which he would impugn the validity of the amendments, he decided to ask for another adjournment. Since an atmosphere of helplessness had been generated in the country by the introduction of these amendments, he reasoned that the Court was extremely unlikely to go beyond a summary disposal of the case in Mrs Gandhi's favour. He had reasoned that a few days would be needed for it to sink in the minds of the people that all was not over with the case and that the amendments could indeed be declared invalid by the Supreme Court. This would raise the hopes of the people which would, in turn, boost the morale of the Supreme Court.

The Amendments are Challenged

It was 11 August, the date fixed for hearing by the Supreme Court of Mrs Gandhi's appeal. Entry to the Chief Justice's Court was restricted to pass-holders. Passes to lawyers could only be issued by the Secretary of the Bar Association and passes to outsiders were issued under the discretionary authority of the Deputy Registrar. These restrictions were unprecedented. All people going to that Court had to pass through a metal detector and a security check. Some Indian newsmen were granted passes. Foreign newsmen, however, were denied passes on the spurious ground that the seats were not enough, although at least half the seats in the Visitors' Gallery went empty.

The Judges entered the Court punctually at 10.30 A.M. in the ceremonial order of their seniority—first, the Chief Justice, followed by Justices Khanna, Mathew, Beg and, finally, Justice Chandrachud.

Mrs Gandhi by this time had made another change in her lawyer. While Kaushal was retained as an assisting counsel, the charge of arguing the appeal was given to Mr Ashok Sen, who was the Law Minister in Nehru's Cabinet. It is ironical that Sen had been "dropped" from the Cabinet by Mrs Gandhi herself when she became the Prime Minister.

As it was Mrs Gandhi's appeal, Sen was first called upon to make his submissions. In the light of the amendments, Sen's submissions were necessarily brief. He submitted that Mrs Gandhi had been convicted by the High Court on extremely technical grounds. Seeking justification for the amendments, Sen said that the case had become an extremely controversial one in which the judiciary had become dangerously embroiled. It was, therefore, to avoid embarrassment to the judiciary, that the Parliament had taken the responsibility on its own shoulders and clarified the issue by amending the Representation of the People Act. Sen read out the relevant portions of the amendments and submitted that it removed the whole basis on which Mrs Gandhi had been found guilty. Sen then also read out the relevant clause of the constitutional amendment which declared the election of the Prime Minister valid and pleaded that the case be disposed of according to the mandate of the constitutional amendment.

It was now Bhushan's turn to make his submissions. He told the Court that he was left with no option but to challenge the constitutional validity of the 39th Amendment. Bhushan told the Court that in Keshavananda Bharati's case, the 13 Member Bench had laid down that "no constitutional amendment could violate the basic features of the Constitution." He would be relying on the dictum of that case in his attack on the amendments.

Incidentally, these were the last five Judges left in the Supreme Court who had been parties to the decision in the Fundamental Rights case of Keshavananda Bharati. Out of these, only Justice Khanna was a party to the majority decision which laid down that Parliament was incompetent to destroy the basic structure of the Constitution, even by a constitutional amendment. The other four judges had held that the Parliament's amending powers were plenary.

Bhushan then told the Court that since a copy of the gazetted amendment had only been made available that very morning, he had not had enough time to study the ramifications of the amendments and thus frame a proper attack on them. He said that he would, therefore, be grateful if the Court adjourned the case for two weeks.

The Chief Justice seemed displeased. He said, "We want to furnish the case as expeditiously as possible. Why don't you start your arguments straightaway ?"

Bhushan: If your Lordships insist, I could start my arguments straightaway, but after two weeks I would be in a much better position to assist you. I can, however, at this moment indicate the line of attack which I will take.

Justice Khanna: Are you going to attack the Election Law Amendment too?

Bhushan: Yes.

The Attorney-General, at this point interjected to say that the decision in Keshvananda's case was too vague and he would like a review of the case to clarify the matter.[4]

Justice Mathew: But which Bench, according to you, should do it? (Since the Keshavananda case had been decided by 13 Judges it could be reviewed only by a Bench of at least 13 Judges.)

The Attorney-General could not give a categorical reply to this.

Bhushan then briefly indicated the line of attack that he would take. He stated that his first ground of attack would be that the amendment went against the principle of Separation of Powers which was a basic feature of the Constitution. "Since the amendment eliminates judicial review in the case of the election dispute of the Prime Minister, it goes against Article 136 of the Constitution which is the ultimate power of the Judiciary."

The second ground of attack of Bhushan was that the amendment had the effect of destroying democracy which, he said, was also a basic feature of the Constitution. "It is not a question of one or two elections, but a matter of principle. If the Parliament can remove one election from the Court's jurisdiction, it could also remove all. If this was granted to the Parliament, this would certainly have the effect of destroying democracy."

The third ground on which he would be challenging the amendment, Bhushan said, was that it destroyed equality, which was surely a basic feature of a Republican Constitution. He said, "Insofar as it places only the election of the Prime Minister beyond judicial review, it discriminates against other people solely on the ground that the person holds a high office."

The Chief Justice then held consultations with the other Judges for a few minutes, and announced that the case would be adjourned for two weeks, i.e., to 25 August. He directed the parties to exchange

[4]For the review of Keshavananda Bharati's case, see Appendix 3.

their written submissions by that date. With this, the Court adjourned.

THE IRE OF THE BAR

The Supreme Court Bar was angered at the indignities to which it had been subjected on 11 August. Firstly, they had to get passes to enter the Chief Justice's court-room, and then they had to go through a stringent personal security check. The Bar Association met some days later and demanded that the Chief Justice withdraw these restrictions. Ashok Sen, Mrs Gandhi's counsel, who was the President of the Association, met the Chief Justice and communicated this demand to him. The Chief Justice said that he would be willing to withdraw the restrictions if he, (Ashok Sen), took personal responsibility for the good conduct of the lawyers. Sen was willing, but the lawyers were not. "We are not children," they said, "that someone has to guarantee our safe conduct."

On 22 August, the Bar Association met again and passed resolution that no member of the Association should participate in, or witness the proceedings in Mrs Gandhi's case because of the restrictions. The resolution threatened that disciplinary action would be taken against any lawyer violating the resolution.

On 23 August, Raj Narain's lawyers went to Tihar Jail to consult him They drafted a petition addressed to the Supreme Court which was signed by Raj Narain. The petition referred to the Bar Association resolution, stating that since all of Raj Narain's lawyers were members of the Association, they would not be able to argue before the Court. It was, therefore, prayed that either the Chief Justice withdraw the restrictions, or that the Court permit Raj Narain himself to argue his own case in person.

This petition was presented to the Deputy Registrar the same afternoon. Although it was Saturday and the Court was not sitting, the petition was immediately transmitted to the Chief Justice. The Chief Justice reacted instantly. At 8.00 P.M., the Chief Justice told the Registrar to announce that all restrictions on entry for the lawyers were withdrawn. Pass requirements would, however, remain for visitors.

The next day being Sunday, the Bar Association could not meet to withdraw their resolution. A meeting was scheduled for 1.00 P.M. on Monday, 25 August. It was expected that the formality of withdrawing the resolution would be completed in that meeting.

4

Validity of the Constitutional Amendment

12

"IT DESTROYS DEMOCRACY"

When the Supreme Court bench assembled on 25 August at 10.30 A.M., Raj Narain was represented only by J.P. Goyal, while all the lawyers of the other side were present. This was so because the Bar Association's resolution that no lawyer should attend the Chief Justice's court had not yet been withdrawn, as they had not had time to meet after the concession of their demands. Bhushan had, therefore, decided not to go to court and Goyal was to plead for an adjournment, pending the withdrawal of the Bar resolution. He did so when called upon to argue.

The Chief Justice, being in no mood to concede any further demands in this case, said that he would like to proceed with the case immediately. This provoked Goyal to give vent to his anger. He exclaimed loudly: "How can we proceed? Your Lordship, the Chief Justice, will have to give an explanation as to why all the members of the Bar were searched on 11 August. Even the lady lawyers were not spared. However, Mulla, a Counsel of Mrs Gandhi, was not searched. The Chief Justice will have to give an explanation for this discrimination.

Chief Justice: Behave yourself Mr Goyal.

Attorney-General: That will be a contempt of court.

Goyal (violently): All right, punish me! Second me to jail. I am ready to face the consequences. But how can we proceed till the Bar association resolution is withdrawan.

The Chief Justice was subdued. He explained, "You see it is such difficult case for us. All of you should help us in our duty." At this juncture, Ashok Sen informed the court that the Bar Association meeting was scheduled to take place at 1.00 P.M. He said that he would inform the court of the decision arrived at after lunch and said that it would be convenient if the case was adjourned till then. The Chief Justice consulted his brother Judges and agreed to adjourn the case till lunch.

The Bar Association met at 1.00 P.M., and in view of the concession of their demand, unanimously agreed to withdraw their resolution.

After lunch, at 2.00 P.M., all the lawyers of both sides trooped into the court room. The Judges arrived and the stage was finally set for the constitutional battle to begin.

The Counsel for the appellant, Sen, was called upon first to make his submissions. Giving a brief history of the case, he told the court that the appellant was found guilty of two corrupt practices by the High Court. He said, "These two charges were very technical in nature and the Legislature in its wisdom retrospectively amended the election law which took care of them. After that, however, the 39th Constitutional Amendment was passed by Parliament, which constitutionally disposed off the case. Seeing that the case had raised a lot of unhealthy controversy, the Constituent body decided to take the responsibility on its own shoulders to avoid embarassment to the judiciary." Sen then read out the provisions of the Constitutional Amendment and ended with the plea that the appeal be disposed of according to the mandate of the amendment.

BHUSHAN'S OPENING ARGUMENTS

It was Bhushan's turn now. Getting to his feet he launched a strong attack on Sen's rationale for justifying the Constitutional Amendment, saying that it was the function of the judiciary to deal with cases, however complicated they may be. "The Constituent body allows the judiciary to handle all sorts of election petitions, but when the Prime Minister's election is set aside, it suddenly feels that this case is too complex for the judiciary."

Coming to the validity of the 39th Amendment, Counsel summarized his three main grounds of attack on the Amendment Act: (1) That it was not an amendment of the Constitution at all. (2) That if it could be called an amendment at all, it destroyed several basic features of the Constitution. (3) That it was passed in an illegal Session of Parliament and was hence infructuous.

The mention of the third ground caused a stir in the court as it was indeed an unexpected and sensational argument. In fact, this argument had occurred to Bhushan only a few days earlier. Although not very optimistic about it being accepted, he had decided to include it as one of the grounds of challenge in order to add to the psychological pressure on the Judges. Briefly explaining his arguments on the third ground, Bhushan said that since a large number of Members of Parliament were illegally detained, all the proceedings of the Monsoon Session of Parliament became illegal and void. This amendment, since it was passed in that Session, was also void, he submitted.

Attorney-General (interjecting)*:* I wonder whether court can go into the question of the legality of the detentions without a writ of *habeas corpus*.

Justice Mathew: Can we have a *habeas corpus* in these circumstances?

Bhushan: I am not asking for the release of the detenus. But the legality of the Session of Parliament will have to be determined.

Chief Justice: We shall have to consider whether we can go into that or not. In any case that question will arise only after your first two points are decided.

Counsel then referred to his second ground of attack, that the amendment destroyed several basic features of the Constitution. He briefly explained what the basic structure theory meant. He said that the doctrine propounded in Keshavananda Bharati's case was that Parliament could not amend the Constitution so as to destroy its identity. Illustrating this, Counsel explained: "Nowadays we hear a lot about transplants of various organs of the body. Suppose all the organs of a person's body were transplanted and only a leg or a hand remained, could one say that it is still the same person. Suppose every part of my friend, Mr Goyal's body was to be transplanted and only his thumb remained, would his identity remain the same? Could his wife still recognise him?"

Chief Justice (relieving his ire at Mr Goyal)*:* Mr Bhushan, do you want his heart transplanted first or his brain?

Counsel: Everything, my Lord; his heart, his brain, his legs, his hands. Only the thumb remains. (Everyone, particularly the Chief Justice was enjoying himself.) It is not the bulk of the transplanted part which matters. Suppose a person's brain were transplanted. A brain weighs...

Chief Justice: 64 ounces.

Counsel: So if these 64 ounces of a person's body were removed, would his identity remain the same?

Amendment is Exercise of Judicial Power

Bhushan then proceeded to elaborate on his initial submissions. He said that in order to determine the validity of the amendment, it would be necessary to find out exactly what had been done by it. He read out the entire text of the 39th Amendment and submitted that it was only clauses 4(4) and 4(5), which were relevant. They read:

> 4(4) No law made by Parliament before the commencement of the Constitution (Thirty-ninth Amendment) Act, 1975, insofar as it relates to election petitions and members connected therewith, shall apply or shall be deemed ever to have applied to or in relation to the election of any such person as is referred to in clause (1) to either House of Parliament and such election shall not be deemed to be void or ever to have become void on any ground on which such election could be declared to be void or has, before the commencement, been declared to be void under any such law and notwithstanding any order made by any court, before such commencement, declaring such election to be void, such election shall continue to be valid in all respects and any such order and any finding on which such order is based shall be and shall be deemed always to have been void and of no effect.
>
> 4(5) Any appeal or cross-appeal against any such order of any court as is referred to in clause (4) pending immediately before the commencement of the Constitution (Thirty-ninth Amendment) Act, 1975, before the Supreme Court shall be disposed of in conformity with the provisions of clause (4).

At this point, Justice Khanna asked Ashok Sen whether he agreed that it was only clauses 4(4) and 4(5) which were relevant in the present case. Sen agreed.

Reading out clause 4(4) very carefully, Bhushan emphasized the words "and such election...of no effect," submitting that this clause clearly declared the election to be valid and the High Court judgment void, and namely an arbitrary exercise of judicial power.

Justice Khanna: Suppose clause (4) had only said, 'No law made by Parliament before the commencement of this Act insofar as it relates to election petitions and matters connected therewith, shall apply or shall be deemed ever to have applied to or in relation to the election of any such person as is referred to in clause (1) to either House of Parliament,' and stopped there, would not the election be, *ipso facto*, valid?

Counsel: No, the High Court judgment would stand, unless it was declared to be void and the election would continue to be void unless it was declared to be valid.

"Judicial Power not with Parliament"

Bhushan's next contention was that judicial power could not be exercised by Parliament in the guise of a constitutional amendment. "The power conferred by Article 368 to Parliament is of amending the Constitution. Parliament can only exercise that power which is expressly conferred to it and no other power. The Constitution lays down the organizational structure of Government and distributes the sovereign power among the various organs. Thus an amendment of the Constitution would be one which alters the structure of the Government or redistributes power among the various organs of Government.

Attorney-General (interjecting): This argument was not raised in Keshavananda Bharati's case and cannot be raised now.

Bhushan: This point had never arisen in any of the previous cases on constitutional amendment, either in Shankari Prasad, Sajjan Singh, Golak Nath or Keshavananda Bharati. It is arising for the first time now because it is the first time that judicial power is being exercised in the guise of a constitutional amendment.

Counsel proceeded to cite some definitions of the Constitution which made it clear that a Constitution dealt with the structure and organization of the Government. "Such being the character of a Constitution, an amendment to it can only redefine the organization of Government and the distribution of power therein. Clause 4(4) doing no such thing cannot be said to be an amendment of the Constitution."

Justice Mathew: Has any Constitutional amendment in the United States ever set aside a judicial decision?

Counsel: As far as I am aware, none.

Justice Mathew: Can Parliament amend the Constitution and give to itself judicial powers?

Counsel: It can, but first it must amend the Constitution to make itself a judicial organ, In that case, Parliament would itself become a judicial organ.

Justice Mathew: The British can pass a Bill of Attainder. This is a judicial function. What is the limitation on the plenary Constituent power of Parliament to perform a judicial function?

Counsel: The position is different in Britain due to historical and other reasons. There being no written Constitution, the British Parliament is sovereign. But since a written Constitution defines the limits of the powers of the Indian Parliament, it can only exercise its powers within those bounds.

Justice Mathew: Can the constituent power not extend to executive, legislative and judicial powers which are all powers granted by the Constitution?

Counsel: The power of amending the Constitution cannot comprehend an executive or judicial power, since they are powers of a radically different nature. The Constituent body being a delegated authority can only exercise the power which has been delegated to it, which is of amending the Constitution.

Counsel then referred to a Ceylon case[1] in which it was held that the power of amending the Constitution was a legislative power. He argued that since the amendment decided merely one particular case, it was the exercise of purely judicial power and the *ultra vires* Article 368 of the Constitution.

Amendment Destroys the Basic Structure

Moving to his next point, Bhushan argued that even if clause 4(4) could be regarded as an exercise of constituent power, it destroyed several basic features of the Constitution. He read out excerpts from the judgment of the seven majority Judges in the Keshavananda Bharati case to establish the proposition that Parliament cannot in exercise of its amending power abrogate or destroy the basic structure or institutional framework of the Constitution. He contended that once this proposition is established, there would be no escape from its compulsion by saying that the concept of basic features was too vague to be understood.

Justice Beg: Mr Bhushan, this concept of basic features does seem very vague and slippery. I feel that all the provisions of the Constitution are equally essential.

Counsel: What in law is not vague or slippery? If everything was cut, dry and crystal clear, we need not have Judges or four Lordship's eminence to apply the law. What about the doctrine that the essential powers of legislation cannot be delegated? What are the 'essential' powers of delegation? Is this not an equally vague doctrine? But it has been interpreted and applied by the court ever since our Constitution came into existence. In fact, Justice Mathew, who although did not agree with the basic structure theory, had said in his judgement—

> I am not dismayed by the suggestion that no yardstick is furnished to the court except the trained judicial perception, for finding

[1] AELR 1964(2) 785, *Bribery Commissioner* v. *Ranasingha.*

It Destroys Democracy

the core or essence of a right, or essential features of the Constitution.... Few Constitutional issues can be presented in black and white terms. What are essential features and non-essential features of the Constitution? Where does the core of a right and the periphery begin? These are not matters of icy certainty; but, for that reason, I am not persuaded to hold that they do not exist, or that they are too elusive for judicial perception. Most of the things in life that are worth talking about are matters of degree and the great Judges are those who are most capable of discerning which of the gradations make genuine difference.

Counsel went on: "What is the difficulty in discerning the basic feature? Anyone who reads the Constitution can easily see that our Constitution is a thoroughly demoratic Constitution where the rule of law is a recognized institution. One can also see that our Constitution is republican, recognizing the sacred principle of equality before law. Thus, it must be held that at least democracy, rule of law, and equality are basic features of our Constitution.

Counsel then read out those parts of the judgments in the Keshavananda Bharati case where the basic features of the Constitution are indicated. All the Judges had given illustrative and not exhaustive lists of the basic features. Most of them had held democracy and equality to be basic.

Bhushan told the court that he was relying on the following as the basic features of the Constitution:

1. Separation of powers between the Legislature, Executive and Judiciary.
2. Democratic character of our polity.
3. Equality before the law and equal protection of the laws.
4. Rule of law and judicial review.
5. Political justice as enshrined in the Preamble of the Constitution.

Before Counsel could start his argument on how several basic features of the Constitution were destroyed by the amendment, Justice Khanna asked a few questions for clarification: (1) Whether election disputes must be settled by the courts of law, and not by any other body? (2) Whether the provision for election petitions is an essential feature of democracy? (3) If the election of the Prime Minister were to be decided by the Chief Justice, Speaker or Vice-President, would the democratic set-up be affected?

Replying to the first question, Counsel said that election disputes could be decided by other bodies if overall supervision of the Judiciary was retained by Article 136.[2] As regards the question of whether election petitions are necessary in a democracy, Counsel said that they would perhaps not be necessary if the conduct of elections was itself vested in a judicial body which enquired into the complaints during the election process itself. In reply to the third question, Counsel said, "Why should only the Prime Minister's election be decided by a special forum? Such arbitrary discrimination, without any rationale, is clearly destructive of the sacred concept of equality."

Justice Mathew: What about elections to the British House of Commons? Who adjudicates the election disputes there?

Niren De: The House itself does it.

Bhushan: The position in Britain may be different due to historical reasons. After gradual evolution, the Parliament there has become supreme. In India, Parliament is not sovereign. Therefore, we cannot compare the situation in Britain to that in India.

Judicial Review Eliminated

Bhushan went on to submit that the first basic feature effected by the amendment was judicial review. "This amendment makes serious inroads into the powers of the judiciary and is thus repugnant to the separation of power envisaged by the Constitution. One of the main functions of the Judiciary in our country has been adjudicating election disputes. In our Parliamentary system, the party who wins the election and comes into power immediately gains control of two of the three wings of the Government, namely, the executive and the legislative. The postulate of democracy is that the continuance of that party in power should depend on the continued support of the people. This can only be ensured by free and fair periodical elections. For the elections to be free and fair, it is necessary that some third party, which has no axe of its own to grind, be there to preserve the purity of elections. That is why the function of adjudicating election disputes has been entrusted to the Judiciary. The 39th Amendment, as it takes away the right of the Judiciary to adjudicate election disputes relating to the Prime Minister makes serious inroads into this power of the judiciary. It is not a matter of one election. It is a matter of principle.

[2]Article 136 gives the Supreme Court the power to entertain special leave petitions against the decisions of all courts and tribunals.

It Destroys Democracy

If the Judiciary's power can be taken away for one election, it can very well be taken away for all elections."

Democracy Destroyed

Proceeding to his next submission, Counsel said, "Clause (4) arbitrarily declares the election of the Prime Minister valid. If such an arbitrary validation of election is possible, then democracy could well be demolished in the country. There are certain norms which have to be obeyed by all candidates. The logic is that an election procured by unfair means is not a fair election. The amendment declares that the Prime Minister's election shall continue to be valid even though she might have bribed voters, used undue influence, coerced her rival candidate!

"The other side says that the Prime Minister is very important. That is no answer, because there would be no end to important members of the ruling party who play an integral part in the lawmaking process of the country. Using unfair means they would do not even have to get a majority of votes. Only the Returning Officers would have to declare them to be the returned candidates. No further argument is possible.

Justice Beg: Could it not be that the unusual excitement and public controversy aroused by this case justified the exercise of this power of amendment?

Counsel: What is the unusual public controversy aroused by this case? It is only that some Opposition leaders were saying that Mrs Gandhi should step down as the Prime Minister till she was cleared by the Supreme Court. Moreover, if principles are sacrificed for expedients, then democracy is finished in the country.

Equality Denied

Counsel's next contention was that the amendment which provides that the election of the Prime Minister and Speaker shall be valid, was seriously repugnant to the principle of equality, which was a basic feature of the Constitution.

Justice Mathew: Equality is a concept which does not admit of any easy definition. Instances could be cited where equal treatment might result in actual injustice. Indeed, justice and equality are not always compatible.

Counsel: I agree that equality is not an absolutely rigid concept and people could justifiably be treated unequally if they were placed in unequal situations. But there has to be a rational relation of the classification to the object sought to be achieved. I agree that the Prime Minister and the Speaker are not ordinary citizens. But this does not mean that unequal treatment in election matters is also justified for them. Why should their election not be open to challenge as everyone else's is? If they have committed corrupt practices, why should their election not be set aside, in the same way as an ordinary candidate's election is? In fact, being leaders of the country there should be stricter standards for them, because if the leaders of the country do not set an example of fair play, then who will?

Justice Beg: Can merely an exception to the rule destroy a basic feature?

Counsel: Equality is a concept to which there would be no exception. Either we have equality or we do not. In fact, Justice Jaganmohan Reddy in his judgment in Keshavananda's case has clearly stated, 'Insofar as the abridgement of the right conferred by Article 14 (equality) is concerned, it would be ultra vires for the reason that a mere violation of this right amounts to taking away or damaging the right.

No Rule of Law

Bhushan's next contention was that the 39th Amendment completely destroyed the rule of law and eliminated judictal review, which were both essential features of the Constitution.

Justice Mathew: If Article 136 were repealed, would it lead to the destruction of a basic feature? (Article 136 provides for petitions of special leave to the Supreme Court against the decisions of all Judicial Tribunals.)

Counsel: Yes. Article 136 is the ultimate provision for overall supervision of the Supreme Court over judicial tribunals. Its repeal would certainly destroy the basic feature of judicial review.

Chief Justice: Can the Constitution be amended so as to exclude the jurisdiction of the Supreme Court in some matters?

Bhushan: Yes, it could. If the Supreme Court was over-burdened with work, some less important matters could be taken away from its jurisdiction and vested in some other body.

Justice Mathew: You are arguing that both judicial review and democracy are basic features. Don't you think that there is a certain inconsistency between the two? Parliament represents the will of the people and when the Judiciary strikes down a legislation, don't you think that is is acting against the will of the people?

Counsel: A Parliament elected by the people on a certain issue might not represent the will of the people on another issue. Since a referendum on every issue is impossible, therefore the people acting through the Constituent Assembly placed certain injunctions on the powers of Parliament. They provided that Parliament could only exercise its powers in a certain manner and created a judiciary to keep the Parliament in check. Therefore, when the Judiciary strikes down a legislation, it is really giving effect to the will of the people.

Justice Khanna: You mean that the Judiciary when it strikes down a legislation is giving effect to the will of the people as represented by the Constituent Assembly.

Counsel: Yes.

Justice Mathew: But Mr Bhushan, don't you think that the Judiciary is an undemocratic institution, as some say, an oligarchic institution?

Counsel: All right, my Lord, we can call it an undemocratic institution, which is necessary for the preservation of democracy.

Continuing his submissions, Counsel said that he was frankly horrified at the manner in which the Amendment gave a go-by to the rule of law ('no law shall apply to the election of the Prime Minister, and that the election would continue to be valid, no matter how it was procured,)

Monsoon Session Illegal

Coming to the third leg of his submissions, Bhushan argued that the Monsoon Session of Parliament in which the amendment was passed was illegal and that all business transacted in that Session had hence become illegal and void.

He told the court that most of the Opposition leaders, who were Members of Parliament, were under detention without trial when the amendment was passed. They were not even supplied the grounds of their detention which is a constitutional necessity under Article 22. Hence the detentions had become unconstitutional.

Counsel was asked by the court whether the detention could be declared illegal without a writ habeas corpus. He replied that he was not asking for the release of the detenues, but if he could prove that on the face of it that detentions were unconstitutional, the court would have to decide whether or not the Parliament was legal.

Justice Mathew: If a statute was presented to the court duly gazetted, how could the Court refuse to accept its validity?

Bhushan: How do we know that it is really the Gazette of

India and that what it enacts has been validly enacted in a proper Session of Parliament?

Counsel quoted from a 1965 judgement of Justice Gajendragadkar.[3] He had observed, "Article 212(1) seems to make it possible for a citizen to call in question in a proper court of law the validity of any proceeding in the legislative chamber if his case is that such proceeding suffers not from an irregularity of procedure, but from an illegality." Amplifying his contention, Counsel said that here there was no irregularity of procedure, but illegality.

He went on: "On 26 June, an emergency was proclaimed by the President on the advice of the Government and a large number of Opposition leaders were detained under MISA. None of them were supplied the grounds of detention. On 27 June, the President, on the advice of the Government, issued an order under Article 359 of the Constitution suspending the rights of citizens to go to court for the enforcement of their fundamental rights.

Counsel said that even though Article 22—which makes it mandatory for the Government to supply the grounds of detention to a detenu—was suspended by a Presidential Order, the Article still remained in the Constitution. He quoted from the judgment of Justice Mathew in the Keshavananda Bharati case where he had said, "A law is a law even if it is not enforceable in a court of law." Thus Counsel argued that although Article 22 was not enforceable, it still remained the law, and the constitutional obligation of the Government for supplying the grounds of detention was not waived by the Presidential Order.

"I agree that if some members of Parliament are legally arrested, then they forfeit their right to attend the Parliament Session. But since here they were not legally arrested, their right remained and their not being given an opportunity to be present in the proceedings of Parliament clearly rendered the proceedings illegal."

Justice Khanna: How many Members of Parliament have been arrested?

Counsel: I am not absolutely certain of that, but that would not make any difference to the illegality of the Session. Even if one Member has been illegally prevented from attending the Session, it would render the proceedings illegal.

With this Bhushan concluded his arguments on the validity of the Constitutional Amendment, after arguing for about five days.

[3]AIR 1965, SC 745, Ref. Powers and Immunities of State Legislature.

13

"PM CAN BE ABOVE THE LAW"

There was no doubt that Bhushan's argument had a significant effect on the Judges. The Mathew-Bhushan confrontation had been described as "a Tartar meeting a Tartar." The change in the Judge's attitude during the course of his argument was also visible to Bhushan. Since foreign newsmen were not allowed entry in the court, they came to Bhushan for briefing at the end of each day's arguments. And each day Bhushan was more convinced of the chances of the amendment being struck down.

THE ATTORNEY-GENERAL'S ARGUMENTS

The other side was shaken by the effect of Bhushan's arguments. Since the validity of a Constitutional Amendment was in question, the Attorney-General, Niren De and the Solicitor General, Lal Narain Sinha were also defending on behalf of the Union Government. The Attorney-General having right of precedence was the first to argue in defence of the amendment. In order to destroy the effect of Bhushan's arguments, De started his arguments with great gusto. He began, "For five days your Lordships have heard Shanti Bhushan impugn the validity of the 39th Constitutional Amendment. On a petty peddling issue, a case is being made out that the 39th Amendment destroys the basic structure of our Constitution. In fact, deciding election disputes had always been a privilege of the Legislature, not only in our country but in almost all democratic countries. Therefore, how can we call Judicial Review of election disputes a feature of the Constitution, let alone a basic feature. Even in the British system where this power has been delegated to the judiciary, the Parliament retains overall supervision and can always interfere when it wants to."

Continuing, the Attorney-General raised a preliminary objection against Bhushan's argument that constituent power did not embrace judicial power. He said that this argument was not raised in Keshavananda Bharati's case and hence could not be raised then. "In Keshavananda's case, the scope and limit of constituent power were examined from every angle, and the only conclusion which emerged was that you cannot destroy the basic structure of the Constitution. What is inserted in the Constitution is solely for the Constituent body to decide and the court cannot pronounce upon it. The judiciary is also a creature of the Constitution, and being so, it cannot say that it does not like a particular provision of the Constitution. As soon as an Article is incorporated in the Constitution, it becomes part of it and the judiciary being a creature of the Constitution has to give effect to it.

Justice Khanna: The Judiciary has to see whether the Parliament has exercised its power within the limits laid down by the Constitution. The argument of the other side is that constitutional law must also come within the concept of law, and the problem before us is whether a law can relate to an individual case.

Counsel: I submit that it can.

At this point, Justice Mathew quoted from Blackstone's Commentaries on the Laws of England in which it was stated,

> Therefore a particular Act of the Legislature to confiscate the goods of Titus or to attaint him of high treason, does not enter into the idea of a municipal law: for the operation of this Act is spent on Titus only and has no relation to the community in general: it is rather a sentence than a law.

De explained that this dealt only with the ordinary law-making powers of the Government. The constituent power stood on a different plane. It was all-embracing and could enact a law for a particular person too. He proceeded to read out excerpts from the judgments of the various Judges in the Keshavananda Bharati case to establish his proposition that the subject-matter was not a limitation on the constituent power. He particularly emphasized the portions of Justice Mathew's judgment where he had observed:

> In other words, irrespective of the subject-matter, the moment a

provision becomes validity embodied in the constitution, it acquires a validity of its own, which is beyond challenge, and the question whether it relates to constitutional law with reference to the subject matter is wholly irrelevant.

These judgments, Counsel contended, hardly left any room for doubt that the subject-matter was not considered a limitation on the amending power. The Parliament in exercise of its amending power could alter the law in any way it liked.

Justice Chandrachud: Clause (4) of the Amendment does not alter the law. It just provides that the election shall be valid.

Counsel: The Constituent body in its wisdom can always declare an election valid.

Justice Khanna: Could the Amendment have been valid, if it had come after the Supreme Court had finally decided on the merits of the case?

Counsel: Yes, it could. If it can be done now it can also be done after the Supreme Court judgment.

Counsel further submitted that the Constitution contained detailed provisions about elections. He said that part 15 of the Constitution had been held in Ponnuswami's case to be a complete Code on Elections. He argued that Articles 324 to 329 dealt with all the aspects of elections to the Legislature and if the Constituent body felt that the elections of the Prime Minister and the Speaker were important enough to stand on a different footing, then it has every right to make special provisions about their elections.

Justice Beg: When Article 329(b) gives Parliament the power to make laws for election to Legislatures, why could they have not made these special provisions about the Prime Minister by ordinary legislation instead of by a constitutional amendment.

Counsel: If the Constituent body thought that the matter was important enough to be taken into their own hands, their wisdom cannot be questioned.

He then proceeded to cite a number of authorities to prove his contention that the Prime Minister and Speaker because of their high offices stood on a different footing from all other people. This being so, the special provisions for the elections would be justified.

"Constituent Power Comprehends All"

De's next contention was that the constituent power was the fountain source of all legislative, executive and judicial powers. For the Constituent body, there was no separation of powers. Therefore, while it was correct to say that the Legislature could not exercise judicial power, the same could not be said for the Constituent body.

Justice Mathew: Mr Bhushan has argued that a case pending in the court cannot be withdrawn and decided by Parliament. You say that all these things can be done by Parliament in exercise of its Constituent power.

Counsel: Yes.

Justice Khanna: Does the Legislature in deciding an election dispute not have to hear the parties concerned?

Counsel: Parliament when it decides an election dispute in its constituent authority does not act as a judicial forum. It is, therefore, not incumbent on it to follow the procedure of a Judicial Tribunal. It may or may not hear the contending parties. The reason is that sometimes when political necessities overwhelm all other considerations, they have to act in a non-judicial manner, even against the principles of natural justice. Discretionary powers must be vested somewhere in the matter of elections to deal with political situations.

Justice Mathew: This court is not concerned with political necessities or demands, nor is the court concerned with the propriety of the Amendment. The Court is only concerned with whether the amending power of Parliament is comprehensive enough to validate an invalid election.

Counsel: The only limitation is of basic features. There is no other limitation.

Judicial Review not Basic

De's next main submission was that Judicial Review in election matters was not a constitutional compulsion even before the 39th Amendment. He said that Article 329(b) of the Constitution clearly empowered the Parliament to lay down the manner in which election disputes would be decided.

Counsel argued that a fair reading of Article 329(b) clearly showed that the intention of the Constitution-makers was to vest the final authority of deciding election disputes in the Legislature. Being so, judicial review of election disputes could hardly be called a feature of the Constitution, let alone a basic feature.

Justice Khanna: Is there anything in Article 329(b) which prevents the Parliament from appointing non-judicial bodies as the authority to decide election disputes?

De: Nothing whatsoever. Power given to Parliament under Article 329(b) is plenary and without limitation.

In support of this contention, he cited Ponnuswami's case[1] in which Justice Fazl Ali had said,

> Strictly speaking, it is the sole right of Legislature to examine and determine all matters relating to the election of its own members.

This reading of Article 329(b), Counsel maintained, was in conformity with the provisions regarding election disputes in almost all democracies, where the final authority in regard to election disputes was the Legislature itself. He read out the provisions in the Constitutions of several democracies—USA, Australia, Japan, France—regarding elections.

In support of the proposition that election disputes do not come within the domain of the judiciary without statutory authorization, Counsel also quoted from an American book, *Corpus Juris*.

He also quoted from "American, Jurisprudence," which says:

> At common law there was no right to contest in a court a public election. The theory being that elections belonged to the political propriety of Government beyond the control of judicial power...

Referring to the provisions in England, Counsel referred to the overall authority of Parliament.

These provisions, asserted the Attorney-General, clearly showed that the prerogative of deciding election disputes always belonged to the Legislature. "The reason for such a provision is that public interest is involved in election disputes. An election dispute is not merely a dispute between two contending parties. It involves the rights of the whole electorate."

He further argued, "The real question to be examined in connection with the violation of election laws is whether violation was deliberate or otherwise. The courts of law are constrained to follow forensic rules, while the Legislature is not. This is why this power vests in the Legislature. If the Legislature felt that a particular violation of the law was not intentional, it would exonerate the person concerned."

Counsel further contended that there were several Articles in the

[1] 1952(3) **SCR** 218.

original Constitution which expressly excluded judicial review from some fields. "Although Article 136 gave the Supreme Court the power to entertain a petition of special leave against the decision of any court or tribunal of the country, Article 136(2) provides an express limitation on the Supreme Court's power in respect of the armed forces' tribunals.

"There have been several amendments too, which have excluded judicial review and which have been upheld by this court. The 20th Amendment by introducing Article 230(a) had directly set aside a court-judgment which had invalidated appointments of certain District Judges. Similarly, the judgments in the Keshavananda Bharati's case on Article 31B and 31C are also of crucial importance. (Article 31B provides that no law put in the Ninth Schedule shall be questioned on the ground of violation of any fundamental right. Article 31C provides that no law made to implement the directive principles could be challenged on the same ground.) The very fact that these Articles were upheld by the Supreme Court makes it impossible for anyone to argue that judicial review is a basic feature of the Constitution."

Judicial Review Merely Abridged

De next contended that even if judicial review was a basic feature, the 39th Amendment merely involved an abridgement of judicial review and not its abrogation. He said, "Keshavananda's case laid down that you can abridge, but cannot destroy a basic feature."

Justice Mathew: Once judicial review is removed, what remains of it?

Justice Chandrachud: The majority view in Keshavananda Bharati seems to bar even touching the basic structure.

Justice Mathew: No, you can touch, but you cannot destroy.

Justice Khanna: What has been said in Keshavananda Bharati is that you cannot change the basic structure.

Counsel: What I am submitting is that the amendment only excludes judicial review in respect of one election. Judicial review in other elections remains exactly as it was. And it is not as if it is the first time that an election has been validated. Elections have been validated ever since our Constitution came into being. The Representation of People Act, 1956 validated some six thousand elections. Apart from that, the Punjab Act of 1952, the Mysore Act of 1957, the Uttar Pradesh Act of 1971 and the Rajasthan Act of 1969, all validated elections. The Rajasthan Act of 1969 had validated a single a election.

This validation had been challenged but was upheld by the Supreme Court. How can the other side argue that the single election cannot be validated?

Counsel also cited instances of England where statutes had validated elections, quoting from Halsbury's Laws of England. Justice Mathew asked him to cite any similar instance in the United States. Counsel quoted from a book on the American Constitutional Law by Trasolini and Shapiro, which said,

> Actually, there have been numerous instances in our Constitutional history, when Supreme Court opinions have been overturned or reversed either by the Court itself or in some other manner.

Counsel then pleaded that the amendment be examined from the practical point of view and not on a theoretical or academic basis.

Justice Khanna: Can we uphold this amendment merely because the offences in this case are technical? Can we, because of the facts of an individual case, uphold a constitutional amendment which is so widely worded?

Counsel replied that the amendment only touched one election and it was thus not very wide in its application.

Equality not Basic

Counsel strongly contested Bhushan's submission that equality was a basic feature of the Constitution. "After the Court has upheld Articles 31B and 31C, it cannot be argued that equality is a basic feature. However, even if equality is a basic feature, we shall see that it has not been violated."

Justice Mathew: The principle of equality permits unequal treatment to people who are situated differently. Is there anything in this case to justify unequal treatment?

Counsel: Can anyone say that the Prime Minister and the Speaker belong to the same category as an ordinary candidate?

Justice Khanna: Is that relevant for the matter of election?

Counsel: Regarding equality, only the classification is subject to scrutiny and not the object of the classification. The object is left solely to the wisdom of the legislature. They may or may not disclose why they were making a particular classification.

The Attorney-General could not complete his arguments, and he had only gone thus far when the court rose on 4 September. When it assembled on 5 September, the Attorney-General was not present. The

Solicitor General, Sinha told the court that De had suddenly suffered an attack of high blood-pressure, on account of which he would not be able to attend the court for some days. The Chief Justice showed his willingness to adjourn the case, but Sinha said he would argue on behalf of the Union till De recovered.

By now it looked as if the Constitutional Amendment would be struck down. De's arguments had not cut much ice with the Judges. On the final day of his arguments, Justice Khanna had said, 'Mr Attorney-General, I think this Constitutional Amendment will have to go. However, the election can be upheld on the basis of the Election Laws Amendments, subject, of course, to what Bhushan has to say about those." This was the position when the Solicitor General began his arguments.

The Solicitor General's Arguments

Beginning his arguments, Sinha briefly outlined his main contentions. He said that the Constitution permitted exclusion of judicial review for implementing the Directive Principles of State policy. "A similar power must necessarily be conceded when such exclusion is needed in the larger interests of the security of the State. The constituent body, legislating for the larger interests of the State, sometimes makes classifications, the validity of which rests on material to which the court had no access and which might be of highly confidential nature, relating to secret forces inside and outside the country. In such cases, the decision has to be a matter of political necessity and cannot be subjected to judicial scrutiny."

Counsel further submitted that judicial review of election disputes was not a constitutional compulsion. "Article 329(b) of the Constitution contemplates that the Parliament could vest the power to entertain election petitions in whatever body it wants, even in itself. In such a case, Parliament could resolve the dispute after receiving a report from a Special Committee. Thus, judicial review could be eliminated without an amendment of the Constitution at all."

Counsel claimed that judicial review could be validly excluded in certain spheres specially in respect of Article 14 (the right of equality). This, he said, was clear from the fact that in the Keshavananda Bharati case, Articles 31B and 31C had been upheld.

Justice: Mathew Is rule of law part of the basic structure of the Constitution? If so, would not equality before law be also basic?

Counsel: There can be rule of law without strict equality. Moreover, sometimes rule of law can be stretched for the security of the State.

Arguing further, Counsel said that sometimes for political expediencies, the Parliament had to make classifications which though wrong in ordinary times were necessary to meet those expediencies. "Life is not mere logic always. The interests of the State sometimes transcend the needs of logic."

Justice Beg: You are in fact saying that there are no limits on the amending power.

Counsel: I am only saying that when Articles 31B and 31C were upheld, one cannot say that exclusion of judicial review regarding equality destroys a basic feature.

Justice Mathew: Keshavananda Bharati's case laid down the principles that the basic features including equality could not be violated. If a case lays down a principle, but goes wrong in its application, the principle alone would be binding and not its application.

Counsel: When their Lordships laid down that judicial review could be excluded in certain fields, they also laid down a principle.

Illustrating his arguments, Counsel said that in Mulki Rules case,[2] the said Rules were struck down by the Andhra Pradesh High Court. "This decision wrought havoc in Andhra Pradesh. So the 32nd Amendment had to be enacted which overturned the effect of the court judgment. Therefore, sometimes political interests have also to be considered in deciding the validity of an enactment."

Justice Beg: Mr Sinha, your argument that this amendment bars judicial review can be against the interests of your client, as it may prevent her from being cleared on the merits.

Counsel: No, my Lord. This amendment clearly bars the court from going into the merits of the case.

Counsel then read out a passage from Justice Khanna's judgment in Keshavananda Bharati's case to reinforce his contention that the constituent power was unlimited. The passage he read out said, "All provisions of the Constitution are subject to the amendatory process and cannot claim exemption from that process by being described as essential features."

At this, Justice Khanna interrupted him and asked him to read the whole paragraph before this. The paragraph read:

So far as the expression 'essential feature' means the basic structure or framework of the Constitution, I have already dealt with the question as to whether the power to amend the Constitution would include within itself the power to change the basic structure or

---

[2] (1970)(1) S.C.R. 115

framework of the Constitution. Apart from that, all provisions of the Constitution are subject to the amendatory process and cannot claim exemption from that process by being described essential features.

Justice Khanna told Sinha that after reading only the extract which Mr Sinha had read, it would seem that he (Justice Khanna) had given Parliament an unlimited power of amending the Constitution, but reading the whole paragraph made it clear that he had not. Therefore, he cautioned Sinha not to read his observations out of context.

Counsel then strongly rebutted Bhushan's arguments that constituent power did not include judicial power. He said that the constituent power included the power to re-adjust the distribution of legislative, judicial and executive power. "The judicial power in a given matter could be transferred to Parliament which can act by a simple majority. Therefore, there can be no valid objection to Parliament exercising judicial power, where it is acting by a two thirds majority."

Justice Mathew: Can the Constituent body exercise judicial power without first re-allocating the powers?

Counsel: If they can do it in two steps, why can't they do it in one?

Amendment an Exercise of Legislative Power

Sinha further submitted that clause (4) did not involve an exercise of judicial power. It only seemed to do so. He said, "Similar objectives can be achieved sometimes by legislative as well as judicial processes. Where the principle is laid down antecedently, its application is made by a judicial process. When the Legislature creates a principle and also works out the result in an individual case, the process is legislative. To enable it to take decisions, the Legislature has full power to collect materials and supplement the information of its members from all sources.

"A court adjudicates validity. The legislature creates validity, even retrospectively. Validation is law-making. A validating legislation does not involve a pronouncement on the correctness of a court judgment. It merely alters the legal position by creating a new law. What has been done by clause (4) is that the entire election law including Section 123 (corrupt practices) has been removed retrospectively for the Prime Minister's election. The result is that since no grounds existed for declaring her election void, the election, by that very fact, became valid.

Justice Mathew: Would retrospective repeal of the law on the basis which a judgment has been rendered, automatically render the judgment void?

Counsel: In my humble submission, it would.

Justice Mathew: If the High Court decides on the basis of a Supreme Court decision and the Supreme Court later overruled its decision on that point of law, does the High Court judgment automatically fall?

Counsel: No, not then.

Justice Mathew: Apart from repealing the Representation of the People Act for the Prime Minister, was any other law enacted on the basis of which the election might have been validated?

Counsel: No.

Justice Mathew: Then according to you, on what basis was the election validated?

Counsel: Because there were no grounds for declaring the election void.

Justice Khanna: Is there any instance where an election has been declared completely valid and not that a particular ground of invalidity has been removed?

Counsel could not cite any instance of this, but he did cite a Ceylon case[3] where the disqualification of a particular person had been removed by an Order in Council.

Justice Mathew: What about Liyanage's case. In that case, the Privy Council had ruled that legislation which was designed to affect a single person was invalid.

Democracy not Affected

Sinha next contended that the Amendment did not in any way affect democracy or the concept of free and fair elections. "Just because judicial scrutiny of a single election is removed, how can one say that the concept of free and fair election has disappeared? One cannot maintain that democracy would be destroyed if the Prime Minister's election was excluded from judicial scrutiny. President Ford of the United States did not come into office by an election. But because of that, can anyone maintain that America is no longer a democracy?"

Fundamental Rights not Basic

Sinha also submitted that fundamental rights were not part of the

[3] 1932 A.C. 260 *Abeyesereka* V *Jayatilake.*

basic structure of the Constitution. Therefore, the issue whether the amendment destroyed the equality became academic. He said that Justice Khanna had excluded fundamental rights from the basic structure. At this point, Justice Khanna interrupted Sinha and asked him to see his observations on page 685 in Keshavananda Bharati case, where he had observed,

> The secular character of the State, according to which the State shall not discriminate against any citizen on the ground of religion only, cannot likewise be done away with.

Justice Khanna told the Solicitor General that here he had unambiguously held Article 15 (a fundamental right) to be basic. How could Counsel then say that he had found none of the fundamental rights basic?

Legality of Session Unquestionable

Sinha then moved to the last leg of his arguments, the validity of the Monsoon Session of Parliament. "The essence of the grievance is not the illegality of the detentions of the Members of Parliament, but the consequent interference with their right of participation in the proceedings of Parliament. When a Member is excluded from participation in the proceedings of the House, the matter concerns Parliament alone, as the grievance is in regard to proceedings within the walls of Parliament. In regard to the rights to be exercised with the walls of the House, the House itself is the Judge."

In support of this proposition, Counsel quoted from May's Parliamentary Practice which says, "It is the right of each House to be the sole Judge of the lawfulness of its proceedings."

He also quoted a case[4] of England in which it was observed: "It seems to follow that the House of Commons has the exclusive power of interpreting the status so far as the regulation of its proceedings within its walls is concerned." It was also observed, "where there is no legal remedy, there is no legal wrong." Relying on this, Counsel submitted that since there was no legal remedy available to the detained Members of Parliament because of the suspension of fundamental rights, therefore it could not be said that their detention was illegal.

Sinha cautioned the Judges on the consequences of

---

[4] 2 Q.B. 271, *Bradlaugh* v. *Gossett*.

Bhushan's arguments. He said, "The detention of Members of Parliament is by a statutory authority. It would be surprising if the statutory authority, by an order which might turn out to be illegal, could prevent the House of Parliament from assembling and functioning. It would mean that if a District Magistrate acting on his own, arrested a Member of Parliament, the House would not be able to function."

He further argued that these arrests have been made possible because of the proclamation of Emergency which was in force. "When an emergency is proclaimed, Parliament has power to approve or disapprove it within two months. If Bhushan's argument is accepted, then the Parliament cannot even assemble to withhold the approval of the Emergency and thus terminate the suspension of fundamental rights."

Sinha further submitted that the detention would not be declared illegal without a formal writ of habeas corpus. He said that the legality of the detentions could not be challenged in this case as a collateral issue. With this, Sinha concluded his arguments.

14

"AMENDMENT IS LIKE A FIRMAN"

Immediately after Sinha concluded, Ashok Sen began his arguments on behalf of Mrs Gandhi. Giving his interpretation of the amendment, Sen said, "Clause 4(4) provides that no law made by Parliament before the 39th Amendment will apply to *election petitions and matters connected therewith* of the Prime Minister. This has been given retrospective effect. So it is clear that *not* all provisions of the election law have ceased to apply to the Prime Minister's election. The Representation of the People Act has eleven parts. It is only part six which deals with disputes regarding elections. Therefore, it is only part six which has ceased to apply to the election of the Prime Minister. Since part six confers the jurisdiction to the High Court to decide election disputes, therefore that jurisdiction has been removed with retrospective effect for the Prime Minister's election. This being so, the judgment which was delivered under part six automatically becomes void. Since the judgment becomes void, the election as a consequence becomes valid. No declaration is required for it.

Justice Mathew: Does it not require adjudication by a Court to say that an order passed by a lower court without jurisdiction is void or would that order automatically be deemed to be void?

Counsel: If the court initially lacks jurisdiction then this order would be automatically void. But if a competent court loses its jurisdiction because of improper exercise of jurisdiction, then it's order would have to be declared void.

Justice Mathew: What is the difference? In both cases the order is void.

Counsel: Both cases are the same, but in the latter case it has to be determined whether or not the court exercised its jurisdiction properly.

Justice Mathew: Who will delare the order void? The Court or the Legislature?

Counsel: If the task is left to the court, then the court. But in the present case, the constituent body has itself declared the order void.

Justice Mathew: What is the meaning of a writ of certiorari[1] if an order made without jurisdiction becomes automatically void?

Counsel: A writ of certiorari is issued to quash a void order.

Justice Mathew: If an order is void automatically, where is the need to quash it?

Counsel: In any case, my contention is that the election dispute in this case has been inquired into and resolved by the Constituent body itself. After the High Court lost its jurisdiction, the Constituent body took it upon itself to decide the validity of the election. After seeing the effect of the amended law regarding corrupt practices, which retrospectively removed the grounds on which the election was declared void the Constituent body finding no infirmity in the election declared it to be valid. As I am submitting that the chapter of corrupt practices still continued to apply to the Prime Minister's election, the Constituent body did take into account the norms provided by the corrupt practices chapter in order to decide the validity of the election.

Counsel then contended that the impugned amendment followed the familiar pattern of all validating Acts. In support of his contention, he cited a few cases. The most recent was one in which the Supreme Court upheld the validation of a single election which had been declared invalid. In this case,[2] the election of one Kanta Kathuria was declared invalid because she was not qualified to contest as a candidate. The Parliament had validated the election by retrospectively removing the disqualification.

Subject-matter no Limitation

Dealing with Bhushan's arguments that judicial power could not be exercised by the Constituent body, Sen contended that the subject-matter of the Constitution placed no restriction on the amending power. Once a provision was validly embodied in the Constitution,

---

[1] "Certiorari" is a writ issued by a court to quash the order of a lower court.

[2] (1970) (2) S.C.R. 835, *Kanta Kathuria, Manak Chand Surana.*

it became a part of the Constitution. "If a provision did not destroy a basic structure, it would be valid, no matter what its subject-matter was. In the hands of the Constituent body, there is no division between legislative and judicial power. A constituent power is different from legislative power and is a sovereign power." Counsel quoted some old cases in which the power of the native Indian princes to issue *firmans* (royal directives) had been upheld. Equating the constituent body to the erstwhile Indian princes, Counsel pleaded that no restriction could be placed on the constituent body's power to exercise judicial authority.

Continuing his arguments, Counsel said, "Even assuming that the constituent authority could not damage the basic structure of judicial power, this limitation would be available only in regard to those powers which were exclusively granted to the judicial organ under Articles 32, 226 and 136. In India, there is no exclusive respository of judicial power. The whole subject of election has been allocated to the Legislature. It is only an accident that Parliament has chosen to entrust the work of deciding election disputes to the High Courts. If, therefore, Parliament withdraws this power from the court, it cannot be regarded as an encroachment of judicial power."

When asked by the court whether the constituent authority, when deciding the election dispute had to follow judicial procedure, Counsel replied that it did not. Advancing a new argument, he contended that a particular function became legislative or judicial depending on whether the legislature or the judiciary was exercising that function. "In this case since the power to provide for the disposal of election disputes has been vested in Parliament by Article 329(b) it became a legislative function."

Justice Mathew: You mean even when the courts decide election cases, they are discharging a legislative function.

Counsel: Yes. In India we do not have a clear demarcation between legislative and judicial powers.

Justice Mathew: Don't bother about separation of powers. Once the power to settle a dispute is given to an authority, how is it exercised?

Counsel: If the authority is the Legislature then it uses a legislative procedure.

Counsel argued that this power had been left to the Legislature because an election dispute is a political question. It was not a controversy between the contending parties. It concerned the public and the whole constituency.

Justice Khanna: An election contest is a dual proceeding. It is a matter involving the public as well as the contesting candidates.

Counsel however, maintained that an election dispute was not between the parties. In support of this he cited a few British cases and also a Supreme Court case.[3] In this case, it was held that an election contest does not mean a contest only between the parties, but creates a situation which the whole constituency is entitled to avail of.

Justice Mathew: What about a suit under Section 92 of the Criminal Procedure Code. The public is interested in this too. But does it cease to be a judicial proceeding because of this? The correct position is that an election dispute lies between the contesting candidates although the public is also an interested party.

Right of Equality Remains

Counsel then advanced another novel argument. He said that the amendment merely protected the Prime Minisiter's election from challenge on the ground of equality. "If a particular statute is protected from challenge under Article 14, it does not mean that the right of equality itself has been destroyed. The guarantee of Article 14 still remains as a fetter against all executive and legislative acts. It is only that it does not operate on the protected Act. The right of equality as such still remains operative as before and if it is a basic feature, the basic feature still continues."

Norms of Elections Left to Parliament

Counsel further submitted that the norms of free and fair elections were not prescribed by the Constitution. "The Constitution only prescribes that there must be elections. Parliament makes all laws regarding elections and also about the determination of election disputes. Post-election scrutiny of election is not a constitutional imperative nor is it a necessary ingredient of free and fair elections. Free and fair elections may be ensured by the various provisions of the R.P. Act under which a candidate may be prosecuted criminally even in the absence of a machinery for contesting the validity of election.

Merely One Election

Counsel's final submission was that the amendments did not affect the

---

[3] AIR 1958, SC 698, *Mallappa Basappa* v. *Basavaraj Ayappa.*

structure of republican democracy, assuming that was a basic feature of the Constitution. He said that the validation of one election cannot alter the character of a democracy. "Parliament and State Legislatures will still be elected by direct election under the laws made by the Parliament. This was just one election out of the 500 odd elections to Parliament which took place in 1971."

This concluded Counsel's arguments in defence of the constitutional amendment.

Kaushal's Arguments

After Ashok Sen concluded his submissions, J.N. Kaushal, the Advocate General of Haryana and the assisting counsel of Mrs Gandhi also made brief submissions in defence of the amendment.

Giving a rationale for the amendment, Kaushal said, "The Constituent body validated it's amendment because it found that the High Court judgment was being used for political purposes by some elements of society. The constituent body had previously seen how this provision for election petitions was used merely to trouble the elected candidates. Your Lordships may just look at the statistics. After the 1967 Lok Sabha Elections, 52 election petitions were filed. Only 7 were allowed in the High Court and the Supreme Court reversed the findings in four of these. So ultimately out of the 52 election petitions, only 3 succeeded. After the 1971 elections, 58 election petitions were filed. Only 3 have been allowed by the High Court. The judgment in one was set aside by the Supreme Court so that upto now only two have succeeded, while four are still pending.

Counsel submitted that the constituent body had validated the Prime Minister's election after seeing how petitions were used to harass the elected candidates.

Counsel did not advance any other new argument. He merely repeated some of the arguments already advanced by the Solicitor General and Sen. This concluded the arguments in defence of the Constitutional amendment.

15

EMERGENCY MEASURE OR TRANQUILLIZER?

Immediately after Kaushal ended his arguments, Bhushan began his rejoinder on the Constitutional Amendment. Analyzing the arguments of the four Counsel of the other side, he said that each of them had treated Clause (4) of the Amendment in a unique manner which was very curious and interesting.

He said, "The Attorney-General has treated it as a sort of homecoming, as if the Parliament was the principal who had delegated its own functions of deciding election disputes to the judiciary and when it found that the judiciary had acted as a reckless agent, it took back the function from it. The Solicitor General, on the other hand, has treated it as an emergency measure. He says that when the constituent body found that forces of chaos and anarchy threatened the security of the country, they enacted the amendment to save the country from these dark forces. Sen has, however, treated it as a relief measure for the Supreme Court. He says that Parliament found that the Supreme Court had suddenly got a case which was too complex and difficult for it to handle. Therefore, the Parliament, like a big brother, took the responsibility of deciding the case on its own shoulders to save the judiciary from the embarrassment of having to take on more than it can chew. Lastly, Kaushal has treated it as a medical measure. He says that it is like a tranquilizer or a sleeping pill for the Prime Minister who was being harassed by a petty election petition.

Their common complaint, he felt, was that the High Court had applied the same judicial yardstick to this case as they were applying to the case of humbler people. Hence Clause (4) was necessitated. He referred to Clause (4) being compared to these *firmans*, and to the argument that an election dispute being a political question was not a matter with which the judiciary could interfere.

Bhushan said that before examining the various questions arising out of Clause (4), the effect of its implementation had to be discussed. "On the interpretation of Clause (4), there is an important divergence of opinion between the Prime Minister's counsel and the Union's counsel. The Solicitor General has said that by Clause (4), parts 6 and 7 of the R.P. Act both become inapplicable to the Prime Minister's election. While Sen has clearly argued that part 6 became inapplicable, part 7 continued to apply. (Part 6 gives jurisdiction to the High Court for deciding election disputes. Part 7 provides for corrupt practices.) So while Sinha has argued that in declaring the election valid, the constituent body did not apply the standards in the section of corrupt practices, but their own standards of free and fair elections, Sen has argued that the constituent body must have applied the standards furnished by the corrupt practice section of the R.P. Act. But what is the reality? A proper interpretation of Clause (4) leaves no room for doubt that the Prime Minister's election has been declared valid just because she was the Prime Minister. It appears that of all the various interpretations awarded to the Amendment, Kaushal's interpretation is nearest to the truth. Mr Kaushal has said that Clause (4) retrospectively removed the High Court's jurisdiction in regard to the Prime Minister's election. The High Court judgment therefore automatically becomes void. Thus far I agree. But Clause (4) declares the election to be valid. This is not a consequence of the removal of the High Court's jurisdiction. The constituent body has arbitrarily declared the election to be valid. It has been argued that the declaration of validity is not arbitrary and some norms of free and fair elections were applied. But after seeing the cavalier manner in which the elections have been declared valid, no one can say that any norms were applied."

Justice Chandrachud: The constituent body may have applied its own norms, which were different from the norms of a judicial body. Suppose it was considered that even if the High Court's ruling was substantially correct, the charges were too technical to justify the invalidation of the Prime Minister's election.

Justice Mathew: No, that cannot be, because if the cross-appeal is considered, then the complexion of the charges changes completely.

Counsel: Exactly, my Lord. The cross-appeal contains allegations of bribery, etc. Who can say that bribery is a technical offence?

Bhushan then advanced several reasons which, he said, showed that the constituent body did not apply any norms while validating the election: He said:

1. It does not merely deprive the High Court of its jurisdiction, but also makes the substantive law inapplicable to the election of the Prime Minister. It flatly declares that the election of the Prime Minister could not have been void on any ground on which it was declared to be void. This means that the election has been made invoidable.

2. If the constituent body applied any norms, they would have said so. Neither the preamble nor the statement of objects and reasons give any clue for that.

3. The amendment was moved on the 7th of August. It received the Presidential assent on the 10th of August. This means that it was passed by both Houses of Parliament and ratified by a majority of the State Legislatures in just 3 days. The evidence in the case and the issues arising in it could not have been considered by all these people within 3 days.

Bhushan then referred to the other side's contention that election disputes came within the domain of Parliament and the court's jurisdiction in election matters stood excluded by Article 329(b) of the Constitution. He pointed out that the original scheme of the Constitution was that under Article 324, the power to appoint election tribunals was vested in the Election Commission, and the jurisdiction of this tribunal was amenable to the jurisdiction of the Supreme Court under Article 136. So the Supreme Court retained overall authority on election matters. The 19th Amendment of the Constitution however took away the Election Commission's power to appoint election tribunals and under Article 329(b), Parliament had conferred the jurisdiction to decide election disputes to the High Court with normal appeals to the Supreme Court.

Justice Mathew: Does the power granted by Article 329(b) to Parliament not exclude the jurisdiction of the Supreme Court under Article 136?

Counsel: I submit not. Whichever body is vested with the jurisdiction regarding election disputes becomes a tribunal within the meaning of Article 136, and its decision is subject to an appeal by special leave in the Supreme Court.

In this connection, Bhushan cited a case of the U.S. Supreme

Court[1] in which it was held, "In exercising the power to judge the election returns and qualifications of its members, the Senate acts as a judicial tribunal."

Regarding the contention of the other side that an election dispute was a political question with which the judiciary could not interfere, Bhushan referred to the American doctrine of political questions, which evaded the issue by saying that the issue raised a political question. "It was thus a way of avoiding a principled decision which could be damaging to the court, or an expedient decision damaging to the principles of the court."

Counsel asserted that in any case, the political questions doctrine had been overthrown in the United States, and that in India, however, the political questions doctrine had never held sway and was rejected in the Privy Purse case.[2]

He quoted from the judgment of Justice Shah where he had said:

> The only forum under our Constitution for determining a legal dispute is the court, which is by training and experience, assisted by properly qualified Advocates, fitted to perform that task. A provision which purports to exclude the jurisdiction of the court in certain matters and deprive the aggrieved party of the normal remedy will be strictly construed.

Counsel pleaded that according to a strict construction, Article 329(b) could not be interpreted to exclude the special jurisdiction of the Supreme Court under Article 136. "Your Lordships will have to see which interpretation is more reasonable: whether the legislature itself which has a vested interest in the outcome of the election dispute, or the judiciary, which is an impartial observer, should have the ultimate say in election disputes."

Bhushan also referred to May's Parliamentary Practice on election disputes in England which says,

> Before the year 1870 controverted elections were tried and determined by the whole House of Commons as mere party questions upon which the strength of the contending factions might be treated. In order to prevent *so notorious a perversion of justice,*

---

[1] Lawyers Edition 867, *David S. Barry* v. *The United States of America*.

[2] AJR 1971, SC 530, *Madhav Rao Scindia* v. *Union of India*.

the House consented to submit the exercise of its privilege to a tribunal constituted by law, which though composed of its own members should be appointed so as to secure impartiality in the administration of justice according to the laws of the land and under the sanction of oaths.

Bhushan argued that there was no reason why Article 329(b) should be given an interpretation which would lead to such a notorious "perversion of justice" when an alternative interpretation was possible.

Coming to the scope of the amending power, Bhushan strongly rebutted Sen's contention that the constituent power was an amalgam of legislative, executive and judicial power. "Mr Sen argued that the constituent power is sovereign and is analogous to the sovereign powers of the native Indian princes which they exercised by *firmans*. The myth that the constituent power is sovereign or unlimited has been conclusively destroyed by the Keshavananda Bharati case. It has been held that there are limitations on the amending power. An amendment under Article 368 means not only a law but a law on a particular subject. This would be a law of a particular kind dealing with the creation of organs of Government and their relation *inter se*."

Justice Mathew said that the Indian Constitution was very long, unlike the US Constitution, and contained many things which did not relate to the organs of Government and the power distribution between them. Counsel, however, totally disagreed.

Justice Mathew: What about Directive Principles of State Policy?

Counsel: They are directions to the organs as to how they will function.

Justice Mathew: Everything is a subject matter of the State. So every law can be included in the Constitution. You can only say that a judicial exercise is not law at all.

Counsel: That is all I want to establish. A purely judicial or a purely executive power cannot be said to be constituent power.

Justice Beg: Would you say that the judicial authority cannot be vested in Parliament?

Counsel: No, I would not say that. I could be vested in Parliament subject to the limitation of basic structure.

Chief Justice: The principle of law is that if a body can create a power, it can also exercise that power.

Counsel: I submit that it is not correct. Let us take an illustration. The Governor has the power to appoint Judicial Magistrates. Does it mean that he can himself exercise the functions of a Judicial Magistrate?

Counsel submitted that if it was established that constituent power did not include judicial power, the only question which remained was whether deciding a particular dispute was an exercise of law-making power or of judicial power. "Mr Sen has conceded that Clause (4) is an exercise of judicial power, although he maintained that judicial power can be exercised by the constituent body. On the other hand, Mr Sinha and Mr Kaushal have submitted that Clause (4) retrospectively takes away the jurisdiction of the High Court and makes the substantive laws relating to corrupt practices inapplicable to the election. Even if this were so, the election would not become valid automatically. When a statutory remedy for enforcing a right is removed, the common law remedy remains, specially when an election has already been held and the validity of it is disputed. Even if the High Court judgment became void by the effect of Clause (4), the election would still remain disputed and the declaration of validity was clearly an exercise of judicial power.

Justice Mathew: When the law no longer applies to election petitions, where is the question of election petitions existing?

Justice Khanna: But the complaint against the election still existed, though it may not be in the form of an election petition.

Counsel: Exactly. Even if the legal remedy in the form of election petitions, has been taken away, it does not follow that the legal right has also been taken away.

Justice Chandrachud: The sole purpose of Clause (4) appears to be to take away the legal right as well as the remedy.

Counsel: If that is so, then it involves shameful destruction of the rule of law.

The Solicitor General at this point intervened to say that the validation of the election was a legislative function in which a decision was taken after considering the relevant material.

Chief Justice: If the election petition does not exist, which material did the constituent body take into consideration?

Sinha: Material collected by the High Court did not exist 'in law.' But it existed 'in fact.' In addition to these facts, the constituent body applied its own intelligence. It was a question of general appraisal as to whether the election has been free and fair or not. It came to the conclusion that the election was free and fair.

Bhushan then referred to De's contention that there were precedents of election validation in England as well as in India. He told the court that in all the validation cases of England cited by

Emergency Measure or Tranquillizer?   179

De, only the disqualification of a person for contesting the election was removed retrospectively. It was not that the claims for both parties were gone into and adjudicated upon. Referring to De's contention that the R.P. Act of 1956 had validated about 6,000 elections, Bhushan said that it was absolutely wrong. He said that the R.P. Act, 1956 did not validate a single election, but merely removed the disqualification which people might have had, and thus allowed them to contest the 1956 elections. Regarding the other four cases cited by De as examples of specific election validations by the Legislature, Counsel said that in none of these, the election as such was declared valid. Only a particular defect of the election was removed by a retrospective change in law.

Counsel labelled as absurd Sinha's arguments that the nature of function depended on the authority which was performing that function. He cited a U.S. Supreme Court case[3] in which it was held that the Senate though a legislative body, was conferred certain powers which were not legislative, but judicial in character. Bhushan also cited an Indian Supreme Court case[4] in which Justice Bhagwati had stated the fact which distinguished a judicial enquiry from legislation. He had said, "That question depends not upon the character of the body but upon the character of a proceeding." Relying on this judgment, Counsel contended that it completely demolished Sen's argument.

Bhushan then came to the second leg of his arguments: that the amendment destroyed several basic features of the Constitution. "I have tried to show that free and fair elections are necessary for democracy, and for free and fair elections it it essential that a candidate resorting to corrupt practices cannot be declared elected. The other side has argued that this amendment affects only one election and all the other elections were still free and fair. Therefore, democracy cannot be destroyed by it. I submit that it is not a matter of one or two elections, it is a matter of principle. If today one unfair election can be declared valid, then tomorrow all the unfair elections can be declared valid.

"The Solicitor General's argument was that the constituent body while determining the fairness of the election had applied its own norms. My reply is twofold. Firstly, it is quite clear that no norms had been applied. Secondly, even if some norms were applied, the application of different norms for different candidates for the same election

---

[3] Lawyers Edition 867, *Barry* v. *United States*.
[4] AIR 1958 SC 578 *Express Newspapers Ltd.* v. *United of India*.

is completely destructive of democracy. If Raj Narain had been elected, the validity of his election would have been tested on the norms prescribed by the R.P. Act. On the other hand, because the Prime Minister was elected, the constituent body decides to apply its own norms to such an election. How can we have a free and fair election when opposing candidates are required to maintain different standards of fairness?

"The other side has also submitted that in all democratic countries, election disputes are decided by the Legislature itself. Let us see the true position. In Britain, upto 1870, controverted elections were tried and determined by the whole House of Commons, but in order to prevent so notorious a perversion of justice, the House consented to grant this power to the courts of law. Thus today, in England, election disputes are decided by the courts. In America, the power of deciding elections was previously considered a political question, but we find that this too has been rejected. So when the House decides an election dispute, it acts as a judicial tribunal which is subject to the appellate jurisdiction of the Supreme Court." He cited a few cases in which the Supreme Court had interfered with the determination of the House.

Regarding his challenge on equality, Bhushan said, "The main argument of the other side on this point was that since Article 31(b) was upheld in Keshavananda Bharati's case, equality cannot be said to be a basic feature. This is not correct because the validity of Article 31(b) was not in question in Keshavananda Bharati's case. Only the 29th Amendment was challenged in that case, which merely inserted two Land Reform Acts in the Ninth Schedule. (Article 31(b) provides that any act inserted in the Ninth Schedule could not be challenged as violative of any fundamental right.) Since the Land Reform Acts related only to the property right, which Mr Justice Khanna held not to be a basic feature, the 29th Amendment was upheld. Lack of equality in the matter of property might not have the same effect on the basic structure as the lack of equality in the matter of elections. Suppose an Act discriminates against people in the matter of dresses. Suppose it provides that some people will have to wear a particular dress and some other people will have to wear a different dress. Although this Act is discriminatory, it probably does not affect the basic structure of the Constitution. But suppose an Act discriminates in the matter of elections and provides that a Muslim will have half a vote, a Christian will have quarter of a vote, a Harijan will have one-tenth of a vote, a Brahmin will have five votes and a Bhumihar like Mr Raj Narain will have 10 votes; would that Act not affect the basic structure of the

Constitution? Can anyone say that democracy will still survive if such an Act came into force?

Counsel further contended that even if Article 14 was not basic, because republican democracy was a basic feature, therefore, equality which flows necessarily from republicanism must be a basic feature of the Constitution.

Justice Mathew: Is not Article 14 the only guarantee of equality?

Counsel: Equality is also guaranteed by the Preamble. Moreover, there could also be an implication of equality in the Constitution. Even if equality in other spheres is not basic, it has to be basic in the matter of status and opportunity, which are mentioned in the Preamble. In this case, the Amendment discriminates merely on the basis of status. Just because the person concerned happens to be the Prime Minister, her election is made immune from all attack. I do not dispute that the Prime Minister is a class by herself. But what is the connection between a person being the Prime Minister and his election being immune from judicial scrutiny? Even the Prime Minister contests an election as an ordinary candidate. What kind of contest is that in which one person can cheat and the other cannot?"

Counsel then referred to Sinha's argument that the amendment was made to save the country from chaos and anarchy. "Mr Sinha has advanced a very strange argument. He says that the consitituent body found that a change in the Prime Minister in these circumstances would lead to chaos and anarchy in the country. The court cannot take notice of this argument. I will not deal in detail with the merits of his claim. I will only say that a democratic Constitution like ours does not contemplate a situation where a single person can become indispensable to the country."

Parliament Session Illegal

When Bhushan began his rejoinder on the legality of the Monsoon Session of Parliament, he was immediately interrupted by Justice Khanna.

Justice Khanna: Suppose an illegal order of detention is issued by a District Magistrate to arrest a Member of Parliament. If what you are saying is correct, this would invalidate the Session. How can a wrong order of a District Magistrate invalidate a session?

Counsel: Because the President, by suspending the Fundamental Rights, has become a party to the continued illegal detention of the Members. The President convenes the Session of Parliament. If he himself becomes a party to an illegal prevention of some Members of

Parliament from attending the Session, then the Session clearly becomes illegal. Otherwise the Government can get the whole Opposition arrested and pass whatever it likes without anyone to oppose it.

With this Bhushan concluded his rejoinder on the validity of the Constitutional Amendment.

As he was ending his arguments, the five Judges were conferring with each other. Two minutes after he had ended, the Chief Justice made a startling announcement. He said, "After hearing both the sides on the validity of the Constitutional Amendment, we have decided to hear counsel of both sides on the merits of the case in order to decide the validity of Constitutional Amendment."

Bhushan was taken aback by this announcement. He was expecting that the Judges would first pronounce on the validity of the Constitutional Amendment before going into the merits of the case. As he was confident that the Constitutional Amendment would be struck down, he wanted to start arguments on the merits of the case only after the Constitutional Amendment was struck down, so that the slate was clean at that time. He protested, "How can the merits of an individual case affect the validity of a Constitutional Amendment? Its validity should depend solely on the limitations imposed by the Constitution. Moreover, since the amendment ousts the jurisdiction of the court to hear the merits of the case, it would be highly improper to go into the merits before deciding on the validity of the Amendment."

Justice Beg also agreed with the Chief Justice and said that an evaluation of the merits of the case was extremely important in order to decide the validity of the Amendment. Bhushan did not persist. Saying that he was duty bound to obey the dictates of the Court, he sat down. So it was on 19 September that Ashok Sen was called upon to make his submissions on the merits of the case.

Giving a historical background of the entire case, Sen started explaining the effect of the Election Laws Amendment on the case. As he was explaining this, Justice Mathew interrupted him and pointed out that these amendments, if they be valid, took care of almost all the charges framed in the petition. Therefore, unless their validity is assailed, it would be pointless to go into the merits of the case. He conferred with the Chief Justice who then called upon Bhushan to make his submissions on the validity of the Election Law Amendments.

5

Validity of the Election Laws Amendment

16

"RULES OF THE GAME CHANGED RETROSPECTIVELY"

Opening his arguments Bhushan told the court that the validity of the Election Law Amendments would depend upon their interpretation. He would advance his interpretations of the amendments and in case they were accepted, he would not challenge the validity of the amendments. He would only assail their validity if his interpretations were rejected by the court.

DEFINITION OF CANDIDATE

Bhushan first read out the change made by the amendment in the statutory definition of candinate in Section 79 of the R.P. Act. The original Section 79(b) of the Act defines a candidate as the person "who has been, or claims to have been, duly nominated as a candidate at any election, and any such person shall be deemed to have been a candidate as from the time when, with the election in prospect, he began to hold himself out as a prospective candidate." The amended definition defines a candidate as a person "Who has been or claims to have been duly nominated as a candidate at any election."

A Wise and Just Amendment

Bhushan submitted that according to him the original definition involved the identification of the person who was the candidate as well as the time from which he was to be regarded as the candidate. "The amended definition has done away with the second part of the definition. Now a person would be regarded as a candidate for the purposes of Section 123 (corrupt practices) from any time." Section 123 provides that a corrupt practice can be committed by a candidate or his election agent or by any other person with the consent of the candidate or his election agent. Counsel argued that previously a candidate could commit a corrupt practice only after he held himself out as a prospective candidate. But after the amendment a corrupt practice can be committed at any time, even 10 or 20 years before a person is nominated as a candidate. I am very happy that the Parliament has made such a wise amendment which makes the law on corrupt practice extremely just."

Justice Beg: What you are interpreting could not have been the intention of Parliament.

Counsel: Why not my Lord? We must assume that Parliament makes fair and just laws.

Justice Beg (smiling): You want us to be legislators.

Counsel: The court never makes the law. It only interprets it.

Justice Mathew: The theory has been discarded long ago. (Citing from his judgment in Keshavananda Bharati's case) "The dictum that judges do not make law, but only interpret it, is a fairy tale. And nowadays we do not believe in fairy tales."

Counsel: At least judges are supposed to interpret the law. Your Lordships will see what will happen if my interpretation is rejected. If the phrase 'corrupt practice committed by a candidate' implies that they must be committed after a person becomes a candidate, then on the same logic section 100(1)(b) which mentions the phrase 'corrupt practice committed by a returned candidate,' would mean a corrupt practice by a candidate after he becomes a returned candidate. (Section 100(1)(b) provides that the High Court shall declare the election of the returned candidate void if it finds that any corrupt practice has been committed by the returned candidate or his election agent.) This would render Section 100(1)(b) quite absurd because obviously no person will commit a corrupt practice after he gets elected and becomes a returned candidate.

Justice Mathew: Section 100 cannot involve the concept of time. That is impossible.

Counsel: If Section 100 does not involve the concept of time, why should there be a concept of time in Section 123? Section 123 only provides that a corrupt practice must be committed by that person, who was a candidate at the election or by any other person with the consent of the candidate. Your Lordships will consider what the situation would be if Section 123 really means that the corrupt practice must be committed by a candidate after he becomes candidate. It would mean that a person can commit all sorts of corrupt practices, bribe all voters, use undue influence, even prevent the rival candidates from filing their nomination papers, before he himself files his nomination papers and he would incur no liability. This would make the provision of the Chapter on Corrupt Practices absolutely redundant. What a candidate would have to do to escape the consequences would just be to file his nomination papers at the very last day. Why should the court give an interpretation which would completely destroy the meaning of the chapter on corrupt practices?

On this point Bhushan made full capital out of the passage read by Justice Mathew from his judgment in Keshavananda Bharati's case where he had said that the view that Judges do not make the law was a fairy tale. Bhushan said, "Your lordships will be making the law in Justice Mathew's opinion and will have to see whether the law is to be reasonable or absurd."

OFFICIAL DUTIES MEAN STATUTORY DUTIES

Bhushan then took up the amendment in Section 123(7) of the R.P. Act. The original Section 123(7) provides that if a candidate obtained or procured any assistance from Government servants belonging to a specified category for the furtherance of the prospects of his election, it would be a corrupt practice. The amendment adds a proviso to Clause (7) saying that "where any person in the service of Government and belonging to the specified class, in the discharge or purported discharge of his official duty, makes any arrangements, or provides any facilities, or does any other act or thing, for, or in relation to any candidate or his election agent, then such arrangements, facilities, or acts shall not be deemed to be assistance for the furtherance of the prospects of the candidate's election."

Bhushan's interpretation of this proviso was that "the official duty" mentioned here would only mean statutory duty (provided by law). He submitted that this interpretation of official duty would not include duty which was assigned by an order of the Government.

Justice Mathew: Can a limitation be imposed on official Government function.

Counsel: A limitation has to be there. If there is no limitation it would mean that if the Government by a circular directed Government officials, such as District Magistrates, Secretaries etc., to organize the election campaign of Ministers, it would be an official Government function and no liability of a corrupt practice would be incurred. It would mean that the Government merely by an administrative order could direct that the entire election campaign of the ruling party, including canvassing for votes, giving speeches etc., be carried out by Government servants.

Interpretation of the '74 Amendment

Bhushan's interpretation of the R.P. Amendment Act, 1974 was the same which he had given in the Allahabad High Court. This amendment about election expenses has provided that any expenditure incurred or authorized in connection with the election of a canditate by the political party or friends and supporters of the candidate would not be included in the candidate's election expenses. Counsel told the court that according to his interpretation the amendment only made it clear that any expenses incurred or authorized by a political party or a friend or supporters of the candidate without the authorization of the candidate or his election agent could be excluded from the candidate's election expenses. "It does not protect expenditure which has been incurred or authorized by a candidate or his election agent. If the correct interpretation is that even if expenditure has been incurred or authorized by the candidate himself, but if it is also authorized by someone else it could be excluded from the election expenses of the candidate, then the limit on expenses would become meaningless. A candidate will only have to ask his party or any other individual to authorize him to spend money and then the candidate can spend any amount of money without being required to show it in his return.

Justice Mathew: If a candidate is spending his own money, the authorization by any other person has no meaning. An authorization has meaning only when the person intends to reimburse the candidate for the amount authorized by him. The candidate need not get authorization from any other person to spend his money.

Counsel: In Chawla's case it has been held that when a candidate participates in a function organized by his party or any other person, he impliedly authorizes the expenditure in connection with that function. Here though the candidate does not reimburse the party with that amount, he still has authorized that expenditure. So authorization need not always carry with it an idea of reimbursement.

After giving his interpretation Bhushan told the court that he would not challenge the validity of these amendments if his interpretations were accepted. Then he would only challenge the validity of other amendments for which he had offered no interpretation. But if his interpretations were rejected, he would challenge the validity of all the election law amendments.

Scope of Attack on Ninth Schedule

Bhushan told the court that since the Election Laws Amendment Act, 1975 and the Representation of People Amendment Act, 1974 were included in the Ninth Schedule by the 39th Amendment, therefore the scope of the challenge on them would have to be seen. Parliament can include any ordinary law in the Ninth Schedule only by a Constitutional Amendment. Any law included in the Ninth Schedule is protected from challenge as being violative of a fundamental right. Bhushan submitted that the Acts included in the Ninth Schedule could still be challenged as destructive of the basic features of the Constitution.

Justice Mathew: Mr Bhushan, how can an ordinary law be struck down as violative of the basic features of the Constitution?

Counsel: Once an Act is included in the Ninth Schedule a challenge on the basis of infringement of fundamental rights is blocked off. Hence an attack on the ground of destruction of basic features of the Constitution is thrown open, because what the constituent body cannot do they cannot do by any means, including the device of the Ninth Schedule. Counsel then read out the judgments of the majority Judges in Keshavananda Bharati's case where they had pronounced on the scope of attack on the Ninth Schedule. Six of these Judges, Chief Justice Sikri, Justices Shelat, Grover, Hegde, Mukherjea and Jaganmohan Reddy had held that the Acts included in the Ninth Schedule could be struck down, if they violated any basic feature of the Constitution. Justice Khanna had not said anything in his judgment about the scope of attack on any Acts included in the Ninth Schedule.

Bhushan submitted that since Justice Khanna had imposed the limitation of basic structure on the amending power it must be assumed that this limitation was also imposed on acts included in the Ninth Schedule. "Let us look at it this way. It is clear that an amendment of the Constitution can be struck down on the basic feature doctrine. Since the inclusion of an Act in the Ninth Schedule is itself an amendment of the Constitution, its validity can be examined on the basic feature doctrine. If it is found that any of the Acts included in the Ninth Schedule violates a basic feature, then that Constitutional Amendment which gives it the protection of the Ninth Schedule can be struck down."

Justice Mathew: Can an ordinary law which is not included in the Ninth Schedule be struck down as violative of a basic feature of the Constitution, although it is not in conflict with any specific provision of the Constitution?

Counsel: Suppose an amendment to the R.P. Act provides that Rs 50,000 would have to be paid for the right of casting a vote. This law does not come in conflict with any specific provision of the Constitution, although it would clearly destroy democracy. Can such a law be upheld? The theory behind the basic feature doctrine is that the Constitution as a whole contains an implication that certain features of the Constitution cannot be destroyed in any way.

Justice Chandrachud: The implied limitation, if there is one, is applicable only to the constituent power, and not to the normal legislative powers of Parliament.

Counsel: If there is an implied limitation on the constituent power, it is because certain features of the Constitution are sacred and cannot be destroyed by any means whatsoever. If there is such a mandate in the Constitution then it must apply to all powers granted by it. How can the Constitution which intends to make certain features permanent, allow them to be destroyed by legislative power?

Justice Mathew: Can directive principles of State policy also illustrate the basic features of the Constitution?

Counsel: Yes.

Justice Mathew: One of the directive principles is that the State shall strive to bring about social and economic justice. Can a law be struck down as being violative of social and economic justice?

Counsel: If the mandate for social and economic justice is regarded as a basic feature of the Constitution, then certainly such a law can be struck down. Suppose the law provides for regressive income-tax rates so that people with an income of Rs 50 would pay 90 per cent as tax, people with an income of Rs 500 would pay 60 per cent, people with income of Rs 5,000 would pay 20 per cent and people with an income of Rs 50,000 would pay no tax. This law would be clearly destructive of social and economic justice and can be struck down.

Justice Khanna: Another directive principle is that the State shall endeavour to bring about prohibition. If a law is made to repeal prohibition in a State can this be struck down as being violative of the basic feature?

Counsel: Sometimes the State may be desperately short of finances, which it needs to provide social security benefits. Therefore to raise more funds it might be essential to repeal prohibition in a State. Then it is a question of paramountacy of two conflicting needs. If prohibition is more essential than social security then a law which repeals prohibition can also be struck down.

Bhushan while maintaining that it would be in the highest degree absurd to hold that what the constituent body could not do by amending the Constitution it could do by putting the Act in the Ninth Schedule, said that the specific Article of the Constitution with which the Election Laws Amendment came into conflict was Article 81. Article 81(1)(a) provides that subject to the provisions of Article 331, the House of People shall consist of not more than 525 members chosen by "direct" elections from the territorial constituencies in the State. Counsel told the court that the direct elections mentioned here must mean free and fair elections and the Election Law Amendments, as they were discriminatory, did not provide for free and fair elections. Therefore even if it was held that the basic structure imposes no limitation on the Ninth Schedule, these laws could be struck down as violative of Article 81.

Counsel then told the court that he would make his submissions on the validity of the election law amendments on the assumption that his interpretations were rejected and that they could be struck down as violative of the basic features. He said that although the retrospectivity of the amendments made them worse, he would submit that even in their prospective effect they destroyed the basic structure of the Constitution.

Dealing first with the amended definition of "candidate," Counsel told the court that it would clearly have the effect of damaging democracy in the country."

Justice Khanna: Suppose this law was made in 1951, could it have been struck down at that time?

Counsel: Yes it could. As it could have the effect of completely destroying the fairness of the elections.

Justice Chandrachud (smiling): But it gives an equal opportunity to everybody to do all these things.

Counsel: Yes, My Lord. So might will be right and the law of the jungle will prevail."

Dealing with the amendment about religious symbols, Bhushan said that this deeming provision added to Section 123(3) created a legal fiction by which even if a religious symbol were allotted to a candidate, it would be deemed not to be a religious symbol. He went on, "Even if a symbol like a portrait of Rama or Christ on a Cross were allotted to a candidate, the election would still be valid. In a religious country like India, the allotment of a religious symbol would have an extremely significant effect on the election results. That is why the R.P. Act, 1951, provided that the use of a religious symbol shall be a corrupt practice. But now this provision is more or less abolished by the amendment which would also lead to the destruction of democracy."

Justice Mathew: But the symbols are allotted by the Election Commission which is an independent body. Why should it allot a religious symbol?

Counsel: The symbol is allotted at the request of the party and it is the normal practice of the Commission to allot symbols which have been asked for by the party. Moreover, the Election Commission is not as independent a body as the judiciary. It is a quasi-judicial body.

Referring to the amendment in Section 123(7) about the discharge of official duties of Government servants, Bhushan said that if his interpretation was rejected, the consequence would be that the party in power could use the entire Government machinery for their electtion work and yet there would be no corrupt practice. "The explanation which has been added to Section 77 (dealing with the ceiling on expenses) that any expenditure incurred by Government servants in the discharge of their official duties would not be regarded as an expenditure of that candidate, makes it very easy for the party in power to use the funds of the State Exchequer for its election campaign. So they cannot only use all Government servants for election purposes, but they can also use all public funds for election purposes without suffering any consequences."

Justice Beg: But you can complain if this power is misused.

Counsel: A law is bad if it allows easy misuse of power. Since this law permits the violation of the fairness of the election, it militates against democracy.

Bhushan then argued on the validity of the amendment in Section 123(3) which added an explanation about the date of appointment and resignation of government servants. In that, it has been explained that the dates specified in the Official Gazette for the appointment, resignation or termination of service of any Government servant shall be conclusive proof of the date of such appointment, resignation or termination of service. Bhushan submitted that this amendment also created a legal fiction by which the Government could specify any date it wanted in the Official Gazette, and that would be deemed to be the correct date of appointment or resignation of a Government servant. "This would allow the Government to use a

Government servant for election purposes, and then specify a fictional date as the date of his resignation, which could be even months after the date on which the person had actually resigned."

Justice Khanna: Can it not mean that if the date is in doubt, the date specified in the Gazette shall be the date which would be taken into account?

Counsel: This does not apply only in doubtful cases. Even if the date of resignation is absolutely beyond doubt, the Government can still specify another date in the Gazette and that date will be deemed to be the correct one.

Bhushan then submitted on the validity of the R.P. Amendment Act, 1974. The validity of this Act (regarding election expenses) was also assailed in the High Court, but the Judge then had not pronounced on it. Bhushan contended that this amendment would have the effect of abolishing the ceiling on election expenses, and would completely stultify the small man's chance of winning elections, and the small man's chances must be the essence of Indian democracy.

Retrospective Effect of the Amendment

Bhushan then assailed the retrospective operation of these amendments.

Justice Mathew: There is no doubt of the unfairness of retrospective laws about corrupt practices. But can you cite some legal authority to impugn their validity, because retrospective legislation is normally permissible.

Counsel: I submit that there is a great difference between retrospective legislation on ordinary matters and retrospective legislation about rules of a contest. The latter would inevitably lead to discrimination against some candidates. Any law which is discriminatory is void because, as I have submitted, equality is a basic feature of the Constitution.

Justice Khanna: What about retrospective laws removing disqualifications? That was upheld in Kanta Kathuria's case. How do you distinguish it from this?

Counsel: In the Kanta Kathuria case, the rules of the election were not changed. Only Kanta Kathuria's disqualifications for contesting the election was retrospectively removed. Therefore, the rival candidate could not complain of any discrimination against him because if Kanta Kathuria had been qualified to contest the election before it took place, the rival candidate could not have done anything more to further the prospects of his election. The only person who could complain would be a person who was similarly situated as Kanta Kathuria before the election took place and was hence unable to contest as he was not qualified. Only he could have challenged the retrospective removal of Kanta Kathuria's disqualification. Here the situation is completely different. If the laws relating to corrupt practices had been different before the elections, Mr Raj Narain could also have taken advantage of those laws. If Government servants could render assistance to candidates in performance of their official duties, then Mr Raj Narain could have asked the State Government of U.P. to depute Government officers to work for his election.

Counsel further argued, "If such retrospective legislation was permissible, the party in power could manipulate laws in such a way so as to always remain in power."

Justice Khanna: Right now we are not concerned about the addition of disqualifications. We are only concerned with the removal of this qualification.

Counsel: No, not now. But if this power is conceded today, then in future such contingencies are bound to arise. If they can retrospectively relax the rules, they can also retrospectively make them stricter. What you are going to lay down in this case will be the law by which the future of such laws will be determined.

Bhushan next contended that the entire Election Laws Amendment Act was meant for a single case and was a colourable piece of legislation. He said, "The election against Mrs Gandhi contains seven charges of corrupt practices. Five of these have been resolved by these Election Laws Amendment Act. Only two minor ones remain. After seeing the timing of this Act, there could be no doubt that this whole Act is meant just for Mrs Gandhi's election. It is only concerned with validating one single election. It is a legislative plan to secure a particular result in a particular dispute, and in the Liyanage case[1] it has been clearly held that such a plan is impermissible."

Bhushan's final submission was that since these amendments were also passed in the same Monsoon Session of Parliament in which several Opposition members were illegally detained, therefore these amendments too were void because of the illegality of the Session.

With a final plea that the Election Laws Amendment Act be struck down as destructive of the basic structure of the Constitution, Bhushan concluded his arguments on the validity of these amendments.

[1] 1967(1) A.C. 259 *Liyanage* v. *Queen.*

After concluding his arguments on the validity of the Election Laws Amendments, Bhushan took up the merits of the case on the assumption that none of his interpretations would be accepted by the court and that the amendments would be held valid. He told the Judges that if his submissions did not find favour with the court, there would be only three issues surviving in the case: the issues of bribery, conveyance of voters and election expenses. He said that he would not press the issues of bribery and conveyance of voters. Thus the only surviving issue on which he would make his submission was the issue of election expenses.

Actually the issue of election expenses too did not survive if Bhushan's interpretation of the R.P. Amendment Act, '74 was rejected by the court. Therefore the reason why he argued only this issue on merits was that the Judges seemed to be more inclined to accept his interpretation of this amendment than they were to accept his interpretation of the other amendments.

Making his submissions on this issue, Bhushan said that the expenditure assessed by the High Court was about Rs 32,000 which was only 3,000 below the prescribed limit. "This assessed expenditure did not include the money spent on the 23 vehicles which are shown to have been used by the District Congress Committee of Rae Bareli. However little be the expenditure on these vehicles it would certainly add upto more than Rs 3,000." Asked by the court as to why this expenditure was not added by Justice Sinha, Bhushan replied, "Justice Sinha has held that since one does not know how many of these vehicles were used in Mrs Gandhi's constituency and what expenditure was incurred on them, he would not estimate any expenditure on them. This is wrong according to Chawla's case. In that case it has been held that if any expenditure is shown to have been evaded in the return of expenses, then it is the duty of the court to make a reasonable estimate of the expenditure and add it to the return. Just because an exact estimate cannot be made, it does not follow that no estimate can be made. The court has to make a reasonable estimate.

Justice Mathew: You mean to say that the return of election expenses is like an income-tax return.

Counsel: Yes, exactly like that. Once it has been shown that the return is not correct, then the income-tax authority has to make a reasonable assessment of the income.

Justice Beg: But how do we know who incurred the expenditure on the vehicles? The party might have incurred this expenditure, or they might even have been provided by friends and supporters of Mrs Gandhi.

Counsel: In Chawla's case it had been laid down that even though an expenditure may not be incurred by a candidate, if it is expressly or impliedly authorized by him or his election agent, it would be treated as his election expense. In this case, Mr Yashpal Kapoor himself got the vehicles released. Therefore, he clearly authorized their use.

Justice Beg: But if a friend or supporter of a candidate spends money on his election, how can the candidate prevent him from doing so?

Counsel: Section 171(b) of the Indian Penal Code makes an expenditure greater than rupees ten by any person for a candidate a penal offence. So if a candidate knows that his friend is incurring expenditure on his election, it is his duty to advise his friend that it is a penal offence. But if his friend persists, then it is his duty to publicly disavow this expenditure and not to take any advantage of it.

Justice Beg: If your interpretation is accepted, then it could be almost impossible to fight an election with this limit.

Counsel: Rs 35,000 is not an insignificant amount. In a poor country like India, if the limit is raised further, the results of the election would be significantly distorted in favour of moneyed people. Only the representatives of rich people would be able to get elected to the Legislatures. The small man would have no chance.

Bhushan submitted that at the very least, one third of the expenditure on the 23 jeeps would have to be included in Mrs Gandhi's election expenses. (He said one third because according to the evidence, the 23 vehicles were used in the three constituencies of Rae Bareli.) Calculating the expenditure on the maintenance, depreciation, petrol and driver of the vehicle, Bhushan contended that at least Rs 4,500 would have been spent on each vehicle during the election. Therefore, on 23 vehicles a total expenditure of Rs 1,03,500 must have been incurred. Even one third of this figure is almost Rs 35,000, and if this is added to Mrs Gandhi's return, the limit is easily exceeded and a corrupt practice is established. With this, Bhushan concluded his arguments on 26 September.

17

"RULES NOT CHANGED, MERELY CLARIFIED"

Since the Attorney-General had not yet recovered from the attack of high blood pressure which he had suffered while making his submissions on the Constitutional Amendments, Sinha took upon himself the task of replying to Bhushan's arguments on the Election Law Amendments.

The Solicitor General's Arguments

Beginning his reply, Sinha said that the first question to be decided was whether the limitation of basic features applied to ordinary legislation too. Arguing that this limitation did not apply to ordinary legislation, Counsel submitted three propositions to support this.

1. The Constitution itself affirmatively creates and negatively restricts legislative power and the only limitation which can be applied to ordinary legislative powers which are specifically granted by the Constitution must be specific limitations, such as the fundamental rights.

2. The limitation of basic features on the amending power has been held in the Keshavananda Bharati case to be ultimately based on the concept and scope of the word "amendment" used in Article 368 and is wholly irrelevant to test the validity of a statute made in exercise of the legislative power granted by Article 245.

3. The terms of the Preamble which are further amplified in the Directive Principles are the ideals to be achieved and not the conditions of validity for legislation. The Preamble or Directive Principles therefore could not import any restriction on the legislative power. The

Preamble only sets out the en sought to be achieved. The means, through which such ends are to be achieved, are left entirely to the will of the Legislature. Counsel further submitted that if this implied limitation of basic features is also applied to ordinary legislation, it would throw the doors open to endless litigation. "Every Bill will have to be submitted to the Judiciary before being voted upon. I submit that the merits of the policy adopted by the Legislature cannot be questioned by the judiciary. A law can only be struck down if it is repugnant to a specific provision of the Constitution or to a direct implication of a specific provision."

Justice Chandrachud: Implied or inherent limitations can arise from the totality of all h e provisions of the Constitution.

Counsel: The implication must arise from some specific provision of the Constitution. Limitation cannot be a matter of speculation. Justice Khanna has clearly rejected the implied limitation theory.

Justice Mathew: Would it not be a paradox if the limitation of basic features is applicable to the constituent power which is a higher power and not to legislative power which is a lower power?

Counsel: My Lord, a power which is affirmatively granted by the Constitution cannot be against the basic features. Moreover, the basic feature theory is so vague that it would be almost impossible to apply it to ordinary legislation. It would be a dangerous extention of Keshavananda Bharati's case to hold that laws inserted in the Ninth Schedule must also satisfy the test of basic features. What has been held in Keshavananda Bharati's case should not be extended now just for the sake of consistency. It is much better for law to be certain than to be logical. Imagine the situation which would arise if Mr Bhushan's contention is upheld. There would be endless litigation. All laws made by Parliament would be challenged as violative of some provision of the Preamble or of the Directive Principles, or of something else.

'74 Amendment Merely Restores Earlier Law

Going on to the actual validity of the amendments, Counsel first took up the Representation of the People Amendment Act, 1974 which deals with expenses. He said that in Section 77 of the Act, "incurred or authorized" means incurred by the candidate or incurred by an authorized agent. "Whatever expenditure is incurred by any person who is not authorized by the candidate to act as his agent, cannot be included in the return of expenses filed by the candidate. In fact that is the ambiguity which is cleared up by this amendment."

Counsel submitted that in order to appreciate the provisions of Section 77 of the Representation of the People Act, one must examine the provisions of the Indian Penal Code. "Section 171H of the Penal Code prohibits people from spending more than a sum of Rs 10 for a candidate's election without his written authorization. It is made a penal offence which is punishable with a fine extending to Rs 500. This provision of the Indian Penal Code prevents any misuse of the law on election expenses. Therefore, the 'authority' contemplated by Section 77 is written authority. In my humble submission, authorization can only be there if the rights and liabilities of a person who is authorized are transferred to the person who authorizes him. Otherwise authorization does not make any sense. Every person can act on his own. It is only when I accept the liabilities which a person may incur that I have authorized him. This carries with it the idea or reimbursement. Unless the person authorized is entitled to be reimbursed by the candidate, there is no authorization."

Justice Mathew: The criminal offence incurred by a person spending money for a candidate under Section 171 of the Penal Code is another matter. The question is whether a person is allowed to spend money for the candidate under Section 77 of the Representation of the People Act.

Counsel: A person who is spending for a candidate without his authority in writing is making himself liable for a criminal offence. If he does not bother about it, it cannot be helped. There is this slight loophole in the law. Law cannot be perfect.

Justice Mathew: Suppose a party sponsors a candidate and spends money for him. Who will be prosecuted under Section 171?

Counsel: The person who is responsible for that expenditure.

Justice Chandrachud: But how can you pinpoint that person?

Counsel: Yes, it would be difficult. But it cannot be helped.

Justice Mathew: So an individual cannot evade Section 171. But a group of persons acting together can.

Chief Justice: Suppose a candidate asks a political party to spend for him. Is that authorization?

Counsel: That is only a request. As long as the political party is acting on its own, there is authorization.

Counsel submitted that the law on election expenses laid down in Chawla's case in 1974 was a clear departure from the law laid down in all the earlier cases. This placed those candidates who had understood the law correctly in 1971 at a disadvantage. That is why Parliament enacted the 1974 Amendment and clarified the position of the law before Chawla's case.

Justice Khanna: Can the court go into the justification behind an amendment? Will it have any effect on its validity?

Counsel: It will have the effect that if the amendment merely clarifies the law as it stood before Chawla's case, then it does not change the law at all. It only disagrees with the interpretation given in Chawla's case.

Definition of Candidate

Sinha then took up the amendment made in Section 79 of the Representation of the People Act which changes the definition of candidate and defines him as a person who has been, or claims to have been, duly nominated as a candidate at an election, thus abolishing the the concept of holding out as a candidate. Counsel argued that this amended definition did away with the legal fiction created by the 'deeming' provision of the earlier definition. "A person shall no longer be 'deemed' to be a candidate from the time he holds himself out as a candidate. So now, either he is a candidate or he is not. Thus the amended definition has removed a lot of unnecessary ambiguity and has made the definition precise and exact."

Counsel strongly contested Bhushan's argument that the injunction on corrupt practice starts applying before a person becomes a candidate. He contended that the amended definition of "candidate" will have to be substituted wherever the word "candidate" occurs. "Since the chapter on corrupt practices provides that they must be committed by a candidate, therefore they must be committed by that person who has been, or claims to have been, duly nominated as a candidate. So now a candidate cannot commit corrupt practice before he has been, or claims to have been, nominated as a candidate.

"Mr Bhushan has argued that this would mean that a candidate can commit all sorts of corrupt practices and undesirable acts before he is nominated, without incurring the liability of a corrupt practice. That is not correct, because the last date for nomination is about a month before the date of election and most corrupt practices can only be committed after this date."

Counsel further argued that Bhushan was wrong in contending that a candidate could get away with bribery if it was committed before nomination. He said, "Section 171(E) of the Penal Code makes bribery at any time a penal offence. Section 8(1) of the Representation of the People Act provides that any person held guilty under Section 171(E) of the Penal Code shall be disqualified from contesting elections for a period of six years from the date of his conviction. Therefore, even though a person committing bribery before nomination does not commit a corrupt practice, he gets disqualified because of Section 8(1) of the Representation of the People Act."

Counsel thus contended that there were few abuses possible even after the amended definition of "candidate." He went on, "But even if there is a slight infirmity in the law, it cannot be helped. Your Lordships will agree that it is a perfectly valid compromise. How can anyone argue that it destroys democracy?"

Official Duty

Sinha next took up the amendment regarding the corrupt practice of procuring the services of Government servants. The amendment provides that any assistance rendered by a Government servant to a candidate as part of his official duty would not be deemed to be assistance for the furtherance of the prospects of a candidate's election. Counsel disputed Bhushan's contention that under this amendment, the Government could impose all sorts of official duties on Government servants to further the prospects of the elections of their party members. He argued that official duty meant duty which could be treated as pertaining to Government. This would include the maintenance of law and order and the provision for security of VIPs. Giving speeches or doing other strictly election work for a candidate would not be regarded as official duties, and whenever such a duty is conferred by the Government, it could always be struck down by the court.

Justice Mathew: What pertains to the Government and what does not, I do not know.

Counsel: Bribery and corruption do not pertain to Government. Law and order pertain to the Government. Official duties will be those which could reasonably be regarded as duties which the Government has to perform. In fact, the concept of official duty is much less vague than the concept of basic features of the Constitution.

Justice Mathew: Executive power is so wide that you can do anything in connection with the election by conferring an official duty through an administrative order.

Counsel: No, my Lord. A line has to be drawn in between.

Justice Mathew: Where will you draw the line? What cannot be done in purported discharge of official duties?

Counsel: Malafide administrative orders cannot bring into existence official duties.

Justice Khanna: So you mean to say that this law should be upheld and each administrative order should be checked to see whether it is proper or not.

Counsel: Yes.

Date of Resignation

Referring to the Explanation added in Section 123(7) of the Act (which provides that the date of appointment or resignation of a Government servant specified in the Official Gazette would be conclusive proof of the date of such appointment or resignation), Sinha then submitted that this again provides finality to the law and removes all ambiguity which the law had before this. Rebutting Bhushan's argument that this provision could be misused by the Government which could specify fictitious dates of the appointment or resignation of Government servants, Counsel said that this was mere speculation, and, in any case, the possibility of abuse of a law was not a ground for striking it down. "It should be assumed that the Government is not mad and will not act in a wholly capricious manner."

Symbols

Going on to the amendment regarding symbols, Sinha argued that since symbols were allotted by the Election Commission, it was not right that the candidate should be made to suffer for the mistake of the Commission. In any case, he said, the Election Commission was an independent body which would on its own see that no religious symbol was allotted to anyone. He, therefore, did not see anything wrong in this amendment.

Amendments do not Change the Law

Arguing then on the retrospectivity which had been conferred on these amendments, Sinha contended that in fact none of these amendments changed the law. "They only clarified what the law was. Hence it is not a question of changing the rules of the game after the game had been played, but only explaining what the correct rules of the game were."

Justice Mathew (smiling): So you have only interpreted the law.

(Interpreting the law is monopoly of the judiciary under the Constitution.)

Counsel further submitted that what had to be seen was whether the corrupt practices were such so as to call for vitiating the election. "Otherwise, setting aside the election would be undemocratic. These amendments by curing the infirmities existing in the earlier law have only given greater effect to democracy."

Justice Khanna: Some American Judges have described all retrospective laws as repressive laws.

Counsel: My Lord, as I have submitted, these amendments have not really changed the law, but only clarified it.

After arguing very briefly on the validity of the Constitutional Amendment again, Sinha concluded his arguments. After Sinha concluded his arguments on behalf of the Union, Ashok Sen began his arguments on behalf of Mrs Gandhi.

SEN'S ARGUMENTS

Arguing first on the effect of the amendment in the definition of "candidate" in the Representation of the People Act, Sen also assailed Bhushan's contention that a corrupt practice could be committed by a candidate even before he fell within the statutory definition of a candidate.

He drew the court's attention to Section 171(c) of the Indian Penal Code which provides that: "Whosoever threatens any candidate or voter, or any person in whom a candidate or voter is interested, with injury of any kind, shall be deemed to interfere with the free exercise of the electoral right of such candidate or voter. . . ."

Counsel also drew the court's attention to Section 171(G) of the Indian Penal Code which provides, "Whoever with intent to affect the result of an election, makes or publishes any statement purporting to be a statement of fact which is false and which he either knows or believes to be false or does not believe to be true, in relation to the personal character or conduct of any candidate, shall be punished with fine."

Counsel argued that if Bhushan was right in his contention that the word "candidate" as it appeared in the chapter on corrupt practices, was only used to identify the person who became the candidate, then in the Indian Penal Code too, it should have been used merely to identify the person who became the candidate. If this is so, your Lordships will see what will happen. Suppose a person 'A' makes or publishes a false statement about another person 'B' who ten years later becomes a candidate, then 'A' becomes liable to penal offence relating to an election under Section 171(G) of the Penal Code, although when he threatened 'B' he had no idea that 'B' would later become a candidate at an election. Thus in effect 'A' would be prosecuted for an offence relating to an election, though he had no idea of the election at that time. Such a result could clearly not have been intended by the Legislature. Therefore, it is clear that whenever the word 'candidate' occurs in the Indian Penal Code, the definition of 'candidate' given in the Representation of the People Act should be strictly applied so that these would be offences only after a person becomes a candidate.

"Moreover, if the word "candidate' is used merely for identification of a candidate, then the words 'election agent' should also have been used merely for identification of the election agent. This would lead to the absurd result that if a corrupt practice was committed by a person with the consent of another person who later becomes the election agent of a candidate, then the election of the candidate would be liable to be set aside. I submit that this could not have been the intention of the Legislature."

Authorization Implies Agency

Making his submission on the interpretation of the term 'authorization', used in the Representation of the People Act, Sen argued, "There is a vital difference between authorization and consent. The principle of agency is involved in authorization. The authorized person becomes an agent of the candidate."

While Counsel was making his submissions on the issue, Justice Beg interrupted to ask him whether there was any evidence that Yashpal Kapoor had acted on the Prime Minister's instructions when he went to Rae Bareli on 7 January and again on 19 January. Counsel replied that there was no evidence whatsoever.

This question of Justice Beg related to a finding of fact of the Allahabad High Court. Though the findings of fact of the High Court were not in issue at all in the Supreme Court, Justice Beg asked several questions on them while Counsel of either side were making their submissions on the amendments. He appeared to be reading the paper books (record of evidence) of the case during the arguments. It is, therefore, not surprising that part of his judgment in this case was a pronouncement on the correctness of the findings of the Allahabad High Court.

Arguing further, Counsel said that authorization meant that

the rights and liabilities of the person authorized become the rights and liabilities of the person who authorized him. "Unless this was so, it would lead to a very odd situation. All sorts of people do odd jobs for the candidates. How can the candidate find out how much expenditure was incurred on these?"

Justice Khanna: Sometimes people do voluntary work not because they are friendly with him, but because they hate the rival candidate.

Counsel: Exactly, my Lord. That is why the word 'authority' has been pointedly used in the Act and not the words 'consent or 'knowledge.'

Counsel submitted that unless the person authorized also has a right to be reimbursed for the amount which he spent for the candidate, there is no authorization.

Justice Mathew: So you mean that the entire expenditure which is liable to be included in the candidate's return must be spent from his own pocket.

Counsel: It has to be, my Lord.

Citing a number of cases to support his contention Counsel submitted that this was where the decision in Chawla's case was wrong and made a clear departure from all previous cases. "Chawla's case laid down the proposition that mere consent or failure to disavow was enough to make an expenditure the candidate's expenditure. This is not a correct proposition according to all previous cases."

Justice Mathew: According to you, can authorization ever be implied?

Counsel: Yes, it can. But implied authorization must be an unequivocal and unambiguous act.

Sen also pleaded that since the amendment did not change the law at all, it had to be valid.

Issue of Expenses

Taking up the issue of expenses, Sen argued that the pleadings in the petition about the expenses alleged to have been incurred by Mrs Gandhi or her election agent were not specific or sufficient. He said that it was not pleaded as to who had incurred and authorized the expenditure, nor had the extent of the expenditure or the things on which it was incurred, been specified.

"However, even assuming that their pleading is correct in law, there is hardly any evidence in this case to show that the expenditure exceeded the prescribed limit. The learned Judge of the High Court after adding Rs 16,000 on the construction of rostrums, and Rs 1,900 on the loudspeakers etc., to the amount shown in the return of expenses, had come to a total of about Rs 32,000. Now, because of the explanation added to Section 77 (that any expenditure incurred by arrangements by a Government servant in the discharge of his official duties shall not be deemed to be expenditure incurred in connection with the election of a candidate), this amount added by the learned Judge would have to go out of the list of expenses. Rostrums and loudspeakers were arranged by Government servants in the discharge of their official duties. So once these expenses are removed from the total reached by the High Court, there would remain a gap of about Rs 22,000 for the ceiling to be reached."

Bhushan's main argument on the expenses issue was that the 23 vehicles used by the DCC of Rae Bareli must have been used in Mrs Gandhi's constituency and the expenditure on these vehicles must be included in her election expenses. Sen submitted that there was a total lack of evidence on the expenditure on these vehicles. "None of the drivers of the vehicles have been examined. This itself shows that their case was not bonafide. Nor has he given any evidence to show the number of days these vehicles were used, or whether they were used in the Prime Minister's constituency-at all."

Justice Khanna: There are three possibilities of how these vehicles could have been used: (1) they were used wholly in the Prime Minister's constituency; (2) they were used partly in her constituency and partly in the other two constituencies; and (3) that all of them were used in the other two constituencies.

Is there any reason for us to accept the third possibility?

Counsel: In the absence of any evidence as to the number of these vehicles used in the Prime Minister's constituency, how can we estimate the expenditure incurred on them for her constitueney?

Justice Chandrachud: If a candidate asks his party to spend money for him, but the party spends money jointly for two or three constituencies, then the question of apportionment of the expenditure would arise.

Counsel: There is no evidence that Mrs Gandhi or Yashpal Kapoor had asked the DCC to use those vehicles in her constituency. The only evidence is that Yashpal Kapoor wrote a letter to the DM to get those vehicles released as they were requisitioned by the DM. This was because the President of the DCC had requested Yashpal Kapoor to get them released as he was unable to find the candidates of the other two constituencies. From just this, we cannot conclude that the vehicles were used in the Prime Minister's constituency.

Giving his interpretation of the amendment about "official duties," Sen said that this was merely to clarify the actual law. "Since it was not clear before the amendment whether any assistance provided to a candidate by a Government servant in the discharge of his official duties could attract a corrupt practice, the Parliament, by this amendment, decided to make things clear. They have conclusively laid down that if any incidental assistance was provided to a candidate by a Government servant in the discharge of his official duties, it would not be deemed to be assistance for the furtherance of the prospects of the candidate's election, and would thus not have the effect of vitiating the election."

Counsel contended that official duties did not merely mean statutory duties, but would include even administrative duties. He said that in England, procuring the assistance of Government servants was not a corrupt practice. Hence, he said, it was in the fitness of things that Parliament had made this amendment in India. Counsel disputed Bhushan's contention that this provision could be Government. He said that in any case, the possibility of abuse of a provision was not a test of its validity.

Issue of Symbols

Explaining the amendment regarding the symbols, Sen said that by this amendment Parliament had made it clear that if a religious symbol was allotted to a candidate because of the negligence of the Election Commission, the candidate would not have to pay the penalty. He said that even if the symbol was allotted at the request of the party, there was no reason why the poor candidate should be made to suffer for the fault of his party. "Being the party's candidate, he has no option but to use the party's symbol. In any case the Election Commission being an independent body will ensure that no religious symbol is allotted to a candidate. But if the Election Commission errs, it cannot be helped. Someone has to take a final decision about whether a symbol is religious or not. If the Commission can make a mistake, so can the courts."

Sen's submissions on the amendment regarding the date of resignation of Government servants were substantially the same as the Solicitor General's. He said that this amendment had provided finality to the law and removed all ambiguity from it.

Spirit of Constitution a Vague Concept

Coming to the most crucial aspects of the case, Sen also submitted that the test of basic features could not be applied to ordinary laws, even if it could be applied to Constitutional Amendments. "The validity of ordinary laws is governed by entirely different provisions like the chapter on Fundamental Rights. Bhushan has argued that the amendments are against the spirit of the Constitution. What is the spirit of the Constitution? Chief Justice Das had said that the spirit behind anything was a very elusive concept. There is no spirit except what the statute says."

Justice Mathew: If the text of basic features can be applied to constitutional amendments, why can't it be applied to ordinary laws as well?

Counsel: The other side has argued that the Election Laws Amendments are against the ideal norms of free and fair election. Now it may be said that the limit of Rs 35,000 on election expenses is too high for a poor country like ours. This makes the election very unfair and is thus against the norms of free and fair elections. But can this be sustained? I submit that the only norms are the statutory norms incorporated in the Representation of the People Act.

Justice Mathew: If we can proceed on the basis that the concept of free and fair election is a valid limitation for a constitutional amendment, then why is it not a valid limitation for an ordinary law?

Counsel: My Lord, for a statute it is not possible to apply that test.

Justice Mathew: But for a constitutional amendment, is it possible to apply it? Take a case where an amendment to the Representation of the People Act provides that people with an income above Rs 20,000 will have two votes. Does this not destroy the basic structure of a democratic State?

Counsel: No, it does not. All these rights are statutory and can be changed by amendment of the statute.

Justice Mathew: We must have some concept of our democracy.

Counsel: Then the validity of laws would be left to the likes and dislikes of the Judges. This concept of basic structure is very difficult to understand.

Justice Mathew: Then the basis feature theory must go even for a constitutional amendment. If equality is a basic feature of the Constitution, then discrimination in voting is not possible. Do you say that free and fair elections are not a basic feature of the Constitution?

Solicitor General (interjecting): The dimensions of the basic structure can be changed. The only condition is that it must not be destroyed. The voting age can be increased to 25 or reduced to 18 without destroying the basic structure.

Sen: The only mandate of the Constitution is that there shall be a Parliament elected by the people. The residual norms of how the elections shall be fought and who shall be able to fight the elections is left to Parliament. This lodging of the power to create residual norms is itself a basic feature of the Constitution and you cannot deny this power to Parliament.

Arguing on the retrospectivity which had been awarded to the amendments, Sen submitted that the Parliament's competence to enact laws was not determined by the prospectivity or retrospectivity of the laws. "If Parliament can enact a law prospectively, it can also enact the same law retrospectively. All that has to be seen is whether the Parliament is competent to enact that law."

This concluded Sen's reply to Bhushan's arguments on the validity of the Election Law Amendments.

Kaushal's Arguments

After Sen, J.N. Kaushal, the assisting counsel for Mrs Gandhi also made brief submissions in defence of the Election Law Amendments. Kaushal urged that this basic feature limitation should not be extended to ordinary legislation, as it would be a dangerous extension of the Keshavananda Bharati case. He pleaded that even though it may logically follow from the majority view of the Keshavananda Bharati case that this limitation should also apply to ordinary legislation, it should not be applied, because a case is an authority only for what it actually decides, and not for what follows logically from it. He cited a Supreme Court case to support his contention. In that case, Justice Hegde had observed, "A case is only an authority for what it actually decides. I entirely deny that it can be quoted for a proposition that may seem logical from it. Such a mode of reasoning assumes that the law is necessarily a logical code, whereas every lawyer must acknowledge that the law is not always logical at all."

Justice Mathew: If other things remained the same, what is the harm in law being logical?

Counsel: If this basic feature limitation is applied to ordinary laws as well, it would open the doors to endless litigation. Thousands of writ petitions will be filed challenging various laws on vague grounds like political justice etc.

Justice Mathew: Article 245 which gives the Parliament power to make laws, uses the words 'subject to the provisions of the Constitution.' Now this must mean subject to the basic structure.

Counsel however maintained thal the words "subject to the provisions of the Constitution" meant subject to the specific provisions of the Constitution.

Arguing on the validity of the amendments, Counsel said that the possibilities of abuse of the amendment suggested by Bhushan were hypothetical. He sought justification for the amendments on the ground that the provisions of the amendment had not been misused in Mrs Gandhi's case at least. "The construction of rostrums was part of the legitimate duties of the State to provided security for the Prime Minister. The date of Yashpal Kapoor's resignation which was specified in the Gazette was also the correct date and not a fictional date. It is clear that the resignation of Yashpal Kapoor was tendered on 13 January, but the learned Judge of the Allahabad High Court has come to the conclusion that the resignation did not take effect till 25 January, because in the eyes of law it does not take effect till it is formally accepted in the name of the President. The very concept of the 'eyes of law' sometimes defeats the purpose of law."

Justice Mathew: Then something must be wrong with the 'eyes of law.'

Kaushal: Yes, my Lord. And that is what has been put right by this amendment.

After briefly reinforcing the submissions of Sen on the expenses issue, Kaushal concluded his arguments.

18

"PARLIAMENT CANNOT INTERPRET THE LAW"

Beginning his rejoinder on the Election Law Amendments, Bhushan said that he would first deal with the other side's contention that the basic feature limitation could not be applied to ordinary legislation. He said, "I have absolutely no quarrel with Sinha's first proposition that there can be no limitation on the powers of Parliament because of some natural rights of Man. He says that the restriction on the Constituent power flows from the use of the word 'amendment' in Article 368. That might be so. But I submit that the basic features of the Constitution certainly cannot be discovered from Article 368. The problem in Keshavananda Bharati's case was to discover the connotation of the word 'amendment' used in Article 368. Just by looking at the word 'amendment' itself, one cannot say whether it was meant to be used in the wide or narrow sense in Article 368. Therefore, to discover the connotation of 'amendment,' the Judges had to look at the rest of the Constitution to discover the intention of the Constitution-makers. The majority found that there were certain basic features which the Constitution-makers intended to be permanent and unamendable by any means. This is why they read a limited meaning into the word 'amendment' used in Article 368."

Justice Mathew: If you assume that certain features of the Constitution are intended to be permanent, then it is easy to import this limitation on the legislative power, but where do you find this in the Constitution?

Counsel read out some passages from some judgments in the Keshavananda Bharati case in support of his contention that certain features of the Constitution were intended to be permanent. He said,

"This was the premise on which the conclusion that the power under Article 368 is limited rests. The other side thinks that this conclusion can stand without the legs on which it rests."

Counsel then dealt with the contention that the basic feature doctrine was too vague to be applied to ordinary legislation. He said, "I fail to understand that if this same vague doctrine can be applied to constitutional amendments, what great difficulty can arise in applying it to ordinary legislation. They say that this will open the gates to a flood of litigation. On the other hand, let us see the consequence of not applying this to ordinary legislation. Does anyone want a law which in the opinion of the Supreme Court is repugnant to the basic features of the Constitution?"

Justice Mathew: Basic features must be there in every Constitution. All legislative power is subject to the Constitution. Basic features are also a part of the Constitution. Why has this argument not been applied to strike down legislation in the USA?

Counsel: Perhaps because of the 'due process' clause in America. The 'due process' clause is sufficient safeguard against any legislation repugnant to the basic feature. (The US Constitution contains a clause that no person shall be denied the 'due process of law.')

Justice Khanna: In America, a lot of retrospective legislation has been struck down because of the 'due process' clause.

Chief Justice: Mr Bhushan, what is your syllogism in regard to legislative power? How do you reach the conclusion that the legislative power is also limited by the basic feature doctrine?

Mr Bhushan did not know what a syllogism was, so he let it go at that time. In the lunch break, he asked me if I knew what a syllogism was. Having been a student of formal logic, I explained that a syllogism was an argument in which a conclusion is derived from two premises taken jointly. He immediately formed his syllogism and presented it before the Chief Justice right after lunch.

He said, "Your Lordships asked me the syllogism for deriving the basic feature limitation on legislative power. This is my syllogism. The proposition established by Keshavananda's case is that there are some basic features of the Constitution which are intended to be permanent. This is my first premise. My second premise is that all legislative power is subject to the provisions of the Constitution. From this the conclusion clearly follows that legislative power is also subject to the restrictions imposed by the basic features of the Constitution.

Chief Justice: But Mr Bhushan, this is *petitio principi* (circular argument).

Bhushan was again out of his depth. He did not know the meaning of this either. He thought it wise to avoid further arguments in formal terms of logic. Trying another line of argument, he said, "I submit that it would be extremely illogical to hold that the Legislature can destroy the basic features of the Constitution, by an ordinary law which can be enacted by a simple majority, while by a constitutional amendment which requires a two-third majority they cannot."

Counsel submitted, "To hold that the basic feature limitation does not apply to ordinary legislation would be so illogical that no expediency can sanction it. Mr Sinha stated that illogic had to be restored to in England to confer legitimacy on illegitimate children. I agree with the Solicitor General that the law can be made illogical for some noble end. Legitimatizing innocent children is certainly a noble end. But in this case what is the innocent illegitimacy, which has to be legitimized? What great end is to be achieved by allowing the Legislature to damage or destory the basic structure of the Constitution? What great purpose is being served by these retrospective amendments except upholding the election of one individual which had been declared invalid by the High Court?

Justice Khanna: We must move out of this sensitive region.

Justice Mathew: No, this argument is very vital for your case. Therefore you must argue it this way. Suppose the majority in Keshavananda Bharati had held that there was some basic structure of the Constitution, but the amending power of the constituent body was plenary. What would you say about legislative power in that case? Would that be subject to the basic features?

Counsel: I submit it would. Because basic features would still constitute implied limitations on legislative power.

Justice Mathew: Suppose some people feel that proportional representation is a basic ingredient of democracy, what would happen then?

Counsel: If the judiciary feels that proportional represenation is absolutely essential for democracy, then the judiciary must see that a law providing for proportional representation is made by the Legislature.

On the amendment in the definition of "candidate," Bhushan gave a cyclostyled compilation of various Election Laws of England, Australia and New Zealand. He told the court that in all these countries, the scheme was that the corrupt practice could be committed at any time either before, during or after the election.

Justice Khanna: Mr Bhushan, do you know that no person has been disqualified for corrupt practices in England since 1921? Not even a single election petition has been filed since then.

Counsel: If the laws are applied properly, then people know that their election will be set aside for any violation of the law. It is only when people think that they can get away without any penalty, that they resort to such practices.

Bhushan rebutted the argument that the object of the Legislature in making this amendment must have been to reduce the liability of a corrupt practice. He said, "We must assume that the intention of the Legislature was honest and just. Why should we assume that the Legislature intended that a candidate could commit all sorts of corrupt practices before filing his nomination papers? The Solicitor General agreed with me that as far as bribery is concerned, it cannot be condoned even if it was done before the nomination of a candidate. He says so, because of the provisions of the Indian Penal Code. So if a candidate commits bribery before his nomination his election would still be set aside through a long and circuitous process. Why should we credit the Legislature with the intention that to achieve the same result they wanted a long and circuitous process to be followed? If the intention was that the candidate's election should be set aside even if bribery was committed before nomination, then there is no reason why my interpretation should not be accepted. Moreover, bribery is not the only corrupt practice. If the interpretation of the other side is acccepted, it would mean that the entire Government machinery can be used by a candidate before he files his nomination papers, without incurring any liability.

"Mr Sen referred to Section 171(C) and Section 171(G) of the IP(C) in order to prove that a corrupt practice could only be committed after the nomination of a person. Let us read Section 171(G). It says,

> Whosoever with intent to affect the result of an election, makes or publishes any statement, purporting to be a statement of fact, which is false, or does not believe to be true, in relation to the personal character or conduct of any candidate, shall be punished with a fine.

What Sen overlooks here is the effect of the crucial words "Whosoever with intent to effect the result of an election." How does it matter if a false statement is published even 10 years before the election? If a person does it with the intention of affecting the result of the election then why should he not be punished even if it is done 20 years before the election. If Sen's interpretation is accepted, it would mean that a candidate can flood the constituency with defamatory posters of the rival candidate just before filing his nomination paper, and get away without any liability.

Bhushan said that the scheme of the R.P. Act was that an election should be set aside even if a corrupt practice was committed without the consent of a candidate if it materially affected the result of the election. "Thus it is clear that the Legislature intended the election to be vitiated, if the result of the election was materially affected by any corrupt practice. With this in view, can it be said that a corrupt practice, however serious, should be condoned if it were committed before the nomination of a candidate?

Justice Khanna: Your contention is that there should be no time limit for corrupt practices. Why is there a time limit for election expenses? (Section 77 provides that a record of election expenses will be maintained from the date of the Presidential Notification calling for the elections.)

Counsel: It is because of practical necessity. It is very difficult to calculate the election expenses unless some time limit is specified. In England too, there is a time-limit for election expenses though other corrupt practices can be committed at any time.

On the amendment about official duties of Government servants, Bhushan said that the Solicitor General had tried to limit the scope of official duties. "He had said that everything cannot come in the category of official duties and the court would have to see whether a duty conferred on a Government servant could be classed as official duty or not." He, however, submitted that any duties for the security of VIPs would be official duties within the meaning of this section. I submit that if the construction of rostrums, as in this case, can be regarded as an official duty, then anything, even if it wholly deals with election work can be regarded as an official duty.

Justice Mathew: If an act can be conceived to be in public interest, and in the process some benefit accrues to a candidate, can this act be said to be an official duty?

Counsel: Everything can be said to be in public interest. It all depends on the point of view. If a person is considered indispensable for the country, then anything done for his benefit can be in the public interest.

Justice Mathew: Is there anything in this amendment which contemplates these facilities for only one party? How can you say that this is discriminatory? If it is applied with an uneven hand and an evil eye, then perhaps you can complain.

Counsel: The power of imposing duties is conferred on the

Government. Normally, the Government should be presumed to act fairly and if it issues an unfair order, that order can be challenged. But the order can also be a secret order. So it may not be possible to challenge it before it is executed. This is exactly the situation in this case. The Blue Book contained secret instructions not known to the outside world. If an order is executed which gives an unfair advantage to a candidate, what is the use of getting it struck down subsequently?

On the amedment regarding the date of resignation of a Government servant Bhushan referred to Kaushal's argument. He said, "Mr Kaushal has said that Yashpal Kapoor submitted his resignation on 13 January which was accepted orally on the same date. It had also been accepted in writing with effect from 14 January. But the learned Judge of the High Court has found that in the eyes of law the resignation did not become valid till 25 January because it was accepted in writing only on that date. Mr Kaushal said that since the eyes of law had begun to see illusions, the Legislature had amended the law and had set the eyes of law right. I wonder when eyes of law can see all sorts of complicated legal matters, what happens to them when they are determining the date on which a Government servant's resignation becomes effective, that the Legislature has to supply them with special glasses. The general law about the date of resignation of a Government servant is quite clear. This amendment gives Government an arbitrary power to specify the date on which a resignation takes effect, however divorced from reality it might be.

Justice Khanna: The amenmdent is like a rule of evidence. It only says what the court will have to take into account in deciding the date of resignation.

Counsel: If there are two principles which can be followed when applying the law, the Legislature can prescribe as to which principle should be followed by the courts. That is a rule of evidence. But here no principle has been prescribed. A judicially determinable matter has been left entirely to the Government.

Going on to amendment regarding symbols, Bhushan said, "The argument of the fault being the Commission's is not correct because the symbol is chosen by the party itself. Although this is not a mandatory rule, the procedure followed is that the party submits a list of three symbols and normally the Commission allots one of these. The alternative submission of Sen was that a candidate should not be made to suffer for the fault of his party. This is also a fallacious argument. A party candidate contests on the label of his party and therefore cannot be divorced from it. If his party is at fault, why should he not suffer for it? Moreover, even if the candidate is not at fault, but it is found that the allotment of a religious symbol substantially affected the result of the election, then there is no reason why the election should not be vitiated. Elections are sometimes vitiated when the returning officer has improperly rejected the nomination papers of some persons, which is also not a fault of the elected candidate.

"Another argument of the other side is that someone has to be conferred the final authority to decide whether a symbol is religious or not. The Election Commission has been conferred this authority. Why should power of deciding whether the symbol is religious or not be conferred to the Election Commission which is a quasi-judicial body instead of the courts? They say that the Election Commission would not allot a religious symbol. Let us look at the peculiar facts of this case. The symbol of cow and calf was the second preference of the Congress Party. Their first preference was a mother with a child in her arms. I do not know what objection the Election Commission could have had to the first preference of the Congress. But by a curious process of reasoning, the Election Commission allotted the second. The reasoning was that since the Congrees (O) had also been allotted its second preference, therefore to ensure equality they were allotting the Congress(R) its second preference too. The only objection to the mother and child symbol could be that children would be attracted to vote on that symbol."

Justice Khanna: But children have no vote.

Counsel: Precisely.

Justice Mathew (smiling): No, they could perhaps induce their mothers to vote on that symbol.

Arguing on the retrospectivity conferred on these amendments, Bhushan ridiculed the other side's contention that the amendment had not changed the law but merely clarified it. "They say that when Parliament found that the judiciary was not interpreting the laws according to the Parliament's intention, they had to move in to interpret them for the benefit of the judiciary. I do not know under which provision of the Constitution the Parliament has been given this power to show the judiciary how to interpret a law. The judiciary is the final interpreter of all laws. The law was as the Supreme Court interpreted it. These amendments have clearly altered the law."

"Mr Sen has submitted that Parliament's competence to make laws is not affected by the retrospectivity given to them. If the Parliament can make a law with prospective effect, it can also do so with retrospective effect. I am surprised that Mr Sen could advance such a grossly erroneous proposition. Let us take the simple case of ex-post facto laws. The Parliament cannot enhance the penalty for a crime retrospectively, though they can certainly enhance it prospectively. I agree that retrospective legislation is possible where it does not come in conflict with any constitutional provision, but retrospective legislation about the rules of a contest is certainly discriminatory."

Bhushan then took up the issue of expenses. He strongly contested Sinha's and Sen's contentions that the word "authorization" used in Section 123 meant a transfer of rights and liabilities of the person who had been authorized, to the candidate who had authorized him.

Counsel said, "Let us take an example. When a person is authorized by an officer to carry on a business, does it mean that he is carrying on the business on behalf of the officer? Are the rights and liabilities of this person transferred to the officers? If authorization is taken to mean a transfer of rights and liabilities, then a ceiling on expenses would become meaningless. A candidate could get any amount of money spent on his election by his friends and supporters merely by refusing the liability. It is also incorrect to say that authorization implies reimbursement. If that is so, it would mean that a friend or supporter of a candidate could give him a cheque of Rs 5 lakhs because most elections are fought on donated money—and the candidate would be free to spend this money on his election."

Justice Mathew: Suppose a person canvasses for his ideals, and his ideals happen to coincide with those of a candidate. If that person spends his money to canvass support for this candidate even though the candidate does not ask for it, will this expenditure have to be included in the candidate's return?

Counsel: It would depend on the facts of the case. If it is found that the refusal of the candidate was a facade and he really consented to the expenditure incurred by that person, then it would have to be included. It could certainly be a difficult question. But just because the application of a particular law can sometimes pose a difficult problem, it does not mean that the law should be given an absurd interpretation.

Justice Mathew: Suppose a juristic person like a company spends money on a candidate. Is it an offence under Section 171(H) of the Penal Code?

Counsel: Yes, it is.

Justice Mathew: How can the company be jailed or hanged?

Counsel: The person responsible for the acts of the company can be punished.

On the expenses issue regarding the 23 vehicles used by the DCC Rae Bareli, Bhushan contested the other side's argument that the petitioner had not discharged his burden by proving the extent of expenditure on the vehicles. He said that once he had shown that these vehicles were used in Mrs Gandhi's constituency with the authorization of Yashpal Kapoor, the burden shifted to the appellant to show exactly how much expenditure was incurred on them. "In this case, I have shown that at least some of these vehicles were used for Mrs Gandhi's election with Kapoor's consent. The expenses on none of these have been included in the return. Now it is their duty to show the exact expenditure incurred on these. In the absence of that, it is the duty of the court to make a reasonable estimate of the expenses likely to have been incurred and add that to the return. Regarding their allegation that we have not tried to examine any of the drivers of the vehicles, your Lordships will appreciate that in theory it is easy to say that this should also have been done, but in practice, it can be extremely difficult. When we managed to locate some of the drivers with great difficulty, they were not willing to give evidence in this case. Nobody wants to give evidence against the Prime Minister. They are all afraid. We cannot drive them from their houses and force them to come to court."

Regarding Sen's allegation that the pleading in the petition about the corrupt practice on the expenses issue was not specific, Bhushan said that pleading must be of a corrupt practice. "The corrupt practice in this case was exceeding the limit of election expenses. The petition has clearly alleged that the appellant exceeded the limit of election expenses. We have also given as many details about the expenses as we could. But I submit that it is not necessary to give the details of every expenditure which was incurred by the appellant. If I can show that the totality of expenses exceeded the limit, then I have proved a corrupt practice."

Bhushan concluded his rejoinder on the Election Law amendments just before the court rose on 9 October. At last the long arguments of the Supreme Court had ended. They had worked continuously for 31 days.

19

THE SUPREME COURT JUDGMENT

As soon as the Supreme Court arguments concluded, Bhushan was asked by some foreign journalists about the prospects of the amendments being struck down. He said that he was sure that the Constitutional Amendments would be struck down, and was also confident of the Election Law Amendments being declared invalid. When questioned about the possibility of the judges being pressurized, Bhushan answered in the affirmative. He was then asked whether he thought they would succumb to the pressure. He said that Judges were trained to resist pressure, but in these extraordinary conditions it would depend on the kind of pressure that was brought to bear upon them. He said, "If I was told that I would be jailed for arguing this case, I could have resisted that pressure. But if I was told that my children would be slaughtered, then, perhaps, the situation would have been otherwise. But in any case I do not think that the Supreme Court Judges will succumb to any pressure."

When Bhushan reached Allahabad after the conclusion of the Supreme Court arguments, he heard that Kanhaiya Lal Misra, the former Advocate-General of U.P., who had also argued Mrs Gandhi's case at the preliminary stages, was very ill. He took the first opportunity to call on him, at which occasion Mrs Gandhi's case was also discussed. Misra's last words to Bhushan were: "Democracy is dead in this country." The very next day he expired.

Incidentally, 9 October, the day the arguments ended, was the last working day before the Court recessed for the Dussehra vacations. Since the Chief Justice, at the conclusion of the hearing, had not said that the judgment in the case was reserved, people

The Supreme Court Judgment

who had witnessed the case were wondering whether, when the Court assembled after the vacations, the Chief Justice would not call upon both the sides to advance their arguments on the merits of the case as they stood before the Election Law Amendments. Everything was possible. They had, after all, decided to hear the case on merits as it stood after the Election Laws Amendments, even before deciding the validity of the 39th Constitutional Amendment. This speculation, however, was put at rest, when the Court assembled after the Dussehra vacations and the Bench began its routine work. Speculation now was about when the judgment would be delivered. Although utmost secrecy was supposed to be maintained, the date leaked out on 2 November. On that day, word went around that the judgment was to be delivered on Monday, 7 November. The official announcement came only when the list of the Court for 7 November was published on the previous evening.

Meanwhile, on the political scene, things were moving. All the State Chief Ministers and all the Central Cabinet Ministers were asked to be present in Delhi on 7 November. On that date, a large number of people had gathered around the Prime Minister's residence where elaborate arrangements had been made for them.

On 7 November, visitors and lawyers started arriving at the Chief Justice's Court from 9.30 A.M. Entry, again, was by passes and no one was allowed to stand. By 10.30 A.M. when the Judges arrived, the Court was filled to capacity. One could almost feel the excitement in the Court. This case was being seen as the last chance to overthrow Mrs Gandhi's dictatorship. There was pin-drop silence as the people waited to hear the Chief Justice.

The Chief Justice announced that an equal amount of time would be given to all the Judges to read out their respective judgments. He was the first to start reading out his judgment. As it is not the convention in the Supreme Court to first announce the operative portion of the judgment, the people had to wait till the end to know the operative order.

The Chief Justice first dealt with the Constitutional Amendment. Within 20 minutes it was clear that he had struck down the Constitutional Amendment. Reporters rushed out in joy to ring up their news services. Their joy was, however, shortlived, as in another 15 minutes it was clear that the Chief Justice had upheld the Election Law Amendments. He finished reading his judgment in 45 minutes. He had accepted the appeal and reversed the High Court's decision because of the Election Law Amendments. The people who had witnessed the proceedings were not greatly surprised at the Chief Justice's decision.

They now held their breaths and waited for Justice Khanna to deliver his judgment.

Justice Khanna was decidedly not at his best when he began his ordeal. He looked slightly worried and his face betrayed a tinge of sadness. He read out his judgment slowly. The people were not surprised when he read out that he had struck down the Constitutional Amendment. They were, however, surprised when he read out that he had upheld the Election Law Amendments and had thus declared Mrs Gandhi's election valid.

The onlookers groaned. All their hopes were shattered. Now it seemed certain that the Election Law Amendments would be upheld by the majority. The fact that the Constitutional Amendment would be struck down was a poor consolation in these circumstances.

It was next Justice Mathew's turn to read out his judgment. In a bold and clear voice, he too declared this Constitutional Amendments invalid, upheld the Election Law Amendments and, therefore, reversed the High Court's decision. The two judgments which now remained were of merely academic interest. By now it seemed that the judgment would be unanimous.

But Justice Beg's judgment was not without surprise. In his 231 page judgment, he did not pronounce at all on the validity of the Constitutional Amendment. By a strange piece of reasoning, he held that the Constitutional Amendment did not bar the courts from going into the merits of the case. Although he did declare the Election Law Amendments valid, he did not stop there. He went on to discuss the correctness of Justice Sinha's judgment on the basis of the unamended laws. Observing that Justice Sinha's judgment contained "manifest errors," Justice Beg disagreed with Justice Sinha's findings on the two issues on which he had found Mrs Gandhi guilty. Observing that these amendments were unnecessary and futile, Justice Beg absolved Mrs Gandhi of all blame, even on the basis of the unamended law.

It was lastly Justice Chandrachud who read out his judgment. His was the shortest judgment. In a 55-page judgment he declared the Constitutional Amendment invalid and the Election Law Amendments valid. Thus he too upheld the validity of Mrs Gandhi's election.

The Supreme Court judgment was greeted with mixed reaction. While the Opposition was disappointed, though not unexpectedly so, there were jubilant celebrations at Mrs Gandhi's house. The "rented crowd" there danced with joy and said that the Supreme Court judgment had vindicated Mrs Gandhi and had shown that she was "innocent" of the corrupt practices declared by the High Court.

The irony of this exercise of back-patting at Mrs Gandhi's house was adroitly brought out by a cartoon published in *Time* magazine. The cartoon depicts Mrs Gandhi sitting on a Judge's desk and saying, "You have been found guilty of election law violations. Do you wish to say anything to the court before sentencing?" She runs from the Judge's chair to the "accused's" position and replies, "Why not get rid of these laws, your honour?," whereupon she moves up again to the Judge's desk to say, "Sounds good to me. Case dismissed. Not guilty."

Raj Narain's lawyers were slightly surprised at the Supreme Court judgment. They were half expecting that the Election Law Amendments would also be declared void. But it was Justice Beg's judgment which had really surprised them. Bhushan was very angry, and he immediately decided to file a review application against this judgment. The review was sought on the ground that Justice Beg, by delivering a judgment on the merits of the case without hearing the parties, had given a go-by to the principles of natural justice.

The review application came up for hearing on 18 December. The same five-member Bench was reconstituted to hear this application.[1] It is sufficient to mention here that the review application was dismissed by the five Judges on the ground that one of them was of the opinion that there were no sufficient grounds for a review. Justice Beg, giving his separate judgment, set out his reasons for delivering a judgment on the merits of the case.

Thus ended what has been perhaps the most sensational case in India's legal history.

The Judgment of the Chief Justice

In his judgment, the Chief Justice first deals with the validity of the Constitutional Amendment. Pronouncing generally on the powers of the constitutent body and of the Legislature, he observes that validation Acts in almost all spheres of legislation are possible in India and the Legislature has power to validate a transaction which has been declared void by the judiciary. All the Sales-tax validation cases and the election validation cases are illustrations of this proposition.

"Constitutent Power is Sovereign"

The Chief Justice further holds that there is no separation of powers for the Constituent body; that the constituent power is sovereign, the power which creates the or ans and distributes the powers.

---

[1]The details of the review application and the judgments on it are given in Appendix 4.

He further says that judicial review is not an essential feature of the Constitution and not a feature at all when it comes to elections.

On the question of equality, the Chief Justice says that the classification made by the Legislature cannot be questioned by the judiciary.

He also rejects the petitioner's contention that free and fair elections was a basic feature of the Constitution. He said that the concept of free and fair elections varied from person to person and the only norms were those provided by the R.P. Act.

The Chief Justice interpreted Clause (4) of the Constitutional Amendment as first, having wiped out not merely the judgment but also the election petition and the law relating thereto. "Secondly, it has deprived the right to raise a dispute about the validity of the election by not having provided another forum. Third, there is no judgment to deal with and no right or dispute to adjudicate upon. Fourth, the constituent power of its own legislative judgment has validated the election."

After all that he has observed about the power of the constituent body, it should have seemed that the Chief Justice would uphold the constitutional amendment. But he does not. With a sudden turn he declares clause (4) of Article 329(A) invalid. The main infirmity in the Amendment, according to him, was that no norms were applied by the constituent body in validating the election. He says that the constituent body could adjudicate the election disputes, but it had to apply some law. In this case all the law relating to the election was retrospectively repealed and there was thus no law which the constituent body could apply. Thus he says that the Amendment offends the rule of law.

The Chief Justice rejects's the petitioner's contention that the Parliament session was illegal. He holds that the legality of the session could only be determined by the Parliament itself. The Court is not competent to pronounce on it.

Interpretation of Election Law Amendments

He then discusses the effect of the Election Law Amendments on the case. The amendment about the definition of "candidate," he says, makes it clear that a person can commit a corrupt practice only after he has been nominated as a candidate. He also rejects the petitioner's argument that the amendment about "official duties" refers merely to statutory duties of Government servants.

Observing that these amendments took care of the two grounds on which the appellant was convicted by the High Court, the Chief Justice proceeds to deal with the expenses issue. About the expenses on the 23 vehicles, he observes that the petitioner had not shown how much expenditure was incurred on these vehicles and in what proportion they were used in three constituencies. He says that there is also no proof that they were authorized by Yashpal Kapoor. He also observes that authorization implies reimbursement of the agent by the principal. For these reasons he holds that Mrs Gandhi had not exceeded the limit of election expenses.

Ordinary Laws not Subject to Basic Structure

On the crucial issue of whether the limitation of basic features would also apply to ordinary laws, the Chief Justice says that the validity of the exercise of legislative power must be determined by the affirmative grant of that power in the Constitution and the negative restrictions imposed by the Constitution. He observes:

> The contentions on behalf of the respondent that ordinary legislative measures are subject like Constitution Amendments to the restrictions of not damaging or destroying basic structure, or basic features are utterly unsound. It has to be appreciated at the threshold that the contention that legislative measures are subject to restrictions of the theory of basic structure or basic features is to equate legislative measures with constitutional amendments.

He further observes, 'The theory of basic structures or basic features is an exercise in imponderables. Basic structures or basic features are indefinable. The legislative entries are the fields of legislation. The pith and substance doctrine has been applied in order to find out legislative competency and eliminate encroachment on legislative entries. If the theory of basic structures or basic features will be applied to legislative measures it will denude Parliament and State Legislatures of the power of legislation and deprive them of laying down legislative policies. This will be encroachment on the separation of powers."

Coming to the Ninth Schedule, the Chief Justice syas that according to the majority view in Keshavananda Bharati, laws inserted in the Ninth Schedule were not open to challenge on the ground of either damage or destruction of the basic features or violation of any fundamental rights. In view of all this, he pronounces the Election Law Amendments valid. Thus the Chief Justice accepts the appeal, sets aside the judgment of the High Court and dismisses the cross-appeal.

The Judgment of Justice Khanna

In his judgment, Justice Khanna first deals with the second phase of Bhushan's attack on the validity of the amendment; that the Parliament session was illegal. Rejecting the contention, he says that the legality of the detention cannot be gone into collaterally in this case. That can only be determined by a writ of Habeas Corpus. Moreover, he says that the detention of an MP is a matter which can only be dealt with by Parliament itself which is the sole judge of the lawfulness of its proceedings.

Interpretation of Constitutional Amendment

Giving his interpretation of the 39th Amendment, Justice Khanna says that Clause(4) of the Amendment retrospectively repeals the Representation of the People Act for the PM's election. The consequence of this is that the High Court judgment becomes void. Although this may be the consequence, it does not become void automatically. The judgment would have to be declared void, he says, by some authority. In this case, the constituent body has been declared void. This is clearly not permissible as the constituent body cannot encroach upon the judicial sphere.

He further holds that free and fair elections—which require that the candidates and their agents should not resort to unfair means or malpractices—are a basic feature of the Constitution.

Forum Necessary to Decide Election Disputes

Justice Khanna says that for free and fair elections it was necessary to have a machinery to resolve election disputes and to investigate the allegations of malpractices.

He says that the vice of the Constitutional Amendment is that "without even prescribing a law and providing a forum for adjudicating upon the grounds advanced by the respondent to challenge the election of the appellant, the constituent authority has declared the election of the appellant to be valid." He says that such an arbitrary conferment of validity is destructive of free and fair elections.

Regarding the Solicitor General's arguments that the constituent body had itself become the forum for deciding the election disputes of the appellant, Justice Khanna observes that there is no material before him which would indicate that the constituent body considered any material in declaring the election to be valid.

He does not pronounce on Bhushan's contention that the

validation of an election could not be a subject matter of a constitutional amendment. Even assuming that it could be, he rejects the arguments of the Solicitor General that an amendment dealing with but one election could only have the effect of damaging the basic structure of the Constitution. He says, "If an amendment striking at the basic structure of the Constitution is not permissible, it would not acquire validity by being related only to one case. To accede to the argument advanced in support of the validity of the amendment would be tantamount to holding that even though it is not permissible to change the basic structure of the Constitution, whenever the authority concerned deems it proper to make such an amendment, it can do so and circumvent the bar to the making of such an amendment by confining it to one case. What is prohibited cannot become permissible because of its being confined to one matter."

In view of all this, he strikes down Clause (4) of Article 329A which was introduced by the 39th Amendment.

Interpretation of the Election Law Amendments

On the interpretation of the amendment in the definition of "candidates," Justice Khanna rejects the petitioner's contention that corrupt practices start applying even before a person falls within the statutory definition of "candidate."

Regarding the amendment about official duties of Government servants too, Justice Khanna rejects the petitioner's contention that the official duty mentioned in the amendment referred merely to statutory duty.

Validity of the Election Law Amendments

Going on to the validity of Election Law Amendments, Justice Khanna does not pronounce on the preliminary question of whether laws included in the Ninth Schedule were subject to the basic feature limitation.

He, however, rejects the petitioner's contention that even in their prospective operation, the Election Law Amendments damage the basic structure of the Constitution. He says that these amendments merely make the law certain. The possibility of abuse suggested by the petitioner was no ground for striking down the amendment. He says that if the power conferred by the amendment was abused by the Government, the courts would not be helpless. So the proper course would be to strike down the action instead of the law.

Dealing with retrospective operation of the amendment, he

observes that the Legislature is allowed to give retrospective effect to the laws unless some specified provision of the Constitution restricts it. He says that retrospective legislation involving election matters has taken place earlier too. Free and fair elections, are not violated by retrospective legislation relating to the elections. Therefore, he says, that the amendments did not affect any basic feature of the Constitution and were thus valid.

Expenses Issue

On the expenses issue, Justice Khanna says that there was not enough evidence to hold that the 23 vehicles or even some of them were used in Mrs Gandhi's constituency nor was it known how much expenditure was incurred on them. So he holds Mrs Gandhi not guilty of a corrupt practice on this issue.

In view of these findings, he accepts the appeal of Mrs Gandhi and dismisses the cross-appeal of Raj Narain.

THE JUDGMENT OF JUSTICE MATHEW

In his judgment, Justice Mathew first deals with the validity of the constitutional amendment. After discussing its validity in a fair amount of detail, he sums up his findings in this way:

> Our Constitution by Article 329B visualizes the resolution of an election dispute on the basis of a petition presented to such authority and in such manner as the appropriate legislature may, by law, provide. The nature of the dispute raised in an election petition is such that it cannot be resolved except by judicial process, namely, by ascertaining the facts relating to the election and applying the pre-existing law. When the amending body held that the election of the appellant was valid, it could not have done so except by ascertaining the facts by judicial process and by applying the law. The result of this process would not be the enactment of constitutional law but the passing of a judgment or sentence. The amending body, though possessed of judicial power, had no competence to exercise it, unless it passed a constitutional law enabling it to do so. If, however, the decision of the amending body to hold the election of the appellant void was the result of the exercise of an 'irresponsible despitic discretion' governed solely by what it deemed political necessity or expediency, then, like a bill of attainder, it was a legislative judgment disposing of a particular

election dispute, and not the enactment of a law resulting in an amendment of the Constitution. And, even if the latter process (the exercise of despitic discretion) could be regarded as an amendment of the Constitution, the amendment would damage or destroy an essential feature of democracy as established by the Constitution, namely, the resolution of election dispute by an authority by the exercise of judicial power by ascertaining the adjudicative facts and applying the relevant law for determining the real representative of the people.

Justice Mathew is thus the only Judge who accepted the argument raised by Bhushan that Clause (4) of Article 329A introduced by the 39th Amendment was not an amendment of the Constitution at all.

Regarding equality, Justice Mathew holds that the majority in Keshavananda Bharati's case did not hold equality to be part of the basic structure of the Constitution and the only logical basis for supporting the validity of Article 31A, 31B and the first part of 31C, was that Article 14 was not a basic feature.

Because of the foreging observations, Justice Mathew strikes down Clause (4) or Article 329A introduced by the amendment.

'Basic Feature Limitation Inapplicable to Ordinary Laws'

On the validity of the Election Law Amendments, Justice Mathew observes:

> I think the inhibition to destroy or damage the basic structure by an amendment of the Constitution flows from the limitation on the power of 'amendment' under Article 368 read into it by the majority in Bharati's case because of their assumption that there are certain fundamental features in the Constitution which its makers intended to remain there in perpetuity. But I do not find any such inhibition so far as the power of Parliament or State Legislatures to pass laws is concerned. Articles 245 and 246 give the power and also provide the limitation upon the power of these organs to pass laws. It is only the specific provisions enacted in the Constitution which could operate as limitations upon that power.

Here it seems that Justice Mathew makes a serious error of reasoning. Although he holds that the limitation in the amending power is because the Constitution makers intended certain features of the Constitution to be permanent, he still holds that the ordinary legislative power of Parliament is not limited by these basic features. If the Constitution intends certain features to be permanent, then it is obvious that there is an implied limitation on the power of any organ of the State to damage those features.

Justice Mathew further holds that the Preamble does not set out the essential features of the Constitution. He says that there are no ideal norms of free and fair elections and the norms are made by the Legislature itself. These norms, he says, can only be tested by some specific provision of the constitution or necessary implications from them, but not on the anvil of the concept of free and fair elections in an ideal democracy. He also says that since democracy is a nebulous concept, one cannot test the validity of laws with reference to the essential elements of an ideal democracy. They can only be tested with reference to the principles of democracy actually incorporated in the Constitution.

Ninth Schedule

Justice Mathew holds that because an ordinary law is not subject to the basic features limitation, it cannot become subject to it because of its inclusion in the Ninth Schedule. He says:

> The concept of a basic structure, as brooding omnipresence in the sky, apart from the specific provisions of the Constitution constituting it, is too vague and indefinite to provide a yardstick to determine the validity of an ordinary law.

He says that Acts did not attain the status of constitutional law merely because they were put in the Ninth Schedule. Therefore, they cannot be challenged on the ground of basic features. "The utmost that can be said is, as I indicated, that even after putting them in the Ninth Schedule, their provisions would be open to challenge on the ground that they took away or abrogated all, or any, of the fundamental rights, and, therefore, damaged or destroyed the basic structure if the fundamental rights or right taken away or abrogated constitute or constitutes a basic structure." He, therefore, holds that the Election Law Amendments were not liable to be challenged on any ground argued by the petitioner and were thus valid. He also did not agree with any of the interpretations of the amendments advanced by Bhushan.

Parliment Session not Illegal

Regarding the illegality of the Monsoon session of Parliament, Justice Mathew says:

> If a statutory authority passess an illegal order of detention and thus prevents a Member of Parliament from attending the House, how can the proceedings of Parliament become illegal for that reason? It is the privilege of Parliament to secure the attendance of persons illegally detained. But what would happen if the privilege is not exercised by Parliament? I do not think that the proceedings of Parliament would become illegal for that reason.

In view of these findings, he accepts Mrs Gandhi's appeal setting aside the order of the High Court and rejects Raj Narain's cross-appeal.

THE JUDGMENT OF JUSTICE BEG

Justice Beg starts his judgment by taking great pains to explain why he considers it important to go into the merits of the case as they stood before the Election Law Amendments. He says:

> The recurring theme of the petitioner's argument was that the Constitutional Amendment and the Election Laws Amendments were instituted entirely to deprive the petitioner of the remedies which he had under the law against an election vitiated by corrupt practices. It was suggested by the petitioner that the law-making powers had been abused by majority in Parliament for the purpose of serving a majority party and personal ends. It was even alleged that the President of India had also become a party to the misuse of the constitutional powers by detaining Members of Parliament and thus disabling them from opposing the amendments.
>
> In the circumstances indicated above, it seemed to me to be absolutely essential for us to call upon the parties defending or assailing the 39th Amendment and the Acts of 1974 and 1975, to take us, inter alia, into the merits of the cases, of the two sides and the findings given by the trying Judge so as to enable us to see how far these findings were justifiable under the law as it stood even before the amendments by the Act of 1974 and 1975, how they were affected by these amendments, and how they were related to the validity of Section 4 of the 39th Amendment.

Going on to deal with the merits of the case, Justice Beg says that he will not disturb the findings of facts of the High Court Judge and that he would only deal with the questions on law involved in the case.

Issue of Yashpal Kapoor

Dealing with the first issue Justice Beg says that there was no evidence to show that Mrs Gandhi had given her consent to Yashpal Kapoor for doing election work for her before 1 February. He also holds that Yashpal Kapoor's resignation became effective in law on the 14 January because of the President's retrospective acceptance with effect from 14 January. In any case, he says that the Amendment puts these issues absolutely beyond doubt. He further holds that there was no reliable evidence to show that Kapoor had done any election work for Mrs Gandhi before 25 January. Therefore, he finds Mrs Gandhi not guilty of corrupt practice on this issue even on the basis of the unamended law.

Issue of Holding Out

Dealing with the question of when Mrs Gandhi held herself out as a candidate, Justice Beg vehemently disagrees with the High Court's findings that Mrs Gandhi's reply to a question in the Press Conference on the 29 December amounted to holding out as a prospective candidate. He says that what was really relevant was Mrs Gandhi's intention in making that statement, and not what other people understood her statement to mean.

Moreover, he says that all uncertainty about holding out has been removed by the amendment in the definition of "candidate" and, therefore, Mrs Gandhi only became a candidate on 1 February. He rejects Bhushan's contention that a corrupt practice could be committed even before a person fell within the statutory definition of a "candidate."

Issue of Rostrums

Regarding the construction of rostrums and the installation of loudspeakers Justice Beg says it did not amount to furtherance of the prospects of Mrs Gandhi's election. They were merely security arrangements which are made by every Government of a civilized country. Secondly, he says that these arrangements were made almost automatically and Mrs Gandhi did not solicit these arrangements. Therefore, this assistance, if any, was not procured at the instance of Mrs Gandhi. Justice Beg also accepts the validity of the Amendment about official duties of Government servants, because, he says, that this Amendment does not change the law but merely clarifies it.

Dealing generally with the validity of the Election Law Amendments, Justice Beg observes that Acts inserted in the Ninth Schedule are not open to challenge on the basic feature doctrine. Moreover, he says that these amendments do not damage the basic structure of the Constitution nor are they against equality. He says that these amendments made a reasonable classification between the Prime Minister and the other people. The Prime Minister, he says, with all the great hazards and trials, which go with his office, is entitled to certain benefits not available to other people.

About Justice Sinha's findings that Mrs Gandhi was not a very truthful witness, Justice Beg says,

> the learned Judge was unduly conscious of the fact that he was dealing with the case of the Prime Minister and he seemed to be anxious not to allow this fact to affect his judgment; nevertheless, when it came to appraising evidence, he applied unequal standards in assessing its worth so as to benefit the election petitioner.

Cross-appeal

Dealing with the issues in the cross-appeal, Justice Beg ignores the issues of bribery and conveyance of voters because they were not raised by the petitioner in the High Court. He also ignores the issue of travel by IAF planes as it was covered by the amendment made about official duties of Government servants.

Dealing with the issue of the cow and calf symbol, Justice Beg says that on the evidence produced in the Court, it was clear that this was not a religious symbol. Moreover, he says that the amendment by providing that a symbol allotted by the Election Commission would not be deemed to be a religious symbol, removed all doubt in the matter.

Dealing with the expenses issue, Justice Beg says that the expenses alleged by the petitioner were incurred by the DCC. Since they have not been shown to be authorized by Mrs Gandhi or Yashpal Kapoor, the limit has not been exceeded. He, therefore, decides this issue in Mrs Gandhi's favour.

Legality of Parliament Session

Regarding the contention of Bhushan that the Parliament Session was illegal, Justice Beg says that the violation of a privilege of Member of Parliament must be considered by Parliament itself. It could not be considered by the court. Moreover, the legality of the detention could not be challenged collaterally in this case. He, therefore, dismisses the attack on the amendment on this ground.

Validity of the Constitutional Amendment

Justice Beg deals last with the validity of the Constitutional Amendment. This, by itself, is strange, because the amendment on the face of it deprives the Supreme Court of its jurisdiction to go into the merits of this case. Therefore, unless he provided another interpretation to the amendment, or declared it invalid, he was precluded from going into the merits of the case. However, this is not strange enough. The way in which he has dealt with the Constitutional amendment is even stranger.

Justice Beg observes that the separation of powers was a basic feature of the Constitution. The constituent power is not an amalgam of legislative, executive and judicial powers. He futher says that the constituent body cannot exercise judicial power without changing the basic structure, but he holds that Clause (4) was not an exercise of judicial power.

In a judgment punctuated by surprises, Justice Beg goes on to say that the basic feature limitation also applies to ordinary legislation. He is thus the only Judge to hold this.

Clause (4) does not Prevent the Court from going into the Merits of the Case

Justice Beg then comes to the most interesting part of his judgment, wherein he gives his reason for believing that Clause (4) did not preclude the Court from going into the merits of the case. In a benevolent gesture towards the petitioner, he observes:

> It is true that the right which the election petitioner claimed is purely a statutory right. The right to come to this Court under section 116A of the Act of 1951 is also a creature of statute and can be taken away retrospectively. But, where this taking away also involves the taking away of the right to be heard by this court on a

grievance, whether justifiable or not, that a minority party is being oppressed by the majority, can we deny the spokesman of the minority even a right to be heard on merits?

I think that this is a basic consideration which must compel us in the light of the principles laid down by us in Keshavananda Bharati's case to hold that we must look into his grievance and determine for ourselves, where his case stood on the law before it was amended.

He further says that if the amendment was nterpreted as barring the jurisdiction of the Supreme Court, then

the original respondent would also be denied an opportunity of asserting her rights under the 1951 Act and of vindicating her stand in the case by showing that there was really no sustainable ground for the findings given by the learned Judge of the High Court against her. We would, therefore, be prevented from doing justice to her case as well, if we were to accept the contention that the 39th Amendment bars our jurisdiction to hear the appeals under Section 116(A) of the Act on merits. The total effect would be that justice would appear to be defeated even if, in fact, it is not so as a result of the alleged bar to our jurisdiction if it were held to be there. Could it be the intention of Parliament that justice should appear to be defeated? I think not.

Proceeding with his curious reasoning, he further observes:

Undoubtedly, Clause (4) of Article 329A could be said to have a political objective, in the context in which it was introduced, and we could perhaps take judicial notice of this context. Even if it was possible to go beyond the statement of objects and reasons and to hold that Clause (4) of Article 329A is there essentially for demonstrating the strong position of the Government and of the Prime Minister of this country to all inside and outside the country, so as to inspire the necessary confidence in and give the necessary political and legal strength to the Government to enable it to go forward boldly to deal with internal economic and law and order problems and international questions. Yet, I fail to see why this could make it necessary to exclude the jurisdiction of this court so as to prevent it from considering a case which would have been over much sooner if we had not been confronted with difficulties, at the very outset, in examining the merits of the case. Speaking for myself, I fail to see what danger to the country could be jeopardized by a consideration and a decision by this court of such a good case as I find that the Prime Minister of this country had on facts and law. Nevertheless, I am prepared to concede that there may be, and was, some very useful political objective to be served by demonstrating the strength and ability of the Government to face the difficulties with which it had been confronted. If that is so, we can certainly see that Clause (4) of Article 329A had a political objective and utility which has been served.

Observing the principle that out of two possible interpretations of a provision, one which prevents it from becoming unconstitutional should be preferred, Justice Beg says:

> If the purpose of Clause (4) of Article 329A was purely to meet the political needs of the country and was only partly revealed by the policy underlying the statement of reasons and objects it seems possible to contend that it was not at all to oust the jurisdiction of the Court. Hence, Article 329A, Clause (5), will not, so understood, bar the jurisdiction of the court to hear and decide the appeals when it says that the appeal shall be disposed of in conformity with the provisions of Clause (4).

What he probably means by this is that since the amendment directs the Court to dispose of the appeal in conformity with Clause (4), that is by declaring the election valid, the court is allowed to deal with the merits as long as the final result is that the election is declared valid. This is what he himself has done.

He, therefore, says that he is disposing of the case in conformity with Clause (4) of Article 329A by declaring the order of the High Court void and the election valid. He thus accepts the appeal of Mrs Gandhi and dismisses the cross-appeal of Raj Narain.

THE JUDGMENT OF JUSTICE CHANDRACHUD

Dealing first with the validity of the Constitutional Amendment, Justice Chandrachud gives his interpretation of Clause (4). He says Clause (4) consists of six parts:

> (1) The laws made by Parliament prior to 10 August 1975, insofar as they relate to election petitions and matters connected

therewith cease to apply the Parliamentary election of Smt Indira Gandhi which took place in 1971.

(2) Such laws are repealed retrospectively insofar as they govern the aforesaid election, with the result that they must never be deemed to have applied to that election.

(3) Such an election cannot be declared to be void on any of the grounds on which it could have been declared to be void under the laws which were in force prior to 10 August 1975.

(4) The election shall not be deemed ever to have become void on any ground on which, prior to 10 August 1975 it was declared to be void.

(5) The election shall continue to be valid in all respects notwithstanding the judgment of any court, which includes the judgment dated 12 June 1975 of the High Court of Allahabad.

(6) The judgment of the Allahabad High Court and any finding on which the judgment and order of that court is based are void and shall be deemed always to have been void.

Constituent Body can Exercise Judicial Power

On the question of whether the constituent body could pronounce upon private disputes, Justice Chandrachud says that what the Constitution ought to contain is not for the courts to decide. The touchstone of the validity of a Constitutional amendment is firstly whether the procedure prescribed by Article 368 is strictly complied with and secondly whether the amendment destroys or damages the basic structure of the Constitution. The subject-matter of the Constitutional Amendments is a question of high policy and Courts are concerned with the interpretation of laws, not with the wisdom of the policy underlying them.

The Basic Features of the Constitution

Justice Chandrachud then lays down what, according to him, are the basic features—democracy, equality, secular character of the State, and rule of law.

He did not agree with Bhushan's contention that the Preamble held the key to the basic structure of the Constitution. He says that the Preamble cannot be regarded as a source of any substantive power or a source of any limitation.

Judicial Review not Basic

Justice Chandrachud holds that Artice 329B of the Constitution can plainly be used by Legislature to exclude judicial review. He further says:

> Since the Constitution, as originally enacted, did not consider that judicial power must intervene in the interests of purity of elections, judicial review cannot be considered to be a part of the basic structure insofar as legislative elections are concerned. The theory of basic structure has to be considered in each individual case, not in the abstract, but in the context of the concrete problem. The problem here is whether under our Constitution, judicial review was considered as an indispensable concomitant of elections to country's legislatures. The answer, plainly, is, no.

Amendment does not Destroy Democracy

Justice Chandrachud holds that the amendment does not destroy democracy. He said that the provisions for election still remain exactly the same as they were before the amendment. The amendment had validated only one election. The validation of a single election does not destroy democracy, he says.

Equality and Rule of Law Negated

Justice Chandrachud, however, accepted Bhushan's contention that the amendment was destructive of equality by discriminating in favour of the Prime Minister. He says that just because a person is a class by herself, it does not mean that the election law should also be different for her. Moreover, since the amendment makes all law relating to elections inapplicable to the Prime Minister's election, it is destructive of the rule of law.

Justice Chandrachud also holds that the amendment had decided a matter of which the courts were lawfully seized. He does not agree that the amending power is an amalgam of legislative, judicial and executive powers.

For these reasons, he strikes down Clause (4) of Article 329A introduced by the Consitutional amendment.

Election Law Amendments Valid

Dealing with the scope of attack on the Election Law Amendments, Justice Chandrachud rejects Bhushan's contention that ordinary laws must also be subject to the basic feature limitation. He says:

> Shri Shanti Bhushan thought it paradoxical that the higher power should be subject to a limitation which will not operate upon a lower power. There is no paradox, because certain limitations operate upon the higher power for the reason that it is higher power. A constitutional amendment has to be passed by a special majority and certain such amendments have to be ratified by the Legislatures of not less than one-half of the States as provided by Article 362(2). An ordinary legislation can be passed by a simple majority. The two powers, though species of the same genus, operate in different fields and are, therefore, subject to different limitations.
>
> No objection can accordingly be taken to the constitutional validity of the two impugned Acts on the ground that they damage or destroy the basic structure. The power to pass these Acts could be exercised retrospectively as much as prospectively.

Expenses Issue

Dealing very briefly with the issue of expenses, Justice Chandrachud observes that the limit of expenses is not shown to have been exceeded in this case. He, therefore, holds Mrs Gandhi not guilty on this issue.

On the question whether the Parliament Session was illegal, he holds that the legality of the detention of Members of Parliament cannot be questioned collaterally in this case.

For these reasons he holds Mrs Gandhi not guilty on any corrupt practice and accepts the appeal reversing the High Court's judgment.

20

EPILOGUE: FROM COURT BATTLE TO ELECTORAL BATTLE

The Supreme Court judgment effectively killed all speculation on the consequences of a verdict against Mrs Gandhi. An adverse verdict by the High Court resulted in the petitioner being jailed. It is indeed difficult to speculate on the fate of the Supreme Court or its judges, if the Supreme Court had given an adverse verdict. Mrs Gandhi had at no time said that she would accept an adverse verdict of the Supreme Court. On 13 July 1975, the reporter of *Sunday Times* of London asked her the following question: "If the Supreme Court upholds the Allahabad High Court judgment setting aside your election, would you step down as Prime Minister?" This was her answer:

> I have sought legal remedy to which every citizen is entitled. The Supreme Court will give its finding. Is it right to speculate on what it will say? It is relevant to note that the Government in the State at that time was an Opposition one and the Minister-in-charge of Police belonged to my constituency and was the election agent of my opponent who later filed the petition.

Again, on 1 August Mrs Gandhi was interviewed by Norman Cousins, Editor of *The Saturday Review* of New York. She was asked as to what she planned to do in the event of an adverse Supreme Court verdict? She again hedged and her reply was substantially the same as her last reply.

The questions put to Mrs Gandhi were only as to whether she

would accept an adverse Supreme Court verdict. It is difficult to imagine why she could not have said that she would accept an adverse verdict, if she really had intentions of doing so. For her, the appeal to the Supreme Court was a matter of convenience—heads I win, tails you lose. Her psychology here was not dissimilar to that of a highwayman who is out to plunder. If the goods can be partaken without a shoot-out, so far so good. Otherwise no holds are barred.

For the Supreme Court too, the Emergency will remain a sad blot on their record. Quite apart from Mrs Gandhi's case, where they laid down the dangerous precedent that retrospective changes were permissible in the Election Law, the worst blemish on their record would be their ruling in the habeas corpus case where they held that during an emergency when fundamental rights are suspended, the rule of law was also suspended. The executive could detain or even shoot anyone without having to provide any explanation. There was no right of life or liberty, they said.

The sordid story of the remaining months of Emergency is well known and need not be told here. The people gave their verdict on it in the March 1977 polls by giving a severe drubbing to the Congress Party. It seems that the people also have their final verdict on Mrs Gandhi's case at the polls. In another straight fight between Mrs Gandhi and Raj Narain, the people of Rae Bareli turned the tables by defeating Mrs Gandhi with 55,000 votes. In an election where the case had also been made a major issue, this amounted to a verdict of the people's court—"guilty."

In retrospect, it is now possible to analyze the long-term effects of the case. Although the immediate effect of the case was the imposition of the Emergency, it seems clear now, that the nation has learnt much from it, and would ultimately be grateful for it. Democracy in the country has emerged immensely stronger after the traumatic experience. After having lost their rights once, the people of India have learnt to value them much more.

The experience of the Emergency also dealt a possibly mortal blow to a dangerous school of thought which was gaining strength before the Emergency: that dictatorship was the best form of government for India. The sour experience of the short spell of dictatorship strengthened the faith of the people in the democratic process.

Apart from these long term gains, there was at least one immediately beneficial effect of the Emergency. There would possibly have been no Janata Party today if Mrs Gandhi had not chosen to crush the Opposition so rudely. The shock greatly hastened the process of unification of the Opposition parties which shed their differences to deal with the common enemy, when their very survival was threatened. Thus the Emergency has helped bring about a two-party system, with each party fully aware of the price of disunity. It is indeed ironical that for all this, the nation has Mrs Gandhi and the Emergency to be grateful for.

Appendix I

TESTIMONY OF YASHPAL KAPOOR

In the oral deposition of a witness, the counsel asks questions which the witness answers. After that the Judge dictates only the answers to the questions. Thus the records of the oral depositions merely contain the answers and not the questions.

In his examination in chief, which was conducted by S.C. Khare, Kapoor stated that he had gone to Rae Bareli on 7 January 1971 with Shri G.L. Nanda, who was then the Railway Minister. Kapoor said that Nanda addressed a public meeting at Munshi Ganj because of the Shahid Mela (Martyrs Day Celebration). "I also went on the platform and paid my tributes to the martyrs. I spoke for only half a minute. I did not mention anything about Respondent No. 1 contesting election to the Lok Sabha from the Rae Bareli constituency, nor any other thing pertaining to elections, as it was not a political meeting." When asked whether this was a private or an official visit, he replied that it was a private visit and he did not charge any TA for it.

About his resignation date, Kapoor said that on 13 January he had conveyed to Mrs Gandhi his final decision to resign from his post. She agreed to it and asked him to meet Haksar, who was then Secretary-in-Charge of the Prime Minister's Secretariat. Kapoor stated, "Some time during that day, I met Shri Haksar in his office and submitted my resignation letter to him." After asking Kapoor whether he had informed Mrs Gandhi about his decision, Haksar told him that as far as he was concerned the matter was all right and that he was relieved from his post.

Giving the reason for putting the date 14 January under his

signature though he signed the transfer of charge report on 13 January, Kapoor said that this was done because in his resignation letter he had requested to be relieved with effect from 14 January.

Kapoor stated that he was sure that Mrs Gandhi decided to contest from Rae Bareli only on 1 February, because on that date while she was at Rae Bareli, members of the DCC met her and requested her to contest from Rae Bareli. After having heard their request, Mrs Gandhi took Shri Kamlapati Tripathi (then President of the UPCC) aside and spoke to him. Kapoor stated that she also consulted him and only thereafter did she announce her decision to contest the election from Rae Bareli.

Kapoor further stated that till 1 February, Mrs Gandhi had not asked him to do any election work for her. Nor did he do any. He, therefore, denied the petitioner's allegation that he had started working for Mrs Gandhi's election much before 1 February.

Kapoor also explained the reason why the return of election expenses showed some items to have been bought in connection with the election before 1 February. He said that these items which included a voters' list were bought by the DCC of Rae Bareli for the benefit of whosoever ultimately become a candidate from there. He had considered it proper to repay the money spent on these accounts to the DCC and had, therefore, included the expenditure on these in the return of election expenses.

CROSS-EXAMINATION

It was then Shanti Bhushan's turn to cross-examine Yashpal Kapoor.

Bhushan first questioned Kapoor about his duration of service in the Prime Minister's Secretariat. Kapoor said that he had been in the Prime Minister's Secretariat since 1951. Counsel then suggested to Kapoor that he had resigned from his post in 1967 in order to work for Mrs Gandhi's election, because he had rejoined the Secretariat just three months later. Kapoor denied that he had resigned in order to work for Mrs Gandhi's election. The reason for his resignation, he maintained, was his desire to enter public life; but he rejoined the Secretariat because Mrs Gandhi was particularly keen about it and she requested him to do so.

Counsel: You resigned in 1967 on the eve of Parliamentary elections. You resigned again in 1971 on the eve of Parliamentary elections. In 1967, you worked in Mrs Gandhi's constituency. In 1971, again you worked in her constituency. Is there any particular reason behind this coincidence?

Kapoor: Everyone wants to get into work which may push him into Parliament or the Legislature of any State.

Kapoor was then questioned about the fact that his name appeared in the voters' list of Rae Bareli which was prepared for the 1971 elections. In this connection, he was asked where he was residing in 1970. He replied that although he had been to Rae Bareli six or seven times, he was residing in Delhi.

Counsel: You concede that during the year 1970 you were not a resident of any town or district of Uttar Pradesh. You would then concede that your residence as mentioned in the copy of the Electoral Roll is wrong?

Kapoor: I will not call it wrong. I remember that when the revision of electoral roll was taking place, I was at Rae Bareli and I was told that my name had been entered in the electoral roll of Rae Bareli.

Counsel: Your answer does not answer the question that was precisely put to you. You still have to answer as to how the description of your residence in the electoral roll is correct when you concede that during that year you were not residing in any town or district of U.P.

Kapoor: I will not be able to anwer this question.

Counsel: Is it not correct that a person who is not a resident of a particular State cannot be elected a member of the Rajya Sabha from that State? (Bhushan was suggesting that Kapoor had got his name enrolled in the voters' list of Rae Bareli so that he could be elected a member of the Rajya Sabha from U.P.)

Kapoor: I don't thing so.

Counsel: Would you kindly read Section 197 of the R.P. Act and then answer as to whether a person who is not a resident of any particular State can be an election of that State?

Kapoor: Since the word used in Section 197 is 'ordinarily resident,' I still maintain that a person who is not a resident of a particular State can be an elector of that State. At the time the electoral rolls were revised, I was a person 'ordinarily resident' of Rae Bareli.

Kapoor was then asked as to how he happened to reach Rae Bareli on 15 January if it was a fact that at that time he did not even know whether Mrs Gandhi would be contesting the election from there. He replied that after resigning from his post, he went to Lucknow and met Kamlapati Tripathi who then told him to go to the eastern districts of U.P., and since Rae Bareli was one of the eastern districts, it was just by chance that he reached there.

Kapoor was then shown the issue of a newspaper dated 22 January 1971. It carried a news item stating that on 15 January Kapoor reached Rae Bareli with a fleet of 70 cars to launch the election campaign of the Prime Minister. Kapoor denied the report, and said that the correspondent who filed it must have played on his imagination to write it.

Kapoor was then asked as to what he did during the period between 14 January and 1 February? He said that he was in Rae Bareli from 14 January to 1 February? He was in Rae Bareli from 14 January to 17 January, from where he went to Sultanpur and Barabanki to do some organizational work. When asked as to where he stayed at both these places, he said that he could not remember.

He further stated that he was in Delhi between 21 January and 26 January. When asked as to whether he had met the Prime Minister during these five days, he replied that he must have met her twice during this period.

It is interesting to note that in his cross-examination the next day, when Kapoor was asked whether he had met Mrs Gandhi between 13 January and 1 February, he stated that he could not remember.

He was also questioned extensively about election expenses. He said that election expenses were being maintained by Shri Gaya Prasad Shukla (a Congress worker) and he did not know much about them. He was then shown a copy of the receipt obtained for the payment made as remuneration to his driver. The receipt showed that the driver had been paid for the period 15 January to 10 March.

Counsel: According to you, you obtained a jeep only on 1 February. Would you explain the remuneration having been paid to the driver for the period prior to 1 February 1971, if you had obtained the jeep only on 1 February and not prior to it?

Kapoor: I paid a salary to the driver for the period from 15 January because Shri Gaya Prasad Shukla told me that the driver had been hired from that date. (According to Kapoor, the jeep was with the DCC of Rae Bareli from 15 January to 1 February.)

Counsel: You are aware that in the return of election expenses only the amounts spent in connection with the election have to be shown. The amount specified in the receipt according to you includes the amount which was not spent on the election. If that was so, why did you include the entire amount shown in this receipt in the election expenses?

Kapoor: I have erred, but I erred on the right side There was a big margin available, I, therefore, saw no harm in including the whole amount specified in the receipt in the election return.

Counsel then asked some questions unconnected with the case in order to damage the credibility of Kapoor. Kapoor answered affirmatively to Counsel's query of whether a property of value not less than Rs 4 lakhs had been purchased by his wife in the Golf Links area of New Delhi. When asked as to where the money for this property had come from, Kapoor said, "When my wife told me that she wanted to purchase the property, I told her that my savings were only Rs 20,000. My father had received Rs 30,000 as gratuity and that amount had also been passed on by him to me, by cheque. I therefore told my wife that I could not make arrangements for the money beyond Rs 50,000. My wife then told me that her mother, who was living with us, had agreed to advance her a sum of little more than Rs 1 lakh. Narang Bank also agreed to advance a sum of a little more than than Rs 1 lakh to my wife for purchasing the building. A family friend of ours gave my wife a little more than Rs 1 lakh. It was thus that the amount of four lakhs and odd was arranged by my wife to purchase the property."

Counsel then asked him about the conditions on which the loans had been obtained? Kapoor said that he was not aware of them. Counsel further asked him whether the building purchased by his wife had been mortgaged by her in favour of any persons from whom the loan was taken. Kapoor was not aware of this either. He was then asked about the covered area of the building. Kapoor said that he had no idea of the covered area as he claimed that he had been to the house just once and that too for a few minutes only.

In the end, Counsel put the case before Kapoor.[1] He suggested that Kapoor had resigned in January 1971 in order to work for Mrs Gandhi's election, and that he had started working right from 14 January or even earlier. Kapoor denied all these suggestions.

After Bhushan ended his cross-examination, Khare requested the Judge to permit him to re-examine Kapoor on one point. Being allowed to do so, Khare elicited from Kapoor that his name was recorded on the electoral roll of Rae Bareli towards the end of 1968 or the beginning of 1969, and that he had cast his vote in the assembly election that took place in 1969 at Rae Bareli.

In his cross-examination on this point, Bhushan asked him as to how he happened to be in Rae Bareli in 1969 on the date of the assembly polls. Kapoor said that he went to Rae Bareli in 1969 specially to cast his vote.

[1]Putting the case before a witness, is suggesting all those facts which the counsel wants the witness to affirm.

Counsel: Were you so keen to exercise your franchise that you went all the way from Delhi to Rae Bareli merely in order to cast your vote?

Kapoor: I was not able to exercise my right of franchise in 1957, 1962 or 1967. So when I came to know that my name as an elector was recorded in Rae Bareli, I just went down to Rae Bareli to exercise my right of franchise.

This ended Kapoor's testimony.

Appendix 2

TESTIMONY OF MRS INDIRA GANDHI

The examination in chief of Mrs Gandhi was led by Khare. He first addressed questions on the facts of the issue of holding out. This was the main issue for which she had been produced in court. What she said on this would be of crucial importance. In reply to his questions, Mrs Gandhi affirmed that she held a Press Conference after the dissolution of the Lok Sabha in December 1970. She could recollect that at the Press Conference, a question was put to her to the effect that a short while ago members of the Opposition Parties had stated that the Prime Minister was changing her constituency from Rae Bareli to Gurgaon. In answer to this question, she recollected having said that she did not intend to contest from Gurgaon.

Khare: Did you in reply to the question put to you in the Press Conference say, "No, I am not."

Mrs Gandhi: I meant specifically that I was not going to contest from Gurgaon. Since it is such a long time, I do not precisely remember, but most probably, while replying to the question I used the words 'No, I am not.' I would add that my reply did not necessarily mean that I would not change my constituency I only meant that I would not contest from Gurgaon constituency.

Being asked whether she had requested or authorized Yashpal Kapoor to announce her candidature from Rae Bareli or to work for her election prior to 1 February, she replied in the negative. "Since I had not made up my mind until 1 February 1971 to contest the election from Rae Bareli, obviously I could not request or authorize any person to do election work for me in that constituency or to announce or propagate that I was to contest from there."

On being questioned about Yashpal Kapoor's resignation date,

Mrs Gandhi stated that in the second week of January 1971, Kapoor had expressed to her his desire to resign. She had told him to think about it as his decision would be final. On 13 January, he had met her and told her "he had made up his mind to resign." She agreed to his being relieved and asked him to contact P.N. Haksar for completion of formalities. She said that according to her understanding, P.N. Haksar as the Secretary-in-Charge of the Prime Minister's Secretariat was competent to accept Kapoor's resignation.

Mrs Gandhi also deposed that she had not issued any specific instructions to the Air Force to place any aeroplanes or helicopters at her disposal for her election tours. Nor did she give any specific directions to the District Magistrate or Superintendent of Police of Rae Bareli to make arrangements for her election meetings.

She said this to repel the charge in the petition that she had "procured" their services for furthering her election prospects.

CROSS-EXAMINATION

Her examination in chief was over in an hour and she was then cross-examined by Bhushan. After asking some preliminary questions about Yashpal Kapoor's work in her Secretariat, Bhushan decided to make use of the letter which had been procured from the Congress office at Jantar Mantar to impeach her credibility.

Counsel showed her three letters written in May 1959 by the Chief Minister of Himachal Pradesh to Mrs Gandhi. She was the Congress President at that time. These letters helped her recollect that a by-election had taken place in a constituency of Himachal Pradesh in 1959.

Counsel: Did you ask the Lt. Governor of Himachal Pradesh to help your candidate in winning the election?

Khare shot up from his chair and objected to the question. The Judge agreed with the objection and dictated the following order:

> Whether the witness did or did not do so in 1959 does not appear to be relevant for the purpose of this case, as this case relates to an election that took place in 1971. The question is accordingly disallowed.

Bhushan immediately clarified that he had not asked this question because it was relevant for the issues in the case. He showed the relevant provisions of the evidence Act which allowed the cross-examining Counsel to ask questions which did not strictly relate to the issues, but which could have the effect of impeaching the credibility of the witness. It was to impeach the credibility of the witness that he had asked this question.

Counsel then showed Mrs Gandhi a letter addressed to her by the Lt. Governor of Himachal Pradesh in 1959. In that letter, the Lt. Governor had informed Mrs Gandhi that the Congress candidate had managed to win the by-election, and that this was the toughest test that Mrs Gandhi had put him to. Mrs Gandhi replied that the statement of the Lt. Governor that she had put him to any test, was incorrect, and added that the word "test" could mean many things. It could also mean a test of maintenance of law and order during the period of the by-election, which was ultimately the responsibility of the Lt. Governor.

In response to a question about Yashpal Kapoor's resignation before the 1967 elections, Mrs Gandhi denied that he had resigned in order to be able to work for her election. She said that Kapoor had told her that he was resigning because he wanted to do political work, and she also thought that Kapoor had worked for the Congress and not specifically for her in 1967. In response to another suggestion, Mrs Gandhi denied that when Kapoor had resigned in 1967, it was decided that he would be reappointed after the elections were over.

Counsel: Did you not ask Mr Kapoor to rejoin the Secretariat after the elections were over?

Mrs Gandhi: I did.

Counsel: Did Mr Kapoor make any formal application for that purpose?

Mrs Gandhi: I do not think so. But Mr Kapoor was looking for some opportunities which were not available in 1967 and I, therefore, felt that he might be interested in rejoiniog my Secretariat. It was for this reason that I asked him to rejoin it.

Coming to Mr Kapoor's resignation in 1971, Counsel suggested that he had resigned in 1971 merely in order to organize the election campaign of Mrs Gandhi.

Mrs Gandhi denied the suggestion and said that at the time when Mr Kapoor resigned, she did not even know that she would be contesting the election from Rae Bareli.

Regarding the date of Kapoor's resignation, Counsel asked her whether she had been shown any paper to indicate that Kapoor had resigned 13 January.

Mrs Gandhi: No. But I had been told that Shri Kapoor was paid his salary only for the period ending on 13 January. Shri P.N. Haksar also told me that Mr Kapoor had resigned on 13 January. There was also the gazette notification regarding the acceptance of the resignation submitted by Shri Kapoor which I had myself seen. Another thing which I would like to mention is that he did not attend my Secretariat from 14 January onwards.

Counsel: How can you remember clearly that Mr Kapoor did not attend the Secretariat from 14 January onwards?

Mrs Gandhi: Because on the 13 of January he had spoken to me about resigning from the job.

Counsel: Did you see the election petition regarding the date of his resignation?

Mrs Gandhi: Yes, but when I saw the election petition I did remember that he had resigned on 13 January. In order to make sure, I had also enquired from Shri Haksar about it.

Counsel: Do you remember any particular event which took place on 13 January 1971 or 13 December, 1970?

Mrs Gandhi: Not unless some indication of the event is given to me.

Counsel: Do you remember any particular event which took place on 18 February 1975 (exactly one month before the date of cross-examination)?

Mrs Gandhi: No, I do not.

Counsel then questioned her about the acceptance of Kapoor's resignation. He asked her whether she had herself formally accepted his resignation. She replied that she had not.

Counsel: Can you recall any instance in which you have asked any person to take charge of any post before an order appointing him to that post was made in writing and signed by the relevant authority? (He asked this question because Haksar had in his deposition stated that he was appointed Deputy Chairman of the Planning Commission by an oral order of Mrs Gandhi.)

Mrs Gandhi: I do not remember of any such instance.

Counsel: Are you aware of any rule authorizing the Secretary-in-Charge of your Secretariat to appoint a person as Officer on Special Duty in your Secretariat?

Mrs Gandhi: I am not aware of any rule investing such authority in the Secretary, but I am also not aware of any rule contrary to it. I have always functioned on the basis that my Secretary was competent to make such appointments.

Being questioned about the date on which she decided to contest from Rae Bareli, Mrs Gandhi said that the final decision in this respect was taken only after she had had talks with Kamlapati

Tripathi and the workers of that area. This was done only on 1 February 1971.

Counsel showed her the newspaper report of 15 January 1971 in which it was stated that the Congress Parliamentary Board had decided that sitting Members of Parliament would contest the elections from their old constituencies. Bhushan was suggesting that since Mrs Gandhi was also a sitting Member of Parliament, this decision would also apply to her, thus fixing her constituency at least on this date. Mrs Gandhi denied that the Congress Parliamentary Board had taken a decision of this nature, and she said that in any case, for the Prime Minister and other prominent leaders, the matter was left to their own choice.

Counsel then showed her her own tour programme, dated 28 January 1971, for Rae Bareli. In this tour programme, 11.30 A.M. was marked out for filing her nomination paper.

Counsel: Was this tour programme issued after obtaining your approval?

Mrs Gandhi: It was. But I do not accept that I decided to file my nomination paper from Rae Bareli on or before 28 January. It was tentatively mentioned in the tour programme so that if I decided to contest from Rae Bareli, the nomination paper could be filed at that time. I was also told that a nomination paper after it was filed could be withdrawn.

Mrs Gandhi was then asked certain formal questions on the issue of Air Force planes and rostrums and barricades. Bhushan then asked her some more questions unrelated to the case to impeach her credibility. These questions related to some gifts which she had received from foreign dignitaries. Most of these questions were disallowed by the Judge.

This ended the cross-examination for the first day. It was resumed the next day.

Counsel: When did you see Mr Kapoor next after 13 January 1971?

Mrs Gandhi: I saw him next at Rae Bareli on 1 February 1971.

Counsel: Mr Kapoor had stated before this court that during the period 21 January 1971 to 26 January 1971, he stayed at Delhi and had met you twice. Is that statement incorrect?

Mrs Gandhi: It may be correct. I meet a very large number of people everyday, so I have no idea about it.

It was now that Counsel decided to play his trump card. Till now, Mrs Gandhi had vehemently maintained that she had not decided to contest from Rae Bareli before 1 February. Her demeanour suggested that she was quite confident that there was no evidence to suggest the contrary.

Counsel: Did the Congress Party take any decision about your constituency?

Mrs Gandhi: The Congress Party did not take any decision about my constituency, but once I had taken the decision, it was deemed to be the Party's decision because the Party had left the matter to me.

Counsel: Did Shri K.N. Joshi, Parliamentary Secretary to the All India Congress Committee, make any announcement regarding your candidature on the 29 January 1971?

Mrs Gandhi: Not within my knowledge.

Counsel then invited her attention to the additional written statement which had been filed by her in August 1972. In the additional written statement she had averred that K.N. Joshi had informed her about the final decision in regard to her consituency which was announced by the All India Congress Committee on 29 January 1971.

For the first time in her deposition Mrs Gandhi squirmed. So far she had been exhuding confidence, but now she was nervous. She said that she could not recollect that fact that day.

Counsel: Are you quite certain that no announcement was made by the All India Congress Committee on 29 January 1971 about your constituency?

Mrs Gandhi: I do not know whether any such announcement was made.

Counsel: Did you read the additional written statement before signing it?

Mrs Gandhi: I did read it before signing it, and to the best of my ability I took care to see that whatever was contained in it was true. I must, however, say that the language contained in the additional written statement is legal language which I find difficult to understand.

Counsel had clearly trapped her here and her explanation did not pass muster in the eyes of the audience or the Judge. Bhushan made full capital out of this in his arguments.

Counsel finally asked Mrs Gandhi some questions about the Maruti Project of her son, Sanjay Gandhi. Most of them were disallowed by the Judge. Nevertheless he did allow some of them.

Counsel: Was the matter of the grant of Letter of Intent to Sanjay Gandhi considered by a sub-Committee presided over by you?

Mrs Gandhi: No.

Counsel: Did the Government of India announce a policy decision that if the project of manufacturing a small car was ever undertaken, it would be in the public sector?

Mrs Gandhi looked hopefully at the Judge as if to say "Do I have to answer this question." The Judge smiled and nodded politely. She would have to answer that question. So she said, "There was discussion in the Government regarding this, but no final decision was taken to that effect."

In 1962 when this matter was being thought over, no person had submitted any design for the completely indigenous production of a small car. "There was, however, later, a proposal in the Industries Ministry, that if anybody came forward with the proposal to manufacture a completely indigenous small car, it may be considered."

Counsel: I suggest that the proposal for the manufacture of a small car in the public sector was given up because Mr Sanjay Gandhi got interested in it.

Mrs Gandhi: That is not true. If the Government wants to go ahead with the manufacture of a small car in the public sector, the Maruti Project would not prevent the Government from doing so.

Counsel: Are you aware that in March 1971 the acquisition of land for Maruti Project was objected to on behalf of the Indian Air Force on the ground that it would constitute a risk to the security of the Explosive Depot at Gurgaon?

Mrs Gandhi: Land was acquired by the Haryana State for Industrial purposes and much construction had come into existence near the Explosive Depot at Gurgaon. Some objection was raised in that connection. But I am not sure whether the objection was raised by the Air Force Authorities or by some Parliamentarians. The objection was not sustained.

Counsel: Are you aware that Maruti Ltd., even though it has not gone into production yet, has already acquired dealership deposits amounting to over Rs 2 crores up to the year 1973-74?

This question was disallowed.

Counsel then put his case before Mrs Gandhi. He suggested that she had decided to contest from Rae Bareli right from the time of the dissolution of the Lok Sabha in 1970 and that Kapoor had started working for her election right from that time. Mrs Gandhi denied these suggestions.

This ended Mrs Gandhi's cross-examination. It lasted only 90 minutes the second day.

Appendix 3

SUPREME COURT REVIEWS THE THE KESHAVANANDA BHARATI CASE

It was some time during the end of October 1975 that Chief Justice A.N. Ray announced the constitution of a 13 member bench (the entire strength of the Supreme Court) for a review of Keshavananda Bharati's case. Ever since the Keshavananda Bharati case had been decided in April 1973, the Government had constantly been trying for a review. The Government's requests had not been headed earlier as no Constitution bench had felt the need to do so. Normally, a case can only be reviewed if its decision creates a serious difficulty in the decision of some other case. Therefore, according to the established procedure, Keshavananda's case could only be reviewed if some constitution bench had difficulty in applying its dictum to some other case before them. Mrs Gandhi's appeal was the first occasion when Keshavananda's case became involved in a big way. But even in Mrs Gandhi's case the bench did not feel that there was sufficient reason for a review. Therefore, the 13 member bench for review was not constituted in pursuance of any reference by a smaller bench, but on the oral directions of the Chief Justice.

PALKHIVALA'S OBJECTIONS

The entire bench assembled in the Chief Justice's courtroom at 11.00 A.M. on 10 November 1975 for the hearings of the review.

At the very outset, Palkhivala, arguing on behalf of the petitioners, raised some preliminary objections against the reconsideration of the Keshavananda Bharati case. Dividing his objections into two parts, Palkhivala asserted that: (1) the Court did not have the legal competence to review the case at that juncture. (2) Assuming that the Court has the discretionary authority of reviewing it, it should not exercise its discretion to review it at that juncture.

Elaborating on the first objection, Palkhivala submitted that in the Keshavananda Bharati case there were six petitions in connection with which the full court had been constituted. He said, "In all these petitions some constitutional amendments were challenged. After deciding on the validity of the amendments and the amending powers of Parliament, the 13 member bench had referred the six petitions for disposal to the Constitutional bench, in the light of the law laid down by the full Court. So, none of the original six petitions were disposed of by the full Court. In fact, two of those five petitions are listed in today's list.

"Suppose that this Court now reviews and reverses the decision of Keshavananda Bharati. What happens then, when the original six petitions come up for hearing. The reversed decision of this Court will be *res judicata*[1] as far as those petitions are concerned. Therefore, those petitions will have to be decided in accordance with the original Keshavananda Bharati decision, the Judges knowing full well that it is an overruled case. Therefore as long as any of those petitions are pending before the Court, this Court cannot review that case."

Justice Untwalia: But that means that if in a High Court, a full bench decides a point of law in connection with a case and asks a division bench to dispose of the case, then as long as those cases are not disposed of, a full bench cannot reconsider the point of law laid down earlier.

Palkhivala: Yes, if the full bench had said that those cases be decided in accordance with its decision, then as long as those cases are pending, the full bench cannot reconsider that point of law. However, in such situations a difficulty might arise; but why should we create a difficulty when we can very easily avoid it. Observe the curious situation that would arise. Suppose this case is overruled. When the original petitions come up for hearing the Judges of the constitution bench would be placed in a very peculiar situation. The mandate of Article 141 commands them to apply the new Keshavananda Bharati, but *res judicata* commands them to apply the old Keshavananda Bharati. What do they do?

Justice Krishna Iyer: What you mean is that the Judges will be

[1] *Res judicata* is a legal principle according to which, if a point of law in a case has been decided, the rest of the case will have to be decided according to that law.

tossed between the horns of dilemma—*res judicata* on one side asking them to apply the old Keshavananda Bharati case, but Article 141 on the other, commending them to apply the new Keshavananda Bharati case.

Palkhivala: Exactly.

Elaborating on his second preliminary objection, Palkhivala said that there were ten different reasons why the court should not reconsider the Keshavananda Bharati case, even if it could, at that juncture. Outlining his reasons he said: "Such a request could not have been entertained for a citizen, so it should not be entertained for the Government. I have no doubt that if a citizen had asked for a review instead of the Government, the request would have been turned down. Thus there is absolutely no reason why this request of the Government should be accepted. And it is only an oral request. This bench has been constituted only on the oral request of the Government."

Chief Justice: No, the request had also come from the petitioners. Ever since the Keshavananda Bharati case, we have been flooded with requests for review from these petitioners.

Palkhivala: I beg your pardon, my Lord. It is impossible that the petitioners had requested a review. Why should they ask for a review which could only damage their case? If the basic feature theory disappears, then no Constitutional amendments can be struck down.

Chief Justice: Even the Tamil Nadu Government had asked for a review.

Tamil Nadu Advocate General: I beg your pardon, my Lord. We never even once asked for a review.

Chief Justice: Well, you were all asking for some Constitutional amendment to be struck down on the basic features. The Government said that it could not understand the theory, so the question arose.

Palkhivala: The question would, of course, arise whenever a Constitutional amendment is to be struck down on that theory, but that does not mean that it should be reviewed. If a principle has to be reviewed every time that it arises, then every case of the Supreme Court would have to be reviewed within a few days.

Going on to his second point, Palkhivala submitted that none of the established principles of jurisprudence could justify such a reconsideration. Citing a few cases of the Supreme Court to support his contention, Palkhivala contended that a case could only be reconsidered if (i) the judgment in that case was manifestly wrong, (ii) that the continuance of the judgment of that case was baneful to public interest. These two conditions must co-exist, he said. He went on, "I challenge the Government to say that there is a manifest error in the judgment. As far as the second condition is concerned, I can't see how by any stretch of imagination, the judgment in that case can be regarded as baneful to public interest. All it says is that there are certain things which are basic and beyond the Parliament's powers of amendment. It says that the Government cannot abolish the rule of law, equality, liberty etc. Can anyone say that the preservation of these values is baneful to public interest? Let the Government tell us which is the amendment which it wants to pass and which is prevented by the Keshavananda Bharati case. In fact if anything, it will be the overruling of this case which will be baneful to public interest."

Justice Beg: Mr Palkhivala, how can you assume that we will overrule that case.

Palkhivala: Then are we going to waste five months of the Supreme Court's time merely to reaffirm an old judgment? We are not a debating society that we argue in order to reaffirm a judgment. Therefore, we have to consider the possibility of it being overruled.

Justice Beg: You see, I don't know what these basic features are.

Palkhivala: With the greatest respect, my Lord, it is inconceivable that the Supreme Court cannot understand its own judgment. If the Supreme Court cannot understand its own judgment, then who will? I have absolutely no doubt in my mind as to what the basic features are, and anybody who reads the judgment carefully cannot have any doubt.

Justice Murtaza Fazal Ali: Mr Palkhivala, it seems that the judgment in Keshavananda Bharati is ambiguous, and by reconsidering it we might only clarify the issues.

Palkhivala: I do not think it is ambiguous, but assuming that it is, we have Judges of enough competence to interpret even ambiguous judgments. Ambiguous judgments involving general principles are interpreted every day by this Honorable Court. What about the dictum that 'the essential powers of legislation' cannot be delegated. What are the essential powers of legislation. Or take the due process clause of America. For 200 years, the US Supreme Court has been interpreting and evolving that principle. Does it have any precise meaning? We can't have cut and dried definitions of general principles. They are not things which can be applied like ⁞mathematical formulae.

Citing cases from England, USA and Australia, Palkhivala

contended that vagueness or lack of definiteness is not a basis for discarding a sound legal principle.

Justice Beg: But I think every Article in the Constitution is basic.

Palkhivala: If you take that view my Lord, I will be the happiest man, because then the Constitution will remain substantially unchanged throughout.

Justice Beg: No, I mean I cannot tell the difference between basic and non-basic features.

Palkhivala: Suppose Article 368 of the Constitution itself said that the basic structure of the Constitution cannot be damaged or destroyed. The judiciary as the interpreter of the Constitution would have had to interpret it. Could it have said that it did not understand the Constitution?

Untwalia: Suppose there is a manifest error, but we are not sure of the baneful effect on public interest. In that case, can we review a judgment.

Palkhivala: My Lord, if a case goes on for five months, is heard by 13 Judges and literally thousands of authorities are quoted in the judgments, can anyone say that there is a manifest error in the judgment?

Laying the 41st Amendment Bill (already passed by the Rajya Sabha) before the Judges, Palkhivala read out the provisions of the Bill which was introduced in Parliament in the monsoon session. It states that any person who has held the office of either President or Prime Minister or Governor shall have life long immunity against all criminal suits for 'personal' acts done either before or during the tenure of office. It also gives immunity while in office against all civil suits to these category of persons. Expressing horror at the provisions of the Bill, Palkhivala said that this was the type of amendment for which the Government wanted unlimited powers.

Palkhivala continued, "When we argued the Keshavananda Bharati case, we were told that the possibility of misuse of power was only hypothetical and we should trust our elected representatives. Today the misuse of power is no longer a hypothetical possibility. It is a stark reality. The 41st Amendment has already been passed by the Rajya Sabha. If this Bill became law, then any person can commit the most heinous crimes, even murder his political opponents, and he has only to have enough political influence to get himself made the Governor of a State even for a day, to get away scot free. With such amendments being passed when Keshavananda Bharati is still good law, consider what will come when it is overruled.

"If the Keshavananda Bharati decision stays, then I have no doubt that this 41st Amendment Bill will not be introduced in the Lok Sabha, but if Keshavananda Bharati is overruled then it is going to be the law of tomorrow. When the Keshavanand Bharati case was being argued, the Government said that we had vested interests and wanted to preserve our property. In the Keshavananda Bharati case, it was decided that property right is not basic. We accept the judgment. There are some interested people who want to distort our stand by connecting us with property. We wish to make it clear that we are not fighting for the property right. Let the Government take away all our property. But what about liberty, what about equality, what about the freedom of speech and dissent. It is for these values that we are fighting."

Proceeding further with his arguments against a review, Palkhivala asserted that the Court would stultify itself and the judicial process would command no respect if the Court struck down a recent Constitution amendment on the basis of Keshavananda Bharati, and, on the immediately following working day sat to consider whether the Keshavananda Bharati case was correctly decided. Enunciating a well-known principle, Palkhivala said, "Justice must not only be done but it must also be seem to be done." This was why we have open courts, where people can see justice being done. What respect and confidence will people have in the highest court of the land if they find it behaving in such a capricious way. Judicial discipline demands that cases should not be reviewed just because the constitution of the Court changes. What will happen to judicial discipline if the Supreme Court fails to observe it?"

Justice Mathew: You can't say that we didn't observe judicial discipline. We struck down the 39th Amendment by respecting the majority decision.

Palkhivala: I never said that you didn't observe judicial discipline. In fact, uptil now the Supreme Court has had the most glorious tradition of observing judicial discipline and it would be very sad if this tradition is broken now.

Palkhivala's next reason against review was that nothing had happened since Keshavananda's case to justify reconsideration because all that had happened since then was the passing of some laws which justified to the hilt the wisdom of the Keshavananda Bharati decision.

"Let us see what the situation was when Keshavananda's case was decided. We had individual liberty, equality, rule of law, freedom of speech and dissent. What do we have now? There is no liberty today. Anyone can be put behind bars for no reason at all, so much so that the latest amendment to MISA says that the grounds of detention cannot be 'permitted' to be disclosed even to the courts. It expressly says that 'no citizen can claim the right of liberty on any grounds of common law, natural law or principles of natural justice.' As a result, thousands of people are languishing in jail without trial. Can anyone say that we have equality after observing the various obnoxious Constitutional amendments which have been enacted. They expressly say that some people will be above the law. This is the atmosphere in the country today in which the Government has the nerve to come and ask for unlimited powers. Can one think of any country where we have such laws as the 41st Amendment Bill proposes?"

Justice Mathew: They might be there in some military dictatorships.

Palkhivala: I meant civilized countries. Of course, if the Government is ruthless enough it can abrogate the Constitution and have such laws. But then let them say that they do not respect the Constitution. Let the people no longer be fooled into believing that everything that is being done is Constitutional.

Justice Beg: Mr Palkhivala, do you remember that famous US Supreme Court decision which led to the civil war? Do you want us to be a party to such a decision?

Palkhivala: That is exactly why I am insisting on not having a review. Because if the Keshavananda Bharati decision is reversed, it might very well lead to a civil war. You cannot suppress the people for long.

Palkhivala again pleaded for the judgment to be given with the utmost caution.

Justice Murtaza Fazl Ali: But we might only clarify and lay down as to what the basic feature is.

Palkhivala: We don't need the full Court of 13 Judges to lay down what the basic structure is. Each Constitution Bench can come to its own conclusion on that. Moreover, that is not the question referred to this Bench. The question referred to this Bench is whether the Parliament's powers are limited by the basic feature theory. And even if this Court does try to clarify, how can we assume that the judgment will be any less ambiguous than in the Keshavananda Bharati case.

Palkhivala then went on to his next point. "This is the most inopportune time to review the case," he submitted, "because only one party is effectively functioning and all Opposition leaders are in jail without trial. With a monstrous press censorship and all dissident voices silenced, how can we have an effective public debate on such an important topic." Commenting on the extent of press censorship,

Palkhivala told the Court that even proceedings and judgments of Courts were not allowed to be published in the newspapers. In his opinion that was gross contempt of court.

Justice Krishna Iyer: Are there any written orders about censorship of court proceedings?

Palkhivala: Yes, there are, and we have enough documentary evidence to prove it to the hilt. The Delhi High Court's judgment on the Habeas Corpus of Mr Kuldip Nayar was not allowed to be published. The only way one heard of it was by tuning in to the BBC which reported parts of it. What I am saying now also will not be reported in tomorrow's newspapers due to censorship. If I say anything about the recent amendments in public, I shall probably be arrested. In fact the only place where there is any freedom of speech in this country is the few hundred square feet of various courtrooms. In fact, I am very grateful to the Government for giving me the opportunity of expressing my views in this court.

Justice Krishna Iyer (amidst laughter)*:* You should thank the Court for this.

Palkhivala: My Lords, I do thank the Court.

Justice Murtaza Fazl Ali: Suppose the Keshavananda Bharati decision had gone against you. Would you not have been entitled to come and ask for a review now. So why should you object to the Government asking for a review?

Palkhivala: Let me answer this without any flippancy, my Lord. If the Keshavananda Bharati decision had gone against us, then there would be no Supreme Court today before which I could come for a review. But supposing that by some stroke of good fortune some part of the Court survived, I would have perhaps been entitled to ask for a review because of its baneful effect on public interest. But here the case is just the opposite. If the decision is reversed, then it will have a baneful effect on public interest.

Mr Palkhivala's next reason against reconsideration was that it would start a pernicious precedent which would gravely impair the continuity of law, and make law dependent on changes in the composition of the Court. In fact, asserted Palkhivala, following the precedent of this case, another full bench would be justified in reviewing this reconsideration soon after the decision in this case. "Such a precedent would seriously erode the judicial discipline, the confidence of the people in the Supreme Court. What has happened in these two and a half years which justifies such a reconsideration?"

Justice Mathew: That is why Jefferson said that the Constitution must be changed every 20 years.

Palkhivala: But certainly not every two years, even if that is true.

Reading out the written submissions of the State of Jammu and Kashmir and Tamil Nadu, Mr Palkhivala asserted that these States had no difficulty in identifying the basic features of the Constitution. Pointing out that in the Keshavananda Bharati case all the States supported the Union Government and it was for the first time now that some States were opposing the Union Government in its plea for overthrowing the basic feature theory, Palkhivala argued that in these circumstances a reconsideration would threaten the integrity and unity of the country.

Justice Mathew: How can it affect the unity or integrity of the country?

Palkhivala: Well, there are some parts of India which do not agree with the Union Government. Now if the basic feature theory is overthrown, the Union Government could and quite likely would abolish some States. This would certainly sow the seeds of disunity and disintegration.

Palkhivala further pleaded that a review would mean reopening and rehearing all that was argued in Keshavananda Bharati. "That would take another five months. So for five months the entire Supreme Court will hear no other case except this. Can we waste five months of the Court's time for reasons which are not absolutely compelling?"

Rounding off his submissions on the preliminary objections, Palkhivala ended with an impassioned plea that the Keshavananda Bharati case should not be reconsidered at that juncture.

Tarkunde's Submissions

Following Palkhivala's arguments, V.M. Tarkunde, Counsel for a detenu, spoke for a few minutes. Supplementing Palkhivala's arguments, Tarkunde said that after examining all the petitions connected with the present case, he had found that all but one of them related to property. Since in Keshavananda Bharati it was made clear that the property right was not basic, the Keshavananda Bharati case could not be invoked in any of those petitions. The only case remaining was a petition challenging the 32nd Constitution Amendment which had replaced the High Court's jurisdiction under Article 226 by an administrative tribunal in connection with the service matters of some Government servants. Tarkunde contended that the case would only be referred to the full court if the Constitution Bench found that Constitutional amendment in question should be struck down on the basis of Keshavananda Bharati. "Without the Keshavananda Bharati case creating any difficulty in any case, how could this case be referred to the full Court." Therefore, Tarkunde contended, the Keshavananda Bharati case should not be reconsidered unless it was found to be presenting an unsurmountable difficulty in some cases. With this plea Tarkunde concluded his brief submissions.

THE ATTORNEY-GENERAL PLEADS FOR A REVIEW

Appearing on behalf of the Union of India which had asked for a review, the Attorney-General Niren De started by arguing that the so-called preliminary objections of Palkhivala are not preliminary at all. "A preliminary objection is one which challenges the legal right of the litigant party to come to the Court, but here the objection is to a 13 member bench being constituted to review the Keshavananda Bharati case. This is not a preliminary objection at all. The decision to review that case was taken by your lordships for good or bad, and it cannot be questioned now on any preliminary objection." Charging that Palkhivala had delivered a political lecture to the Supreme Court, De said that the situation in the country was absolutely "pell mell" following incoherent decision in the Keshavananda Bharati case. "Every constitutional amendment is being challenged in the High Courts all over the country. Everybody was giving a different interpretation to the decision. In these circumstances, it is essential that the Court clears up the issues."

On being asked by the Bench as to whether any baneful effect flowed from the judgment of Keshavananda Bharati, De replied that the question about the limits of the Constitution amending powers of Parliament surely could not be divorced from public interest.

Justice Khanna: Has the theory of basic features impeded any legislation about socio-economic measures?

Mr De: Socio-economic measures are not the only thing, important as they are. The very structure of Government is the fundamental object of the amending process. You don't need the amending power for non-essential features of the Constitution.

Justice Untwalia: Is there any example where the Government wanted to amend the Constitution in public interest and has been prevented by the basic feature theory?

De: Take the case of the 39th Amendment.

Justice Untwalia: I am talking of amendments in public interest.

De: The point is that the Parliament doesn't know what it can do. It doesn't know where it stands. We must know where we stand.

De pleaded that the case be reconsidered as there were many fundamental issues involved in the case.

Justice Krishna Iyer: The same plea can be advanced the very next day after reconsideration. You can still say that it is very important and must be reconsidered. The point is, what has really happened to justify a second look at the ruling?

De told the court that there was a tremendous amount of uncertainty in the country about the meaning of the basic structure theory.

Justice Krishna Iyer: Are you asking for a clarification of the basic structure, or do you want us to annihilate the theory?

De: Mr Palkhivala has raised preliminary objection that we can't go into that case. At least the Court can go into it to clarify it.

Justice Bhagwati: This is a matter of application of the case. Every Judge can have his own view as to what the basic stracture is. We need not review the case for that.

De: All over India, litigation is going on, on the concept of basic structure. Are we going to tolerate a situation where different High Courts give different judgments on the same concept?

Justice Krishna Iyer: Are you assuming that after reconsideration we will get a homogenized version?

Mr De said that even amongst the Supreme Court Judges, opinion was divided as to what was decided in the Keshavananda Bharati case. Justice Mathew has not held that equality is basic.

Justice Mathew: I have said that I do not know whether the majority in Keshavananda Bharati held equality to be basic.

De: It did not. If the Supreme Court itself cannot find out as to what the judgment was, how do you expect the High Courts to find out.

Justice Chandrachud: There will always be difference of opinion in every case. You cannot prevent that.

At this note the Court rose for the day.

The Bench is Dissolved

The next day, that is, 12 November 1975 the visitors' gallery was also allotted to the lawyers because there were insufficient seats for lawyers. However, the visitors did not miss much. As soon as the 13 Judges assembled and the Attorney-General was about to continue, the Chief Justice made a startling annoucement. "This bench is dissolved," he said. "For two days the arguments have gone into the air. These cases will now go to the constitution bench." With a pointed reference to the Andhra Pradesh case about the service matters, the Chief Justice said that the Constitution Bench could refer it back to the full court if it had any difficulty with the Keshavananda case. With this, the Court rose and the bench was dissolved.

Appendix 4

REVIEW APPLICATION AGAINST JUSTICE BEG'S JUDGMENT

The review application against Justice Beg's judgment was heard —by the same five Judges who had heard the appeal—on 18 December between 3.30 and 4.00 P.M., the time at which miscellaneous matters are heard.

Appearing on behalf of the applicant, Shanti Bhushan read out the text of the review application. The main grievances was that Justice Beg had dealt with the merits of the case without hearing the arguments on them. After giving a history of the arguments on the Supreme Court, the petition stated, "On the morning of Friday, 19 September 1975, when the petitioner's counsel concluded his rejoinder on the validity of the Constitutional Amendment, the Court said that before pronouncing judgment on the validity of the Constitutional Amendment, it would hear arguments on the merits of the appeal. It asked A.K. Sen, Counsel for the appellant, to start arguments on the merits which he promptly did. After Sen had given an introduction to the issues arising in the appeal, but before he could make his submissions on these issues, or refer to the evidence on them, or even read the reasonings and findings of the High Court on these issues, Justice Mathew interrupted him and observed that in view of the Election Laws (Amendment) Act 1975, there was no occasion to enter into the merits of the issues decided by the High Court unless the Court first heard the arguments on the validity of the Election Laws (Amendment) Act. His Lordship further observed that as the Amendment Act must be presumed to be valid till the contrary was proved by the petitioner, he should be called upon to start arguments on the validity of that. The Court, thereafter, directed the petitioner's counsel to address the arguments on the validity of the Election Laws (Amendment) Act.

"The hearing which continued thereafter was, therefore, confined only to the validity and interpretation of the provisions of the Election Laws Amendment Act and the issue relating to expenses, and it was made clear to the counsel that arguments on the merits of the other issues would be heard, if at all, only at a later stage if the provisions of the Election Laws (Amendment) Act were either held to be invalid or inapplicable."

"It is true that when the validity of the Thirty-ninth Constitution (Amendment) Act was being argued by the parties and the learned Solicitor General was defending the Constitutional amendment on the ground that the same had become necessary in order to prevent any arguments being made on sensitive issues arising out of the allegation of corrupt practices against the holder of the high office of Prime Minister, Hon'ble Mr Justice Beg did make observations that such an argument may not be in the interests of the Prime Minister herself as it may deprive her of an opportunity of getting herself exonerated on the facts. This suggestion was, however, not accepted either by the Solicitor General or by the counsel who argued the case on behalf of Mrs Indira Gandhi and they continued to defend the impugned clause (4) of the Constitutional (Amendment) Act.

"It was in these circumstances that the petitioner's counsel was not given an opportunity to make any submission on the correctness of the findings of the High Court, or on the merits of the other issues on the basis of the law as it existed at the time when the High Court decided the case.

"While the Hon'ble Chief Justice A.N. Ray, Hon'ble Justice Khanna, Hon'ble Justice Mathew and Hon'ble Justice Chandrachud have only decided the points on which the parties' counsels were permitted to argue, to the surprise of the petitioner, it was found that Hon'ble Justice Beg had entered into the merits of the issues decided by the High Court in contravention of the principles of natural justice, and without giving any opportunity to the parties to address arguments on those questions.

"Hon'ble Mr Justice Beg has also on pages 9 and 10 of his judgment made the following observations:

> If that election was not really void and had been wrongly held by the Trial Court to be vitiated, it did not need to be validated at all. In that event, a purported validation would be an exercise in

futility before this court had decided these appeals. Could it not be said that the intended validation was premature inasmuch as it proceeded on a basically erroneous premise that the original respondent's election was invalid when the question of its validity was subjudice in this court? How could such a premise be assumed to be correct before this court had gone into the merits and decided the appeals pending before it? Such an inquiry is not irrelevant if the very nature and purpose of the exercise of a power are put in issue by both sides.

"Neither had the petitioner's counsel advanced any contention that the Constitutional Amendment was invalid on the ground that it was premature, or that it was not necessary at all, nor could the validity of the 39th Amendment of the Constitution depend on the correctness or otherwise of the different findings of the High Court.

"In fact, the validity of the amendments to the election laws neither were, nor could be challenged merely on the grounds that they were either not necessary or not justified. As stated earlier, Hon'ble Justice Beg had not persisted in his query relating to the Trial Court's findings when he was informed by Mr Raj Narain's counsel, that it would require going into considerable evidence and a number of witnesses and circumstances, and would require protracted hearing, and that if the same was to be done, it had to be indicated as to whether the appellant's counsel or the petitioner's counsel would be heard first. Hon'ble Justice Khanna after conferring with Hon'ble Justice Beg, had then made it clear that they would not be entering into a discussion of the correctness of the findings of the High Court of the other issues at the stage. It is respectfully submitted therefore that the discussion of the merits of the issues on which counsels were not permitted to argue involves a serious breach of the principles of natural justice and had led to very palpable errors in the various observations made.

"On page 40 of his judgment, Hon'ble Justice Beg has recorded the finding that Shri Yashpal Kapoor had visited Rae Bareli on 7 January 1971, accompanying Shri Gulzari Lal Nanda, Railway Minister, in connection with his own official duties whereas Shri Yashpal Kapoor himself in his oral evidence before the High Court had clearly stated that: 'On 7th January 1971, I went along with the Railway Minister in my private capacity. I, therefore, did not charge any T.A., for these journeys.'

The application, therefore, prayed that the Hon'ble Court be pleased to:

(a) review its judgment dated 7.11.1975;

(b) clarify that the parties were not required or permitted to make their submissions on the merits of the various issues arising in the election petition except those which were not covered by the retrospective provisions of the Election Laws (Amendment) Act, 1975;

(c) expunge the findings from the judgment of the Hon'ble Justice Beg from page 19 beginning with the words 'On Issue No. 1 the case set up in paragraph 5 of the petition is . . . and ending with the sentence 'the learned Judge also cited the following case where it was decided that a cow is not a religious symbol . . .' on page 89;

(d) also expunge the other observations from the judgment of Hon'ble Mr Justice Beg which have been set out in the body of the application."

Justice Beg: Your only grievance is that we did not hear complete arguments on the merits of the case.

Bhushan: Yes. It is a total negation of the principles of natural justice to decide on the merits of the case without hearing the arguments of either side. We were asked to restrain ourselves from arguing on the merits by Justice Khanna and Justice Mathew.

Justice Beg: Well, you can submit your written submissions now and we will consider them.

Bhushan: Written submissions would not be enough, oral arguments would be necessary.

Chief Justice: No, we cannot go into it now.

With this, the court rose and reserved judgment on the review application.

The judgment came the next day. The order signed by all the five Judges was a very small one. It said: "In view of the fact that one of us (Justice Beg) is of the opinion that there is no sufficient ground for reviewing the judgment, this review application is dismissed."

This order is so strange that it invites comment. The order dismisses the review application merely because Justice Beg is of the opinion that there is no ground for reviewing the judgment. This is an obviously erroneous principle of law. If five Judges had heard the arguments, it was the duty of each of them to give their individual opinions on the application. It was clearly unjustified to leave the decision to just one of them.

Justice Beg delivered a much longer judgment. In his judgment he said that he had indicated to the parties that he regarded consideration of the merits of the case essential for a just and proper decision and disposal of the appeals. He further says,

> Indeed, the direction given by His Lordship, the Chief Justice, to the parties to address their arguments on merits, after those on the constitutional amendment, necessarily meant, I think, that a consideration of merits could not be separated from the question of validity of the amendments of the election laws.

It was the contention of the petitioner's counsel that the respondent in the High Court, being in the advantageous and powerful position of the Prime Minister of the country, supported by a large majority in Parliament, had obtained a change of laws in her favour so as to convert a defeat into a victory. It was, therefore, essential for the decision of this issue raised by the learned counsel for the election petitioner himself to convince us that the case of election petitioner, according to the laws as they stood at the time when the election was held, was bound to succeed on merits.

Justice Beg agreed that he had gone into the merits of the case in much more detail than his brother Judges. He observes:

> I found that there was no alteration of the election laws, except in one respect, and, therefore, there could be no question of an alteration of 'the rules of the game' to the disadvantage of the election petitioner. Once I had reached this conclusion, it was not possible to avoid considering findings on merits. Learned Counsel for the election petitioner had conceded, no doubt in the interests of his client, that the findings of the learned trial Judge were unsustainable if the amendments were rejected. I do not think that I could possibly decide the case on this concession after reaching a conclusion, possibly not anticipated by the learned counsel for the election petitioner, that the election laws were not really changed except in one respect.
>
> It may be difficult for learned counsel sometimes to anticipate and meet the requirements of every learned Judge of this court when there are five of us hearing arguments. It is, however, the duty of counsel who raise issues, which may necessitate consideration of questions of fact and law, to satisfy the requirements of any one of us who may be of opinion, as I am, that these issues could not possibly be decided properly without considering findings of fact and the application of law to them.

It seems, from the petition now before us, that the greatest concern of the election petitioner and his learned counsel is not the result of the election petition or the common conclusions reached by all the five learned Judges, with which no fault has been found in this petition, but that the merits of the case, on facts, were examined at all by me. If this is part of a political game, I think that it is high time that it was realized by everyone that courts are not meant for political tactics or propaganda.

In the end, giving a left-handed compliment to Bhushan, he observed: "Learned counsel for the election petitioner also seemed to complain that my judgment contained some remarks indicating that he did not discharge his professional duties towards his client satisfactorily. If that is so, I would like to remove this grievance by saying that he discharged his duty towards his client so well that he succeeded in averting a closer and more detailed scrutiny by all of us of the pleadings, the evidence, and the patently erroneous conclusions of the trial Judge in this case."

With this Justice Beg concluded his judgment on the review application.

Appendix 5

REPRESENTATION OF PEOPLE ACT, 1951
PART VII, SECTION 123

"123. Corrupt practices.—The following shall be deemed to be corrupt practices for the purposes of this Act:

(1) 'Bribery' that is to say,—

(A) any gift, offer or promise by a candidate or his agent or by any other person with the consent of a candidate or his election agent of any gratification, to any person whomsoever, with the object, directly or indirectly of inducing—

(a) a person to stand or not to stand as, to withdraw or not to withdraw from being a candidate at an election, or

(b) an elector to vote or refrain from voting at an election or as a reward to—

(i) a person for having so stood, or not stood, or for having withdrawn or not having withdrawn his candidature; or

(ii) an elector for having voted or refrained from voting.

(B) the receipt of, or agreement to receive, any gratification, whether as a motive or a reward—

(a) by a person for standing or not standing as, or for withdrawing or not withdrawing from being, a candidate; or

(b) by any person whomsoever for himself or any other person for voting or refraining from voting, or inducing or attempting to induce any elector to vote or refrain from voting, or any candidate to withdraw or not to withdraw his candidature.

Explanation: For the purposes of this clause the term 'gratification' is not restricted to pecuniary gratifications or gratifications estimated in money and it includes all forms of entertainment and all forms of employment for reward but it does not include the payment of any expenses *bona fide* incurred at, or for the purpose of, any election and duly entered in the account expenses referred to in Section 78.

(2) Undue influence, that is to say, any direct or indirect interference or attempt to interfere on the part of the candidate or his agent, or of any other person with the consent of the candidate or his election agent, with the free exercise of any electoral right:

Provided that—

(a) without prejudice to the generality of the provisions of this clause any such person as is referred to therein who—

(i) threatens any candidate or any elector, or any person in whom a candidate or any elector is interested, with injury of any kind including social ostracism and ex-communication or expulsion from any caste or community; or

(ii) induces or attempts to induce a candidate or an elector to believe that he, or any person in whom he is interested, will become or will be rendered an object of divine displeasure or spiritual censure,

shall be deemed to interfere with the free exercise of the electoral right of such candidate or elector within the meaning of this clause;

(b) a declaration of public policy, or a promise of public action, or the mere exercise of a legal right without intent to interfere with an electoral right, shall be deemed to be interference within the meaning of this clause.

(3) The appeal by a candidate or his agent or by any other person with the consent of a candidate or his election agent to vote or refrain from voting for any person on the ground of his religion, race, caste, community or language or the use of or appeal to religious symbols or the use of, or appeal to, national symbols, such as the national flag or the national emblem, for the furtherance of the prospects of the election of that candidate or for prejudicially affecting the election of any candidate.

(3A) The promotion of, or attempt to promote, feelings of enmity or hatred between different classes of citizens of India on grounds of religion, race, caste, community, or language, by a candidate or his agent or any other person with the consent of a candidate or his election agent for the furtherance of the prospects of the election of that candidate or for prejudicially affecting the election of any candidate.

(4) The publication by a candidate or his agent or by any other person, with the consent of a candidate or his election agent, of any statement of fact which is false, and which he either believes to be

false or does not believe to be true, in relation to the personal character or conduct of any candidate, or in relation to the candidature, or withdrawal, of any candidate, being a statement reasonably calculated to prejudice the prospects of that candidate's election.

(5) The hiring or procuring, whether on payment or otherwise, of any vehicle or vessel by a candidate or his agent or by any other person with the consent of a candidate or his election agent, or the use of such vehicle or vessel for the free conveyance of any elector (other than the candidate himself, the members of his family or his agent) to or from any polling station provided under Section 25 or a place fixed under sub-section (1) of Section 29 for the poll:

Provided that the hiring of a vehicle or vessel by an elector or by several electors at their joint costs for the purpose of conveying him or them to and from any such polling station or place fixed for the poll shall not be deemed to be a corrupt practice under this clause if the vehicle or vessel so hired is a vehicle or vessel not propelled by mechanical power:

Provided further that the use of any public transport vehicle or vessel or any tramcar or railway carriage by any elector at his own cost for the purpose of going to or coming from any such polling station or place fixed for the poll shall not be deemed to be a corrupt practice under this clause.

Explanation: In this clause, the expression "vehicle" means any vehicle used or capable of being used for the purpose of road transport, whether propelled by mechanical power or otherwise and whether used for drawing other vehicles or otherwise.

(6) The incurring or authorizing of expenditure in contravention of Section 77.

(7) The obtaining or procuring or abetting or attempting to obtain or procure by a candidate or his agent or, by any other person with the consent of a candidate or his election agent, any assistance (other than the giving of vote) for the furtherance of the prospects of that candidate's election, from any person in the service of the Government and belonging to any of the the following classes, namely:

    (a) gazetted officers;
    (b) stipendiary judges and magistrates;
    (c) members of the armed forces of the Union;
    (d) members of the police forces;
    (e) excise officers;
    (f) revenue officers other than village revenue officers known as

lambardars, malguzars, patels, deshmukhs or by any other name, whose duty is to collect land revenue and who are remunerated by a share of, or commission on, the amount of land revenue collected by them but who do not discharge any police functions; and

(g) such other class of persons in the service of the Government as may be prescribed.

Explanation: (1) In this section the expression 'agent' includes an election agent, a polling agent and any person who is held to have acted as an agent in connection with the election with the consent of the candidate.

(2) For the purpose of Clause (7), a person shall be deemed to assist in the furtherance of the prospects of a candidate's election if he acts as an election agent of that candidate."

Appendix 6

THE REPRESENTATION OF PEOPLE (AMENDMENT) ACT, 1974
No. 58 of 1974

"An Act further to amend the Representation of the People Act. 1951.

BE it enacted by Parliament in the Twenty-fifth Year of the Republic of India as follows:

1. (1) This Act may be called the Representation of the People (Amendment) Act, 1974.

(2) It shall be deemed to have come into force on the 19th day of October, 1974.

2. In section 77 of the Representation of the People Act, 1951, in sub-section (1), the following Explanations shall be inserted at the end, namely:

Explanation 1: Notwithstanding any judgment, order or decision of any court to the contrary, any expenditure incurred or authorized in connection with the election of a candidate by a political party or by any other association or body of persons or by any individual (other than the candidate or his election agent) shall not be deemed to be, and shall not ever be deemed to have been, expenditure in connection with the election incurred or authorized by the candidate or by his election agent for the purposes of this sub-section:

Provided that nothing contained in this Explanation shall affect—

(a) any judgment, order or decision of the Supreme Court whereby the election of a candidate to the House of the People or to the Legislative Assembly of a State has been declared void or set aside before the commencement of the Representation of the People (Amendment) Ordinance, 1974;

(b) any judgment, order or decision of a High Court whereby the election of any such candidate has been declared void or set aside before the commencement of the said Ordinance if no appeal has been preferred to the Supreme Court against such judgment, order or decision of the High Court before such commencement and the period of limitation for filing such appeal has expired before such commencement.

Explanation 2: For the purposes of Explanation 1, 'political party' shall have the same meaning as in the Election Symbols (Reservation and Allotment) Order, 1968, as for the time being in force."

Appendix 7

THE ELECTION LAWS (AMENDMENT) ACT, 1975
No. 40 of 1975

An Act further to amend the Representation of the People Act, 1951 and the Indian Penal Code.

BE it enacted by Parliament in the Twenty-sixth Year of the Republic of India as follows:—

Short title. 1. This Act may be called the Election Laws (Amendment) Act, 1975.

43 of 1951
Substitution of new section for Section 8A
2. In the Representation of the People Act, 1951 (hereinafter referred to as the principal Act), for Section 8A, the following section shall be substituted, namely:—

"8A. (1) The case of every person found guilty of a corrupt practice by an order under section 99 shall be submitted, as soon as may be, after such order takes effect, by such authority as the Central Government may specify in this behalf, to the President for determination of the question as to whether such person shall be disqualified and if so, for what period:

Disqualification on ground of corrupt practices

Provided that the period for which any person may be disqualified under this sub-section shall in no case exceed six years from the date on which the order made in relation to him under Section 99 takes effect.

(2) Any person who stands disqualified under section 8A of this Act as it stood immediately before the commencement of the Election Laws (Amendment) Act, 1975, may, if the period of such disqualification has not expired, submit a petition to the President for the removal of such disqualification for the unexpired portion of the said period.

(3) Before giving his decision on any question mentioned in sub-section (1) or on any petition submitted under sub-section (2), the President shall obtain the opinion of the Election Commission on such question or petition and shall act according to such opinion."

Amendment of Section 11

3. In section 11 of the principal Act, after the words "under this Chapter", the brackets, words, figure and letter "(except under Section 8A)" shall be inserted.

Amendment of Section 11A.

4. Section 11A of the principal Act shall be re-numbered as sub-section (1) thereof and—

(a) in the sub-section as so re-numbered, clause (b) shall be omitted; and

(b) after the sub-section as so re-numbered, the following sub-sections shall be inserted, namely:

"(2) Any person disqualified by a decision of the President under sub-section (1) of Section 8A for any period shall be disqualified for the same period for voting at any election.

(3) The decision of the President on a petition submitted by any person under sub-section (2) of Section 8A in respect of any disqualification for being chosen as, and for being, a member of either House of Parliament or of the Legislative Assembly or Legislative Council of a State shall, so far as may be, apply in respect of the disqualification for voting at any election incurred by him under clause (b) of sub-section (1) of section 11A of this Act as it stood immediately before the commencement of the Election Laws (Amendment) Act, 1975, as if such decision were a decision in respect of the said disqualification for voting also."

Amendment of Section 11B.	5. In Section 11B of the principal Act, for the words "any disqualification under this Chapter", the words, brackets, figures and letter "any disqualification under sub-section (1) of Section 11A" shall be substituted.
Amendment of Section 77.	6. In Section 77 of the principal Act, in sub-section (1),—

    (a) for the words "the date of publication of the notification calling the election", the words "the date on which he has been nominated" shall be substituted;

    (b) after Explanation 2, the following Explanation shall be inserted, namely:

"*Explanation 3:* For the removal of doubt, it is hereby declared that any expenditure incurred in respect of any arrangements made, facilities provided or any other act or thing done by any person in the service of the Government and belonging to any of the classes mentioned in clause (7) of Section 123 in the discharge or purported discharge of his official duty as mentioned in the proviso to that clause shall not be deemed to be expenditure in connection with the election incurred or authorized by a candidate or by his election agent for the purposes of this sub-section."

Amendment of Section 79.	7. In Section 79 of the principal Act, for clause (b), the following clause shall be substituted, namely:

    '(b) "candidate" means a person who has been or claims to have been duly nominated as a candidate at any election.'

m : n dment Section 123.	8. In section 123 of the principal Act,

    (a) in clause (3), the following proviso shall be inserted at the end, namely:

"Provided that no symbol allotted under this Act to a candidate shall be deemed to be a religious symbol or a national symbol for the purposes of this clause.";

    (b) in clause (7), the following proviso shall be inserted at the end, namely:—

"Provided that where any person, in the service of the Government and belonging to any of the classes aforesaid, in the discharge or purported discharge of his official duty, makes any arrangements or provides any facilities or does any other act or thing, for, to, or in relation to any candidate or his agent or any other person acting with the consent of the candidate or his election agent, (whether by reason of the office held by the candidate or for any other reason), such arrangements, facilities or act or thing shall not be deemed to be assistance for the furtherance of the prospects of that candidate's election.";

(c) in the Explanation at the end, the following shall be added, namely:

"(3) For the purposes of clause (7), notwithstanding anything contained in any other law, the publication in the Official Gazette of the appointment, resignation, termination of service, dismissal or removal from service of a person in the service of the Central Government (including a person serving in connection with the administration of a Union territory) or of a State Government shall be conclusive proof—

(i) of such appointment, resignation, termination of service, dismissal or removal from service, as the case may be, and

(ii) where the date of taking effect of such appointment, resignation, termination of service, dismissal or removal from service, as the case may be, is stated in such publication, also of the fact that such person was appointed with effect from the said date, or in the case of resignation, termination of service, dismissal or removal from service, such person ceased to be in such service with effect from the said date."

Amendment of Section 171A of Act 45 of 1860.

9. In the Indian Penal Code, in Section 171A, for clause (a), the following clause shall be substituted, namely:

'(a) "candidate" means a person who has been nominated as a candidate at any election;'.

Amendments to have retrospective effect.

10. The amendments made by Sections 6, 7 and 8 of this Act in the principal Act shall also have retrospective operation so as to apply to and in relation

to any election held before the commencement of this Act to either House of Parliament or to either House or the House of the Legislature of a State—

(i) in respect of which any election petition may be prescribed after the commencement of this Act; or

(ii) in respect of which any election petition is in any High Court immediately before such commencement; or

(iii) in respect of which any election petition has been decided by any High Court before such commencement but no appeal has been preferred to the Supreme Court against the decision of the High Court before such commencement and the period of limitation for filing such appeal has not expired before such commencement; or

(iv) in respect of which appeal from any order of any High Court made in any election petition under Section 98 or Section 99 of the principal Act is pending before the Supreme Court immediately before such commencement.

Appendix 8

THE CONSTITUTION (THIRTY-NINTH AMENDMENT) ACT, 1975

An Act further to amend the Constitution of India.

BE it enacted by Parliament in the Twenty-sixth Year of the Republic of India as follows:

Short title. 1. This Act may be called the Constitution (Thirty-ninth Amendment) Act, 1975.

Substitution of new article for article 71. 2. For article 71 of the Constitution, the following article shall be substituted, namely:

Matter relating to or connected with the election of a President or Vice-President. "71. (1) Subject to the provisions of this Constitution, Parliament may by law regulate any matter relating to or connected with the election of a President or Vice-President, including the grounds on which such election may be questioned:

Provided that the election of a person as President or Vice-President shall not be called in question on the ground of existence of any vacancy for whatever reason among the members of the electoral college electing him.

(2) All doubts and disputes arising out of or in connection with the election of a President or Vice-President shall be inquired into and decided by such authority or body and in such manner as may be provided for by or under any law referred to in clause (1).

(3) The validity of any such law as is referred to in clause (1) and the decision of any authority or body under such law shall not be called in question in any court.

(4) If the election of a person as President or Vice-President is declared void under any such law as is referred to in clause (1), acts done by him in the exercise and performance of the powers and duties of the office of President or Vice-President, as the case may be, on or before the date of such declaration shall not be invalidated by reason of that declaration."

Amendment of article 329.

3. In article 329 of the Constitution, for the words "Notwithstanding any thing in this Constitution—", the words figures and letter "Notwithstanding anything in this Constitution but subject to the provisions of article 329A—" shall be substituted.

Insertion of new article 329A.

4. In Part XV of the Constitution, after article 329, the following article shall be inserted, namely:

"329A. (1) Subject to provisions of Chapter II of Part V except sub-clause (e) of clause (1) of article 102, no election

Special provision as to elections to Parliament in the case of Prime Minister and Speaker.

(a) to either House of Parliament of a person who holds the office of Prime Minister at the time of such election or is appointed as Prime Minister after such election;

(b) to the House of the People of a person who holds the office of Speaker of that House at the time of such election or who is chosen as the Speaker for that House after such election;

shall be called in question, except before such authority not being any such authority as is referred to in clause (b) of article 329 or body and in such manner as may be provided for by or under any law made by Parliament and any such law may provide for all other matters relating to doubts and disputes in relation to such election including the grounds on which such election may be questioned.

(2) The validity of any such law as is referred to in clause (1) and the decision of any authority or

body under such law shall be called in question in any court.

(3) Where any person is appointed as Prime Minister or, as the case may be, chosen to the office of the Speaker of the House of the People, while an election petition preferred to in clause (b) of article 329 in respect of his election to either House of Parliament or, as the case may be, to the House of the People is pending, such election petition shall abate upon such person to the office of the Speaker of the House of the People, but such election may be called in question under any such law as is referred to in clause (1).

(4) No law made by Parliament before the commencement of the Constitution (Thirty-ninth Amendment) Act, 1975, insofar as it relates to election petitions and matter connected therewith, shall apply or shall be deemed ever to have applied to or in relation to the election of any such person as is referred to in clause (1) to either House of Parliament and such election shall not be deemed to be void or ever to have become void or has, before such Commencement, declaring such election to be void, such election shall continue to be valid in all respects and any such order and any finding on which such order is based shall be and shall be deemed always to have been void and of no effect.

(5) Any appeal or cross appeal against any such order of any court as is referred to in clause (4) pending immediately before the commencement of the Constitution (Thirty-ninth Amendment) Act, 1975, before the Supreme Court shall be disposed of in conformity with the provisions of clause (4).

(6) The provisions of this article shall have effect notwithstanding anything contained in this Constitution."

INDEX

Act of the Legislature, 156
Advani, L.K., 44, 59, 129
Adwaitanand, bribery issue against, 5, 7-8, 10, 12, 60
Air Force Plane issue, 40, 58, 60; Bhushan's arguments on, 28-31, 87; Khare's arguments on, 62-63; verdict on, 98
Akhil Bharatiya Ram Rajya Parishad and symbol issue, 52
Alagiriswamy, Justice, 18-19
Ali, Justice, Murtaza Fazal, 259, 262
Allahabad High Court Judgement, 94-104; CID's manoeuvrings behind 94-95; rumour of CIA's role in, 95; Congress MP's visit about, 94; dramatic scene in, 23-26 ; people's speculation about, 93; press reaction to, 109-111; and stay order, 97-98

Bahuguna, H.N., 33
Ballot paper, charges of chemical treatment of, 5, 8, 60; Justice Broom's investigation on, 12
Banarsi Das, 44, 59
Barooah, Devkant, 108, 112, 114
Beg, Justice, 38, 138, 148, 151, 153, 163, 177, 186, 192, 195-96, 204, 222-23, 231-36, 259-60, 268, 271-73
Bhagwati, Justice, 17, 35, 54, 81, 179, 266
Bhushan, Shanti, 4, 7-8, 12-13, 18, 20-21, 24, 45, 56, 58, 77, 88-90, 93-95, 99, 107, 108, 111, 113, 117, 120-23, 130-33, 136-58, 167, 169, 173-82, 187-96, 200, 203-04, 206, 208, 210-20, 244, 247, 250, 268, 271
Blackstone, Commentaries on the Laws of England, 156
"Blue Book," 15, 16, 26, 31-33, 64, 76, 85-88
Bosu, Jyotirmoy, 23, 59
Brandt, Willy, 122
Broom, W. Justice, 10, 11, 13, 14, 60

Candidate, amendment definition of, 185-87, 197; definition according to R.P. Act, 42, 185, 200-01; Bhushan's views on, 213; Sen's arguments on, 203-04
Changla, M.C., 126
Chandrachud, Justice, 138, 157, 160, 178, 190-91, 198-99, 206, 236-39, 266
Chandra Sekhar, 50, 69, 104, 108, 112, 174
Charan Singh, 128
Chavan, Y.B., 108, 127
Chawla's Case, 17, 18, 34, 35, 41, 54-57, 76, 81, 82, 86, 188, 195-200, 205
Chenna Reddy's case, 41
Congress (O), *charkha* symbol allotted to, 4, 52
Congress Party, and Allahabad High Court, 108; decision of Mrs Gandhi's constituency announced

by, 45; and "India is Indira" resolution, 112; press reaction to, 113; religious symbol allotted to, 4, 52, 77-78, 90

Congress split (1969), 3

Constitution, basic features of, 149

Constitutional (20th) Amendment Act, 160

Constitution (Thirty-ninth Amendment) Act 1975, 134-37, 146, 152, 221, 269-70; attack on 9th schedule of, 189-92; Attorney-General's arguments on, 155-57; Ashok Sen's arguments on, 169-72; Bhushan's arguments on the validity of, 82-85; Bhushan's rejoinder, 173-81

Dadachandji, J.B., 113-14

Das, S.R., Chief Justice, 208

De, Niren, 18, 54, 80, 96, 150, 152-53, 155, 159, 162, 178-79, 265-66

Desai, Morarji, 94, 115, 128

Dharia, Mohan, 108, 112, 135

Directive Principles of State Policy, 162, 177, 197

District Congress Committee of Rae Bareli, election expenses incurred by, 34, 42, 69, 195

Dwivedi, Dr R.S., 38, 91, 92

Election Commission symbol to Congress (R), 4, 52, 77-78, 90-91, 132, 175, 192, 207

Election expenses, 17-18, 33-34, 82-85, 195-96; Allahabad High Court verdict on, 100-01; Bhushan's arguments on, 80-81, 85-86; Khare's arguments on, 75-76; Sen's arguments on, 205-07

Election Laws, 8

Election Laws Amendment Act (1975), 185-93, 280-84; Bhushan assails retrospective operation of, 144-45, 193-96, 211, 219; Kaushal's arguments on, 209-10; Sinha's argument on, 197-98; review application against Beg's Judgement, 268-73; Supreme Court's Judgement, 221-23

Election Laws (Amendment) Bill, introduction in Parliament, 132-37; approval of, 134

Election petition, and Air Force Plane Issue, 28-31; amendment application and opposition, 13; Blue Book issue, 32-33 (see also Blue Book); Bhushan's final draft of, 7-8; DCC bank account, 42; Bhushan's arguments on interrogations, 13; holding out issue, 42-45; Haksar's witness, 20-21; Justice Broome frames issues for, 10-11; Justice Broome deletes Yashpal Kapoor issue, 13; Justice Broome's decision on interrogations, 11; Kapoor's testimony in, 21, 243-48; Mrs Gandhi's Counsel's objection on interrogations, 11-12; Mrs Gandhi's arrival in court, 24; Mrs Gandhi's decision to appear as a witness, 21; Mrs Gandhi's testimony in, 24-26, 249-55; Mrs Gandhi's reply to the charges, 10; notices to Mrs Gandhi and Swami Adwaitanand, 10; privilege issue, 15-16; Raj Narain's plea to deliver interrogations, 11; rostrum issue, 31-32; Yashpal Kapoor's resignation issue, 46-51; Vehicles issue, 40-42

Elections of 1951 and symbol issue, 52; Niren De's experience in, 80

Elections of 1967, 4

Elections of 1971, announcement of, 3; nomination filing dates, 4; percentage of votes of Mrs Gandhi and Raj Narain, 5

Elections of 1977, 96; Congress Party's defeat in, 241

Emergency, proclamation of, 129, 130, 154; debate in Parliament about, 131-32

Evidence Act, 16

Fundamental Rights, suspension of, 130; Sinha's arguments on, 165-166

Index

Gajendragadkar, Justice, 154
Gandhi, Indira, Allahabad High Court verdict against, 96-104; appeal to the Supreme Court, 109; attack on opposition, 111; Boat Club rally, 114-15; changing her constituency from Rae Bareli to Gurgaon, 3, 43; charges of corrupt practices against, 194; Coimbatore speech against Raj Narain's candidature from Rae Bareli, 4, 72; credibility assailed, 45; decision about her constituency announced by AICC, 74-75; election expenses filed on behalf of, 39-40, 151; evidence in the Court, 8-10, 24-26, 249-55; Interview to the *Sunday Review* on Supreme Court verdict, 240-41; letter from Himachal Pradesh Lt. Governor to, 22-45; letter from Kanhaya Lal Mishra to, 25; nomination papers filed by, 4; polling date for her constituency, 5; press conference regarding elections, 3, 43; resignation issue, 107-09; total expenditure on the vehicles, 41-42; tour programme of, 4, 72-74
Gandhi, Rajiv, 24
Gandhi, Sanjay, 114, 254-55
Gandhi, Sonia, 24
Gayatri Devi, Maharani, 63
Giri, V.V., testimony before the Supreme Court, 23; Supreme Court observation of, 75
Gokhale, H.R., 75, 107, 132
Golak Nath, 147
Goyal, J.P., 114, 143
Grand alliance, formation of, 3; Mrs Gandhi's attack on, 3
Great Britain, Bill of Attainder in, 147; May's parliamentary practice on election disputes in, 176-77
Grover, Justice, 15n, 189
Gupta, M.C., 22, 96-97

Habeas Corpus, 145
Haksar, P.N., 20, 22, 47-48, 66-67, 118, 243, 250

Halsburys, Laws of England, 161
Hegde, Justice, 11, 15, 189, 209
Hindustan Times, comment on the Allahabad High Court, 110; comment on the Congress Party's resolution on "Indira is India," 113; reports on holding out issue, 43
Holding out issue, 24-25; Allahabad High Court verdict on, 101; Bhushan's arguments on, 42-45, 88-90; decision about her constituency announced by AICC, 45; Khare's arguments on, 70-72; Mrs Gandhi's Coimbatore speech, 44; newspaper reports on, 43; Opposition leaders' evidence on, 43-44; R.P. Act defines, 42; Supreme Court example on, 43; tour programme and, 44

Indian Express on holding out issue, 43
Indian Penal Code, 196, 199, 200-01, 203, 214
Indira Hatao programme, 5, 70, 111, 114
Iyer, Krishna, Justice, 113-14, 116-17, 119, 121-22, 124, 263, 266

Janta Party and victory in 1977 elections, 96
Joshi, K.N., 254
Judicial review, elimination of, 150-51

Kackar, 16
Kanta Kathuria Case, 108, 112, 193-94
Kanthamma, Mrs Lakshmi, 112
Kapoor, Yashpal, resignation issue, 31, 33, 40-42, 118, 196, 202, 204, 206; allegations against, 7, 10; allegation of purchasing a house in New Delhi, 50; as election agent of Mrs Gandhi, 4; Allahabad High Court verdict, 102-04; Bhushan's arguments on, 46-47, 90, 216; Haksar's recorded evidence, 20, 47; interrogations related to, 12, 13; Kaushal's arguments, 210; Khare's

arguments on, 66-70; Supreme Court verdict on, 50; Supreme Court's judgement on his services used, 14-15; testimony of, 21-24, 243-48
Kathuria, Kanta, 169
Kaul, R.K., 16
Khanna, Justice, 11, 137-39, 146, 149, 153-66, 170, 178, 180-81, 189, 191, 193, 194, 198, 202, 203, 205-06, 212-13, 215, 221, 226-27, 270
Khare, S.C., 11-13, 16, 21, 24, 33, 58, 59, 63-64, 66-95, 97, 243, 249
Kaushal, J.N., assisting Counsel for Mrs Gandhi, 131-32, 138, 172, 174, 178, 209-10, 216
Kaushalya, 79
Keshavananda Bharati Case, 37-38, 57, 81, 84, 138, 145, 147-49, 152, 154, 156, 160-63, 166, 180, 187, 189, 197-199, 209-213, 229; Niren De's arguments, 265-66; Palkhivala's objection, 256-64; Tarkunde's submission on, 264-65
Khader Sharif's case, 89

Lt. Governor of Himachal Pradesh, role of, 22, 45, 250, 251; Khare's arguments on, 72
Limaye, Madhu, 23, 59, 129
Lokur, Justice B.N, retirement of, 15

Madhok, Balraj, 12
MISA, 128, 154
Manna Lal, harrassment of, 95
Maruti Project, 46, 254-55
Mathew, Justice, 18-19, 38, 138-39, 145, 165, 169, 171, 177-78, 181-82, 186-95, 198-99, 201-02, 205, 208-18, 228-31, 262-66
Mehta, Ashok, 124, 129
Mishra, D.P., 122
Misra, Govind, affair of, 23
Mishra, Pandit Kanhaya Lal, 220; death of, 21; letter to Mrs Gandhi, 25
Mishra, Shyam Nandan, 23, 129
Modi, Piloo, 23, 25, 59, 108, 111-12, 129

Mukherjea, Justice, 189
Mulki Rules Case, 163
Mysore Act of 1957, 160

Nanda, Gulzarilal, 48, 68, 243, 270
Narain, Raj, 24, 44, 56, 58, 59, 65, 72, 83, 84, 87, 107, 108, 115-16, 119, 128, 140, 180, 194; allegations of chemical treatment of ballot papers, 5; candidature from Rae Bareli, 4; election petition against Mrs Gandhi, 7-9 (*see also* Election Petition); victory in 1977 elections, 241; votes polled by, 5
Narayan, Jayaprakash, 112, 115; appeal to armed forces, 127; arrest of, 128; in jail, 26
National Herald, reports on holdinig out issue, 43
Nationalization of Banks, 5
Nayar, R.P., 94
Nehru, Jawaharlal, 80
Nijilingappa, S., 44, 59, 72
Nixon Presidential tapes issue, example of, 18-19

Official duties of Government servants, Bhushan's arguments, 192; Sen's interpretation of the amendment about, 207; Sinha's argument on, 201-02
Opposition Party, Ramlila Ground rally, 115, 127; slogan of "Indira Hatao," 5; *Satyagraha* plan, 127

Palkhivala, Mrs Gandhi's legal adviser 107, 109, 117-22, 129-31, 256-64
Parekh, Justice, 94
Parliament, dissolution of, 3, 13; Govind Mishra's affair in, 23
Parliament Monsoon Session, illegality of, 194; Bhushan's arguments on the illegality of, 153-54, 181-82; Sinha's arguments, 166-69; Supreme Court verdict, 234; Justice Mathews' judgement, 231
Patnaik, Biju, 63
Pillai Committee Report on travel arrangements for VIPs, 98
Political leaders' arrest, 128-29

Index

Ponnuswami's case, 159
Porwar, T.C., 22
Presidential Notification, 4, 88, 90
Press Censorship, 129
Punjab Act of 1952, 160

Rajagopalachari, 4, 90
Rajasthan Act of 1969, 160
Rajmata of Gwalior, 63
Ram, Jagjivan, 108, 127, 131
Ram Dhan, 108, 112
Ram Rajya Parishad and election symbol, 78
Ray, A.N., 15, 18-19, 38, 127, 136, 269
Ray, Rabi, 23, 24, 59
Ray, S.S., 75, 107, 111
Reddy, Brahmananda, 127
Reddy, Justice Jag Mohan, 14, 152, 189
Representation of People's Act, 1951, 7, 192; and symbol issue, 51
Representation of People's Act, 1956, 160, 179
Representation of People's Amendment Act, 1974, 26, 28, 30, 34, 193, 274-77; Bhushan's interpretation of, 188-89; definition of a candidate, 42; interpretation of, 34-40; Sinha on the validity of, 198-200
Rostrum issue, 39; Bhushan's arguments on, 31, 72, 87-88; Khare's arguments, 63-64; judgement on, 98
Rule of the Conduct of Election Rules, 1961, 78

Sapru, B.N., 95-96
Sarkaria, Justice, 17-19
Saxena, S.S., 15
Sen, Ashok, Mrs Gandhi's counsel, 138, 140, 144, 146, 169-72, 178, 182, 203-09, 214, 217, 219, 268
Shastri, Pattabhiram, 79
Shastri, Raghbar Lal, 78
Shelat, Justice, 15n, 189
Sher Singh, Prof, 50, 69, 104
Sikri, Justice, 189
Singh, Dal Bahadur, 42, 77

Sinha, Justice Jag Mohan Lal, 16, 21, 23-24, 32, 52, 55, 58-59, 63, 66, 71, 73-75, 78, 83, 86-87, 89, 91-92, 195, 222; Allahabad High Court verdict by, 93-104; attempt to bribe, 94; rumours about his death, 110; slogans against, 108
Sinha, Lal Narain, Solicitor General, 155, 162-64, 166-69, 178, 197-202
Shukla, Gaya Prasad, 41, 77, 246
Singh, T.N., 64, 65, 67
Srivastava, Justice K.N., retirement of, 15-16
Srivastava, R.C., 7, 10, 22, 66, 96, 97, 113
State Electricity Board and Bombay High Court verdict, 56
State Privilege Issue, 15-16, 26; Supreme Court ruling on, 18-19
Statesman, comment on Congress Parliamentary Party resolution, 113; reaction on the Allahabad verdict, 110; reports on holding out issue, 43
Sunday Times, comment on Supreme Court judgement, 240
Supreme Court, Mrs Gandhi's appeal to, 109; Mrs Gandhi's stay application to, 113-14; Bhushan's arguments on, 120-23; conditional stay to Mrs Gandhi, 124-27; reaction to the conditional stay, 126-27; Palkhivala's arguments, 117-20; Palkhivala's rejoinder, 123-24; interpretation of Article 327, 37
Supreme Court Judges supersession issue, 15n
Swatantra Bharat, report of Kapoor in, 49
Symbol issue, 4; definition according to R.P. Act, 51; Allahabad High Court verdict, 99-100; Bhushan-Khare arguments, 90-91; Bhushan's arguments, 216-17; Bhushan's arguments on the amendment about, 191-92; Khare's arguments on, 77-79; oral testimony of Pandits, 78-79; passage from

Gandhi's book *Go-Sewa*, 53; Sen's arguments on, 207; Sinha's arguments, 202; Supreme Court ruling on, 52-53, 91

Tarkunde, V.M., Counsel for a detenu, 264-66
Tewari, J.N., 58
Thakur, Karpoori, 44
Tripathi, Kamlapati, 104, 244-45

United States, constitutional amendment in, 147
Untwalia, Justice, 18-19, 257, 260, 265

Uttar Pradesh Act of 1971, 160

Vaidyalingam, Justice, 12
Vajpayee, Atal Behari, 129
Vehicles issue, 40-42, 60, 85; arguments on 76-77
Verghese, B.G., 113
Vijay Kumar, 107
Voters, petition relating to the bribery of, 53

Wilberforce, William, 82

Y.S. Parmar's case, 30